W9-AUX-689

China Since Tiananmen

AN EAST GATE READER

Reflecting recent proposals by the National Endowment for the Humanities calling for more analysis of primary materials by students, M.E. Sharpe is pleased to announce the East Gate Readers. These readers are primary source textbooks that are expressly designed to afford undergraduate students the opportunity to read and interpret original and varied materials from Asia. These core texts will allow students to fit "raw data" into an overall analytical framework. To help in this process, each volume in the East Gate Readers contains annotations and introductions by an esteemed scholar in the field.

The inaugural East Gate Reader, *China Since Tiananmen*, presents a selection of key *primary* documents from the Chinese and Hong Kong press. The 109 documents portray deepening rifts over riveting social and political changes that have emerged in China since the epochal events of June 1989.

• **The documents are organized into sections on politics, economics, society and culture, and science and technology, each with a brief but helpful introduction by the editor.**

• **Included are revelations of profound social changes in Chinese society involving crime, AIDS, the proliferation of new media, and other critical issues.**

• **Features an historical chronology of the post-Tiananmen period and a biographical glossary of major political figures in the Chinese Communist Party and the military.**

The post-Tiananmen era in China has been one of explosive change and considerable social turmoil. *China Since Tiananmen* places students at the center of the conflicts precipitated by these changes and encourages them to analyze the events in thoughtful and original ways.

AN EAST GATE READER

China Since Tiananmen

POLITICAL, ECONOMIC, AND SOCIAL CONFLICTS

Lawrence R. Sullivan, Editor

An East Gate Book

M.E. Sharpe

ARMONK, NEW YORK
LONDON, ENGLAND

An East Gate Book

Copyright © 1995 by M. E. Sharpe, Inc.

All rights reserved. No part of this book may be reproduced in any form without written permission from the publisher, M. E. Sharpe, Inc., 80 Business Park Drive, Armonk, New York 10504.

Cover calligraphy by Nancy Liu

Library of Congress Cataloging-in-Publication Data

China since Tiananmen : political, economic, and social conflicts—an East Gate reader / Lawrence R. Sullivan, editor.
p.   cm.
"An East Gate book"
Includes bibliographical references and index.
ISBN 1-56324-538-8 (hc.)   —   ISBN 1-56324-539-6 (pbk.)
1. China—History—1976–
2. China—Politics and government—1976–
I. Sullivan, Lawrence R.
DS779.2.C454   1995
951.05′8—dc20   94-45362
CIP

Printed in the United States of America

The paper used in this publication meets the minimum requirements of American National Standard for Information Sciences— Permanence of Paper for Printed Library Materials, ANSI Z 39.48-1984.

BM (c)   10   9   8   7   6   5   4   3   2   1
BM (p)   10   9   8   7   6   5   4   3   2

For Nancy Liu

Contents

E. Corruption and Political Responsibility

Acknowledgments

I am grateful for the editorial and research assistance of Nancy Hearst, the very capable Fairbank Center China librarian at Harvard University; to Doug Merwin, the senior editor at M. E. Sharpe, who first suggested this project; and to Angela Piliouras and the staff at M. E. Sharpe for their tireless work in rapidly preparing this volume for publication. Thanks are also due to the School of International and Public Affairs, Columbia University, to Adelphi University for its financial assistance, and to Dr. Peter Dimandopoulous.

Introduction

China: 1989–1994

China is today a study in contrasts. At one and the same time it is the world's third largest economy and a country still ruled by the iron dictatorship of the Chinese Communist Party (CCP). In the spring of 1989, an unprecedented popular movement in Beijing and other cities peacefully challenged the authority of the government, only to be crushed by military force. Since then, the Chinese leadership has been obsessed with maintaining control. But it has also encouraged unprecedented economic growth and tolerated social freedoms that over the past five years have produced an increasingly diverse country.

The documents in this volume have been selected and arranged to illustrate the contrasting images and perspectives on contemporary China from 1989 to 1994. They are divided into four parts: Politics, Economics, Society and Culture, and Science and Technology. Most are drawn from the mainland Chinese press. But because the media in China are still tightly controlled, many are taken from sources in Hong Kong. Speeches and documents from the CCP have been edited to ensure readability, though a few are reproduced in full to give readers the flavor of Chinese political discourse. A historical chronology and biographical glossary provide the historical background on events and personages that have influenced China from 1989 to 1994. A map and organizational charts of the Chinese government are also included to assist the inquiring reader. Finally, the editor has added a series of footnotes to explain obscure events and esoteric Chinese Communist terminology.

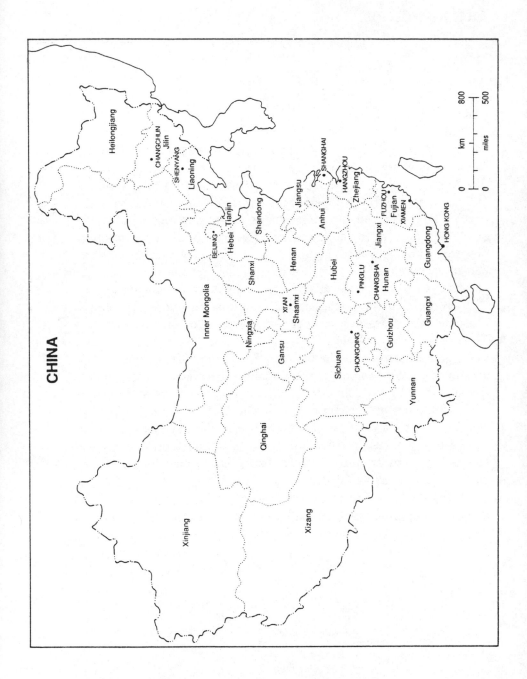

Part I

Politics

This section documents political developments in China since the military crackdown on the pro-democracy movement in Beijing on June 4, 1989. In the immediate aftermath of China's greatest political crisis since the communist takeover in 1949, the regime attempted to regain the legitimacy lost during one night's carnage by the People's Liberation Army that resulted in over 1,000 civilian deaths.[1] Chinese government propaganda defended the crackdown on both the domestic and international fronts (Documents 1 and 4), and warned that any recurrence of popular protests would be summarily crushed (Document 2). Meanwhile, remnant democratic forces in China tried to recover from their devastating defeat by appealing to the government for reconciliation and accommodation (Document 3).

The political fallout from the Tiananmen crisis shaped much of China's political landscape after 1989. The official line after June 1989 was that the country should unite against internal and "outside" enemies that threatened to subvert China's socialist system (Documents 5 and 6). Extensive organizational measures were adopted to squelch political conflicts within the Chinese Communist Party and the People's Liberation Army (Documents 11, 12, 15, 16, 17, 18, and 19) and to tighten control over colleges, factories, and villages (Documents 20, 21, 22, and 23). The lessons of the 1989 pro-democracy movement (and the collapse of communism in Eastern Europe and the Soviet

---

[1]For an extensive documentary analysis of the 1989 pro-democracy movement, see *Beijing Spring, 1989: Confrontation and Conflict, The Basic Documents,* Michel Oksenberg, Lawrence R. Sullivan, and Marc Lambert, editors (Armonk, N.Y.: M.E. Sharpe, 1990), and *China's Search for Democracy: The Student and the Mass Movement of 1989,* Suzanne Ogden, Kathleen Hartford, Lawrence R. Sullivan, and David Zweig, editors (Armonk, N.Y.: M.E. Sharpe, 1992).

Union that quickly followed) was that a ruling Communist Party could not tolerate liberalization. As for remnant leftists in the CCP left over from the Cultural Revolution (1966–76), the events in June 1989 offered a golden opportunity to reclaim their political standing (Documents 7 and 14).

Despite the leadership's claim that "stability" was China's overriding concern, political and ideological conflicts at the central level and below were vented throughout the 1989–94 period. The documents in Part One capture the ongoing battle in the party over the political structure in China and relations with the outside world, especially the West. Hard-line Communists resisted any and all proposals for political reform that could undermine the one-party dictatorship and denounced Western cultural and political influence in China (Documents 9, 14, and 25). Moderate elements in the party, though forced on the defensive by the 1989 crackdown, appealed for incremental institutional changes and advocated even greater openness to the West (Documents 8, 10, and 13). Both sides agreed that unless high-level corruption was curbed, the country faced severe political instability (Documents 27 and 28). And some among the leadership even feared that China confronted a breakup similar to that of Yugoslavia (Document 26).

Unsettling political developments were also apparent at the popular level. A growing nostalgia for the puritanical era of Mao Zedong (Documents 32 and 33) was reinforced by growing public derision for current CCP leaders, including party patriarch Deng Xiaoping (Document 29). The government did promise vigorous prosecution of corrupt officials (Documents 27 and 28) and announced greater legal protection of the citizenry (Documents 24, 30, and 31). CCP leaders praised government responsiveness in deciding on major policy initiatives, such as construction of the Three Gorges Dam on the Yangtze River (Document 35). But critics argued that the sudden and arbitrary decision to build the dam in 1992 demonstrated that the party leadership was insulated from popular interests more than ever (Documents 34).

The pariah status that China faced internationally after June 1989 quickly abated as the PRC rebuilt its ties with Japan, Europe, and the United States. Throughout the early 1990s, China's foreign policy issues gradually shifted from staving off international protests over human rights abuses to confronting the collapse of communism in

Russia and Eastern Europe (Documents 36 and 37). Despite Tiananmen, China consistently won renewal from the United States for its Most Favored Nation trading status. But conflicts over Chinese missile sales to international trouble spots (Documents 38 and 39) kept U.S.–China relations on thin ice. China engaged in intense negotiations with the British over the political future of Hong Kong (Documents 40 and 41) and with authorities on Taiwan (Documents 42 and 43), but without any foreseeable resolution.

A. Aftermath of June 4, 1989

1
Thoughts after Reading *A Day in Martial Law*

Lu Zhengcao

Source: Beijing, *Renmin ribao (People's Daily),*[1] February 20, 1990, p. 3, translated in *Foreign Broadcast Information Service, China,* hereafter *FBIS,* March 16, 1990, supplement.

Lately I read a good book that I would like to recommend to the readers. It is entitled *A Day in Martial Law.*

At first I did not expect too much from this book. . . . Surprisingly, once I started reading it, I did not want to put it down. I even hope everyone inside and outside China will read it.

The book gives the most faithful account of martial law in Beijing. . . . The articles are all eyewitness accounts; nothing is hearsay.

The disturbance that occurred as spring turned into summer last year [i.e., the 1989 democracy movement] involved such a wide scope and so many people and was so complicated that even Beijing residents, cadres, and students do not understand it all or know its nature, let alone those far from Beijing. In addition, some formed their view just from what they saw at one time or at one place, or even from rumor. Some are resistant to writings on the martial law due to misled public opinion. I think that all kind and upright people who are willing to understand the truth of the martial law, including our students and teachers, should throw away their prejudice and read this book with an open mind.

---

[1]*People's Daily* is the official organ of the Chinese Communist Party (CCP) Central Committee, the party's nominal executive organ.

From *A Day in Martial Law* we know that the People's Liberation Army [PLA] endured humiliation in order to carry out their important mission and was highly disciplined during the complicated and dangerous struggle. They would rather suffer injury or even sacrifice themselves than hurt the masses who did not know what really had happened. The piece "Three Days and Nights of Arduous Endurance" reveals that the proceeding motorcade [of soldiers who initially tried to enter the city after the declaration of martial law on May 19, 1989] was encircled by a large crowd. They spit on the faces of the soldiers; hit them on their heads and faces, causing bleeding; and yelled insults at them. For more than thirty hours, the soldiers had no water to drink or food to eat and could not even go to the washroom. Many of them fainted from heatstroke. Even so, they remained cool-headed and silent. From beginning to end, no soldier yelled or fought back, and gradually they won the trust and understanding of the vast masses and students. The associate driver that others called "baby" in "I am Not a 'Baby,' I Am a Soldier" was a nineteen-year-old recruit named Liu Xingmao. When his platoon leader was injured, Liu volunteered to stay behind. After nine hours of life-and-death struggle, the armored vehicle he heroically drove [on the night of June 3, 1989] finally entered Tiananmen Square.

Another thing that impressed me quite a bit is that this book correctly portrays the image of Beijingers and students. In "Sister Ma," we see the beautiful heart of a kind, simple, and honest Beijing working woman who ignored the danger of being beaten and even begged the rioters, miraculously rescuing a general who was seriously injured after a beating. To her, this soldier of about fifty years of age was like her "father." When she went to the hospital to visit this soldier whom she had saved, she found out he was Major General Zhang Kun. Their conversation was extremely touching. Zhang held Sister Ma's hands tight and said with feeling, "Beijing residents are all good people! You are a good person! You saved my life. I am so grateful to you!" Sister Ma stopped him and said, "Please do not say that. You came to Beijing to carry out an assignment. You did so for the good of the country and the people. We residents of Beijing also wish the country the best and that the people live good days. Your goal and ours are the same. So do not thank me, nor say that I saved your life. Soldiers and we, the masses, are one family, and as long as you are safe and well I can rest assured. And this is my greatest wish!" This conversation is so simple and honest. We can see it as a conversation between the troops and the people of Beijing. . . .

A general, sweeping view is that this disturbance was caused by "restless" students. Actually most university students had good intentions, but events developed contrary to their expectation and an impasse developed. The vast majority of university students had not expected and did not want to see it happen that way. Many articles in *A Day in Martial Law* describe this phenomenon: The troops were encircled and attacked, and it was the students who helped them out of the predicament. . . . In "The First Armored Vehicle that Entered [Tiananmen] Square," the first armored vehicle escaped being burnt thanks to the protection of students.

On this major and complicated disturbance that took place last year, we must maintain the viewpoint of concrete analysis on concrete questions. Having read *A Day in Martial Law* and analyzed and synthesized its eyewitness accounts, one naturally comes to this conclusion: Our Army is truly a great people's Army, and our people are truly a great people. It is because of our Army, people, and students that the disturbance in the capital was calmed down and the situation in China returned to normal so quickly. Without these basic conditions, the situation today could not be so good.

People will ask: If everything is so good, why did the disturbance start at all? This is not hard to understand, and with the passage of time, we can see it more clearly. Those who planned and whipped up the disturbance behind the scenes were so-called elites protected by reactionary forces in and outside China. They had without reservation accepted Western liberal thinking and tried to overturn socialist China. Naturally, there have been many faults and unsatisfactory performance in the work of our party and government. Those "elites" manipulated them and tried to confuse and poison the people's minds. They spread rumors in and outside China and stirred up some simple-minded, childish students and masses who did not know the truth. The bad elements that hit, smashed, looted, and burned were only a small handful of thugs and scum in the crowd. This point is clear in *A Day in Martial Law*. Now some of the "elites" have fled abroad to beg pity from reactionary forces. They pass their days by condemning their motherland. They are no more than a few flies that meet failure everywhere.

The lesson from this disturbance is bitter. Because we had abandoned our ideological base, bourgeois liberalization[2] flooded to the point of calamity. A microclimate was even formed in China that echoed the international microclimate. Together they set off this storm in our capital and caused undue damage to our nation and people who try hard to maintain stability and prosperity. However, genuine gold is forged in fire, and the hero is born from adversity. It is in this riot and under new historical conditions that we know better how trustworthy and reliable our Army, people, and students are. This is a firm guarantee for China to continue its stability and unity, to adhere to the Four Cardinal Principles[3] and the deepening of reform, and for the socialist banner of China to flutter.

---

[2]"Bourgeois liberalization" *(zichanjieji ziyouhua)* is the catchall term used by the CCP to describe Western influence in China and proposals for political reform by Chinese who challenge the dictatorship of the Chinese Communist Party.

[3]First articulated in 1979 by China's paramount leader Deng Xiaoping, the Four Cardinal Principles (also known as the Four Upholds) are adherence to socialism, the dictatorship of the proletariat, the leadership of the CCP, and subscribing to Marxism-Leninism-Mao Zedong Thought.

2
Fearful of the Eastward Movement of the European Wind, the CCP Steps Up Its Rule of Force

Ho Po-shi

Source: Hong Kong, *Tang tai (Contemporary)*, 14, March 3, 1990, pp. 7, 8, *FBIS*, March 8, 1990.

The CCP has recently decided to establish antiriot forces in various large population centers, and also demanded that the troops all over the country be unified in absolute obedience to party leadership.

With drastic changes in the Soviet and East European situation, the CCP is increasingly worried about the possibility of sudden changes within the country. This can be perceived from a range of recent maneuvers by the CCP. For instance:

Establishing for the First Time a Nationwide
Antiriot System

First: establishing antiriot forces at population centers nationwide—a move the CCP has never attempted in the 40 years of its rule. A document issued by the CCP central authorities concerning setting up nationwide antiriot forces specifies that an antiriot force system be set up at provincial, prefectural, and key county levels, starting with the provincial level. This intriguing move of setting up a central-to-local hierarchical antiriot force system has never been seen before. This illustrates that the CCP relies increasingly on force to maintain itself, and, from here, we can see that the CCP is extremely worried about changes in the Soviet Union and Eastern Europe. When the antiriot force is established, the CCP's dictatorship system will have one additional suppression arm, and will look like this: the Army, militia, Armed Police Force and antiriot force.

Second: Secretary General of the Central Military Commission[1] Yang Baibing issued an order at a meeting in the Beijing Military Region that "the entire Army must remain extremely alert." He also demanded that unity between field armies[2] be strengthened. The PLA's *Jiefangjun bao [Liberation Army Daily]* has also pointed out that hostile forces within and without the country had vainly attempted to infiltrate the Army in order to instigate military personnel to join in the turmoil. This was the reason Yang Baibing called on the entire Army to "forever remain extremely alert."

The Demand That the Whole Country Absolutely
Obey the Party

Third: issuing to the whole party a document entitled "Concerning Certain Problems on Strengthening and Improving Political and Ideological Work in the Army under the New Situation." The document was meant to be circulated within the Army for the purposes of unify-

---

[1]The party organ in charge of the PLA whose chairman serves as China's commander-in-chief.

[2]China is divided into seven military regions that are under the command of separate and relatively independent field armies. In this sense, China still lacks a fully unified military similar to that of the United States or the former Soviet Union.

ing thinking in the Army and strengthening the absolute control of the CCP over the Army. The reason the army document is now issued party-wide . . . is that the whole party must now learn from the Army and obey the absolute leadership of the party. This, in fact, means a strengthening of the CCP's control over government organs at various levels across the country.

Fourth: demanding that the Public Security Ministry strengthen the intelligence work of special agents as well as monitor reactionary organizations within and without the country in coordination with suppression measures. Recently, the CCP Central Commission of Political Science and Law issued a circular demanding that the public security, procuratorate, and court systems of governments at various levels step up suppression of the democracy movement in order to prevent the appearance of East European- and Soviet-style mass movements. . . .

Strengthening Ideological Control

Concerning raising ideological understanding, the circular says: "Courts at various levels must educate the wide mass of cadres and policemen in fully recognizing the acute, complicated, and long-term nature of the struggle between infiltration and anti-infiltration, subversion and antisubversion, peaceful evolution[3] and anti–peaceful evolution, in fully understanding the adherence to the Four Cardinal Principles. They must also be educated in the arduous and long-term nature of the struggle against bourgeois liberalization as well as the extreme importance of a stable political situation to rectification, improvement, and reform and opening up."

The circular makes three suggestions concerning the adoption of effective measures:

Stepping Up Intelligence Work

—Strengthen intelligence work and be fully ready for any sudden occurrences. Strengthen the construction of command centers at provinces, prefectures, and key counties; organize as quickly as possible and strengthen antiriot police force and tactical units of

---

[3]"Peaceful evolution" *(heping yanbian)* is the CCP's term for purported efforts by the West, especially the United States, to overturn the Communist dictatorship in China by ideological and cultural subversion.

the Armed Police Force in order to raise their overall combat power and quick response capability.

—Highlight the struggle against subversion, infiltration, and sabotage; resolutely expose and strike at hostile forces outside of the country as well as sabotage within our country by reactionary organizations and various counterrevolutionaries within the country.

—Strengthen and improve ideological and political work to ensure the loyalty of public security forces and the Armed Police Force to the party and socialism, and to guarantee that "the handles of knives" are in the hands of the reliable.

Public security departments must do well in the above-mentioned ideological and administrative preparations. Courts at various levels must also strengthen the "dictatorship" functions of judicial work. The circular states that the people's court, as part of the state machine, is an important instrument for the people's dictatorship. Political and legal work must be subsumed under party leadership. Under the current situation, "courts must strengthen the consciousness of class struggle and dictatorship," take as top priority the defending of the party leadership and the socialist system, and exercise fully the functions of "knives." The circular stresses severe punishment for manufacturing "political turmoil" and "counterrevolutionary cases," and also emphasizes that there should be no "kind hearts or soft hands."

From its repeated stress on the "handles of knives," we can see that the CCP, apart from the emphasis on "the barrels of guns," has added "knives" in order to consolidate its political power.

Spare No Effort in Replenishing Servicemen; Military Expenditures This Year Will Not Be Cut

Fifth: spare no effort to increase the number of enlistments to strengthen troop strength. In a publicity outline document for the recent issuance of the 1990 enlistment order, the Central Military Commission mentioned that various levels must build up a concept for the prevention and struggle against the peaceful evolution and forestall elements of the democratic movement from "mingling in the Army." The document says: "In some places people lack the understanding of international situations and have a relatively weak concept of national defense. This affects youths' motivation for military service. It should be seen that the current world is moving from confrontation to dialogue, from tension to relaxation. But this does not mean that international confrontation has disappeared and the whole world is all but peaceful. The international anti-China forces are still harboring intentions to put us to death, and there is no change in Western capitalists' vain attempt to pursue peaceful evolution as well as wage subversive and splittist wars in our country.[4] The security of our country must be supported by the necessary national defense power." The document also says that "in this year's enlistment work, special attention must be given to strictly prevent being inducted into the Army those who supported or participated in [the 1989] Beijing turmoil and counterrevolutionary rebellion; unlawful elements who beat, smash, loot, and burn people or things; and those imbued with serious bourgeois liberalized thinking or who harbor dissatisfaction with the CCP and the socialist system."

Moreover, as revealed by financial departments, to increase troop strength, the financial plan to be submitted to the National People's Congress[5] this March will not cut the national defense budget. Under the condition that there will be no significant increases in gross financial expenditure, expenditures of other departments will be cut but the national defense budget will not be affected.[6]

---

[4]"Splittism" refers to possible separatist movements among China's non-Han minorities. See Part Three, Section D.

[5]China's nominal parliament.

[6]Since 1989 China's national defense budget has been substantially increased, sometimes by as much as 20 percent a year.

3
"Peace Charter" as Drafted by Qin Yongmin

Source: Hong Kong, *Lien ho pao (United Daily),* November 15, 1993, *FBIS,* November 16, 1993.

Over the past ten years and more, great changes have occurred in the economic structure of the [Chinese] mainland, and we deeply appreciate this.

However, as the historical facts of the contemporary world have fully shown, the rapid development of the market economy inevitably requires the adoption of political pluralization and democracy.

In the current world situation, the Cold War has come to an end, and great changes leading to a new order have taken place.

All Chinese people are concerned about China's future peaceful development. It is in these circumstances that we put forward this charter.

There are various precedents of changes in political systems in Chinese and world history, and this makes us worry about the next stage of the historical process in China: As political pluralization and democracy is an irresistible necessity of history, we have to ask ourselves whether this will proceed in China in a peaceful form or in a non-peaceful form.

We deeply believe that people of historical insight in the government authorities of mainland China are also aware of this issue and its urgency. Historical experiences, positive and negative, especially the events occurring in the former Soviet Union and Eastern Europe, are sufficient to prompt all the ruling and opposition parties which are still full of antagonism toward each other in the mainland of our country to reach the following consensus of opinion:

The historic change in the Chinese mainland from monocracy to democratic politics through pluralization can be made peacefully in an orderly way from top to bottom only when the government authorities have sincerity, and only thus can its negative effects, that is, the destructive effects on the people's socioeconomic life, be reduced to the minimum!

It should be pointed out that the overwhelming trend of the world and the unprecedentedly strong democratic forces in the international community have turned China's peaceful change into the common desire of the general public and have brought about various conditions necessary for such change. Today, the international and domestic situation, from any aspect, does not allow a repetition of a tragedy like the June 4 [1989] Incident. At the same time, justice and rationality also hope that the uncontrollable situation of social management that preceded the June 4 Incident does not recur.

As the critical point of the current issue, the change will inevitably produce a certain impact on the upper class and some people with vested interests in Chinese society and will thus make them hold a negative and resistant attitude toward the change; at the same time, some victimized strata and individuals under the current system may tend to assume an extremely radical attitude. These two tendencies will, to a certain degree, negatively affect the peaceful and orderly political structural transformation.

The key to the issue between the two sides of the Taiwan Strait [i.e., the People's Republic of China and Taiwan, the Republic of China] does not lie in when and in what form reunification can be effected; instead, it lies in on what foundation and according to what consensus of opinion reunification is effected.[1]

It is against the above-mentioned historical background that we, a group of Chinese citizens full of the lofty sense of our mission, are bold enough to call the whole nation from top to bottom on both the ruling and opposition sides:

Let us follow the principle of "placing the interests of the whole nation above everything else," remove all previous ill will, respect each other, accommodate each other, compromise with each other, jointly discuss state affairs, realize the great reconciliation of the Chinese nation, and join hands in accomplishing the transformation of the political system in the Chinese mainland and realizing the great cause of peacefully reunifying the two sides of the Taiwan Strait!

We want to particularly remind people on both the ruling and opposition sides: In order to prevent the intensification of the contradictions, which will inevitably bring the inevitable process of political change out of control and will thus draw the country into an anarchical situation, the authorities should now begin to prevent such a vista by adopting every possible means. In particular, the government authorities of the Chinese mainland are responsible for taking the initiative in adopting measures to gradually ease the situation. They should grasp the current favorable opportunity to take the initiative in adapting themselves to the laws of historical development. Otherwise, they must bear the greatest historical responsibility for the appearance of the various possible situations mentioned above.

First, we hold that the mainland government, as the representative of China and a permanent member of the UN Security Council, is obliged to observe all resolutions on human rights adopted by the United Nations and should immediately formulate laws and regulations

---

[1]See Part I, Section G for documents on the reunification issue.

on the people's personal freedom, freedom of speech, of correspondence, of the press, of assembly, of association (including a step to lift the ban on organizing political parties), of procession, of demonstration, and the freedom to enter and leave the country according to contemporary international standards and should immediately abolish "counterrevolutionary crime"[2] in order to guarantee the Chinese people's human rights. All this should be strictly put into practice under international supervision and under the supervision of the people at home and abroad.

As a goodwill response, we call on the masses to keep their inalienable right of assembly, procession, and demonstration within the current lawful level allowed by the authorities in order to reduce social shocks in starting a peaceful transition led by politics.

Second, we call on the mainland government authorities to show their grand boldness of vision in guiding the historic change by formulating and implementing strategic measures for the transition from an autocracy to pluralism and for the establishment and perfection of democratic politics, thus creating the conditions for always keeping the process of transforming the political system within a scope that the central government can control and adjust.

Third, under the preconditions that the mainland government accepts the above two points, we call on the entire people and all progressive forces inside and outside the country to respect the fact that the mainland government is the sole force that has the ability to guide peaceful change in the mainland and to positively cooperate with the mainland authorities by providing various feasible and constructive proposals for them and casting aside insignificant conflicts of interest, thus forming a benign and mutually beneficial relationship with the authorities in order to jointly advance the process of reconciliation.

Fourth, we urge the mainland government to take the first necessary step for reconciliation, that is, to immediately redress the wrongs done in the June 4 Incident, release all political prisoners jailed for involvement in the June 4 Incident or for other reasons, and issue appropriate pensions or compensation to the families of victims killed in the June 4 Incident and to other people who suffered political persecution.

We call on the victims and their families and all social circles to

---

[2]The catchall term used by the Chinese government for any and all critics of the regime.

show an attitude of looking to the future and to discontinue putting blame on the authorities for the June 4 Incident and other political incidents once the mainland government really shows sincerity for reconciliation.

Fifth, we appeal to the CCP and its government to lift all laws and restrictions on political figures in exile and to allow all students, scholars, trade union leaders, and other people who are living in exile abroad to return home.

We firmly believe that China's problems can be resolved only within its own territory. Hence, we call on all those who genuinely want to dedicate themselves to the motherland to immediately return home and take part in China's economic modernization and political democratization.

Sixth, the day of the formulation and implementation of a law of association based on modern international standards and the lifting of the ban on political parties will be the time for all nonviolent political groups and parties at home and abroad to legally apply for registration. By then, all social groups and political parties should vigorously register at the relevant departments. Today, we call on all quarters to take openness, legality, and nonviolence as their principles, tactically and artistically launch an ideological movement that will not lead to social turbulence, and regard this as the proper and most limited means of pressure required to strive for human rights and a democratic movement.

Seventh, we urge the government across the Taiwan Strait to immediately conduct direct talks. We believe that the cohesive force of the Chinese nation is sufficient for the peaceful reunification of Taiwan and the mainland. Therefore, we appeal to the mainland authorities to officially give up the idea of resorting to force; treat the Taiwan KMT [Kuomintang], Democratic Progressive Party,[3] and other political parties on an equal footing; and when the conditions are ripe, welcome Taiwan's political and government figures to develop their careers on the mainland. We also urge the Taiwan government, various circles, and the public to treat the mainland's political parties, including the Communist Party, equally, allow them to develop in Taiwan, and eventually fulfill the mission of social and political reunification. We also hope that the Taiwan Democratic Progressive Party will give up its position of "Taiwan independence" and take an active part in

---

[3]The largest opposition party on Taiwan.

the democratic and progressive cause of the whole of China, including the mainland, Taiwan, Hong Kong, and Macao.

Eighth, we appeal to the mainland government to fully respect the autonomy of the Hong Kong and Macao people. The return of Hong Kong and Macao to the motherland [in 1997 and 1999, respectively] should be handled in light of the principle of sovereignty to the center with administration to the locality and fully respecting the people's choice of social, political, and economic systems and their way of life.

Ninth, we call on people of all nationalities across the country to make concerted efforts to maintain the unity of the Chinese nation. We urge the government to handle the questions of minority nationalities based on international standards, fully respect the autonomy of the minority nationalities, and give up the outdated ideas of resorting to violence to maintain great unity.

Tenth, on the basis of the acceptance of the above-mentioned articles by various parties, the mainland government above all, we propose a round table conference as quickly as possible, attended by figures from the government, various circles, and the public at home and abroad, including the mainland, Taiwan, Hong Kong, Macao, and minority nationalities, to jointly discuss and determine peaceful transformation at the next stage and the peaceful reunification of both sides of the Taiwan Strait.

4
Right to Development: A Basic Human Right

Gu Chunde

Source: Beijing, *Beijing Review,* #19, May 10–16, 1993, *FBIS,* May 12, 1993.

The concept of human rights is multifaceted and includes the right to subsistence and development as well as civil and political rights and economic, social, and cultural rights.

Among these fundamental human rights, the right to development and political rights are closely related. Different understandings of their relationship give rise to disputes between the developing and the developed countries.

The right to development means that each nation and individual has an equal right to develop. As stated in the [UN] Declaration on the Right to Development: "The right to development is an inalienable human right by virtue of which every human person and all peoples are entitled to participate in, contribute to, and enjoy economic, social, cultural and political development, in which all human rights and fundamental freedoms can be fully realized."

Political rights refer to a citizen's ability to participate in state political activities, manage state affairs, and hold public office. The right to development and political rights are individual as well as collective human rights.

The right to development was raised in the 1960s by developing countries. In the early 1950s, when the United Nations Commission on Human Rights was established to draft a human rights covenant, differences on basic concepts appeared between Eastern and Western countries. At that time, the socialist and newly independent countries believed that such a covenant should include economic, social, and cultural rights. However, the Western countries, headed by the United States, opposed this. They held that, according to their domestic conditions and laws, they could not guarantee economic, social, and cultural rights, and that these rights are beyond the function of capitalist states. As a result, the United Nations had to adopt two covenants: the International Covenant on Civil and Political Rights and the International Covenant on Economic, Social and Cultural Rights, artificially separating civil and political rights from economic, social, and cultural rights.

At the end of the 1960s, developing countries put forward a list of human rights that included the right to development. Some Western countries took a clear stand in opposition. They said that development is not a right, but only an opportunity, an economic goal. However, after long efforts by developing countries, the UN General Assembly finally passed the Declaration on the Right to Development in 1986.

Seeing that the right to development had been accepted by most countries, Western countries were forced to change their tactics and began to distort the relationship between the right to development and political rights. In fact, they denied that the right to development was a basic human right. At many international meetings, their delegates claimed that democracy and individual freedom were the preconditions for development and stressed free elections and the establishment of democratic mechanisms. The United States' representatives told the UN Human Rights Commission that sustained economic growth needs a free market and a system that can guarantee individual rights and political freedom, and that economic development should be based on freely elected governments, respect for human rights, and administrative efficiency. They also said that civil and political rights cannot be equated with economic rights. By emphasizing individual freedom and civil and political rights as preconditions for economic and social development, the West appeared to be denying the right to development.

Contrary to the Western view, the developing countries emphasize that political rights and the right to development are united and guarantee each other. The precondition of the right to development, if it exists, is the right to national self-determination rather than individual freedoms and democratic mechanisms. Those countries that have not yet won their national independence have first to realize national self-determination, including full sovereignty over all their natural wealth and resources. Only with national independence can they master their own destinies and exercise the right to subsistence and development and seek economic, social, and cultural progress as sovereign states.

For already independent but underdeveloped states, in order to guarantee their people's subsistence and consolidate their independence, they should give top priority to economic, social, and cultural development. For this reason, representatives from developing countries have repeatedly appealed to have development rights. They insist that people without enough to eat and wear cannot exercise civil and political rights. No political system, however widely representative or democratic, can be established in a country suffering from abject poverty. Ending poverty and social instability is a precondition for promoting human rights. This explains the correct relationship between political rights and the right to development, and shows that the most important task for developing countries is to end poverty and backwardness and guarantee subsistence and development.

Not only in theory, but in practice also, developing countries should emphasize economic, social, and cultural development first. This conforms to their national conditions and their people's desires.

Since the 1960s, nations in Asia, Africa, and Latin America have won independence and achieved economic, social, and cultural progress to some extent. Generally speaking, however, their economic, cultural, and educational sectors are still relatively backward and their people are threatened by poverty, hunger, disease, and death. For example, 60 percent of the people in sub-Sahara Africa cannot obtain the necessities of life. In this situation, the right to subsistence and development naturally becomes the foremost human right. A developing country's representative once said that to a hungry person, democracy, human rights, and freedom are but hollow words.

The 1968 Proclamation of Teheran proclaimed that civil and political rights cannot be fully realized without enjoying economic, social, and cultural rights. A resolution concerning new concepts of human rights adopted by the UN General Assembly in 1977 reaffirmed this stand. The 1980 African Charter on Human and People's Rights also stressed that the right to development decides political rights, and that economic, social, and cultural rights will guarantee the exercise of civil and political rights.

Of course, this does not mean that the developing countries can ignore individual civil and political rights. Political rights can stimulate people's enthusiasm and initiative. The realization of the right to development will provide a material foundation for the exercise of political rights. As the UN resolution concerning new human rights concepts points out, the implementation, promotion, and protection of civil and political rights as well as economic, social, and cultural rights should be given equal attention and urgent consideration.

B. Leadership and Ideology

5
Report by Comrade Jiang Zemin, General Secretary of the CCP Central Committee, on Behalf of the CCP Central Committee and State Council[1]

Source: Beijing, *Beijing Television Service,* September 29, 1989, *FBIS,* October 2, 1989.

Comrades and friends [applause]:

We have solemnly gathered here to celebrate the fortieth anniversary of the founding of the PRC [People's Republic of China]. On behalf of the CCP Central Committee and the State Council, I wish to pay our respects to workers, peasants, and intellectuals of all nationalities, various democratic parties,[2] and patriotic personages of various circles who have contributed to socialist construction on various fronts throughout the country; to pay our respects to the Chinese People's Liberation Army [PLA], the Armed Police Force, and the people's police that have rendered historic meritorious service in defending the People's Republic and the socialist cause; to extend our cordial regards to our compatriots in Hong Kong, Macao, and Taiwan, and abroad who have worked for the reunification of the motherland and the revitalization of China; and to express our heartfelt thanks to all foreign friends and people of various countries who have good relations with us and who support our modernization drive [applause].

The turmoil and rebellion that occurred in late spring and early summer this year was a result of the combination of the international

---

[1]The State Council is the top executive body of the Chinese government.

[2]The eight noncommunist parties in China that are allowed to exist but that exert virtually no power within the political structure monopolized by the CCP.

climate and the domestic climate. Hostile forces at home and abroad created this turmoil to overthrow the leadership of the CCP, subvert the socialist system, and turn China into a bourgeois republic and into an appendage of big Western capitalist powers once again. The victory and nature of this struggle represent an acute opposition between the Four Cardinal Principles and bourgeois liberalization, and it is a political struggle bearing on the life and death of our party, state, and nation. It is also a serious class struggle. We have won this struggle. Thus, we have defended the achievements made by countless martyrs who had struggled, and by many other people who had vowed to struggle, for the survival and liberation of the Chinese nation over more than a century. . . . Comrade Zhao Ziyang [the former CCP General Secretary, ousted in June 1989] committed the serious mistake of supporting the turmoil and splitting the party. It was precisely by firmly correcting his mistake that our party won the victory in this struggle. The significance of the victory has already been understood by an increasing number of people. We must carry this struggle through to the end. We should educate and unite with the overwhelming majority of people, isolate and deal blows to an extremely small number of hostile elements, thoroughly investigate all counterrevolutionary conspiratorial activities, eliminate any hidden perils, and draw a profound lesson from all this. We can say with certainty that any attempts by hostile forces at home and abroad to turn China into an appendage and any attempts by hostile forces at home to reverse the verdict on the turmoil and counterrevolutionary rebellion will certainly come to naught.

While celebrating the fortieth anniversary of the founding of the People's Republic of China, we are recalling the past, looking forward to the future, and keeping China in mind and the whole world in view, and are full of confidence in the socialist cause and in the future of the communism of mankind [applause].

Let us, under the leadership of the Chinese Communist Party, strengthen unity with all democratic parties, personages without party affiliation, and all patriotic people; enhance the great unity of the people of all nationalities in the country; heighten our national spirit; and firmly and valiantly advance along the socialist road, so as to win still greater victories in our socialist cause [applause].

To give full play to the spirit of patriotism and uphold the principle of independence and self-reliance is a fundamental way to successfully accomplish the Chinese revolution and China's socialist construction. In modern China, patriotism and socialism are essentially united. History has proved that, in most cases, patriots who resolutely defend the dignity of the Chinese nation and yearn for our country's prosperity finally become faithful socialists or the dependable friends of socialism. Patriotism and the self-reliant spirit of the Chinese people lend major strength to our socialist modernization.

Our socialist cause has consolidated and developed in the process of stopping the efforts of antagonistic foreign forces to isolate, blockade, and provoke our country. The Chinese people have never bowed to any foreign pressure and never will, nor will China give up the road of socialism and national independence in return for the alms of others. . . . Here, I would like to focus on existing important problems in the work of the party and the state that should receive special attention in order to achieve unity in understanding:

1. Regarding the unity between upholding the Four Cardinal Principles and upholding the reform and open policy:

The Four Cardinal Principles are the foundation of the nation, whereas reform and opening to the outside world are means of strengthening the nation. The whole party and people of all nationalities throughout the country are aware of this. Numerous facts tell us that there are two opposing views with regard to reform and opening to the outside world. The party Central Committee and Comrade Deng Xiaoping have consistently advocated that the socialist road, the people's democratic dictatorship, the leadership of the CCP, and Marxism-Leninism-Mao Zedong Thought [the Four Cardinal Principles] must be upheld while carrying out reform and opening to the outside world. They add that reform and opening to the outside must improve the socialist system. The other kind of reform and opening—advocated by people who uphold bourgeois liberalization and demand total Westernization for China—is divorced from and is opposed to the Four Cardinal Principles. The essence of such reform and opening is to establish a capitalist system. That is, to bring China into the capitalist system of the West. We must draw a clear line of demarcation between these two types of reform and opening to the outside world. Under the present circumstances, the acute antagonism between the Four Cardinal Principles and bourgeois liberalization finds expression to a large extent in whether the socialist orientation should be upheld while making reform and opening to the outside world. In formulating principles, policies, measures, and programs for socialist modernization and in implementing them, we must firmly integrate the Four Cardinal Principles with reform and opening to the outside world. We must stick to the Four Cardinal Principles in all fields of work. We must do a good job in correctly carrying out the reform and open policy and in improving our country's socialist economic and political system so as to promote the rapid and smooth development of the national economy and other social undertakings.

2. Regarding the strategic plan for China's economic development and the efforts to improve the economic environment and rectify the economic order:

Based on a proposal by Comrade Deng Xiaoping, our party formulated three steps to realize the strategic goal for achieving socialist modernization and economic development. The first step is to double the gross national product reached in 1980 and solve the problem of clothing and food for the people. The second step is to double the gross national product by the end of this century and achieve a comparatively well-off level for the people's life.[3] The third step is to basically achieve modernization by the middle of the next century and achieve per capita gross national product of the intermediate developed countries, so that the people live a fairly rich life. Then we will continue to advance on this basis. This strategic goal shows neither our strong desire for quick results nor a state of inertia; instead, it conforms to China's realities. We can reach this goal after making efforts. In reaching this strategic goal, we must resolutely develop education as a first priority. We must shift economic development step by step into the orbit of relying on scientific and technological progress and continuous increase in productivity. It is necessary to strictly control population growth, improve the quality of the population growth, improve the quality of the population, use resources in a rational way, and pay attention to the preservation of the ecological environment. All this is of great importance.

We have basically carried out the first step toward our goal and are carrying out the second step, which is the most crucial. To fulfill this task, we must now resolutely continue to implement the policy of improving the economic environment and rectifying the economic

---

[3]China's 1993 per capita income is about $370.

order and continue to deepen reform. In three years or a little more, we must strive to fundamentally alleviate the excess of total social demand over total supply, eliminate inflation step by step, and extricate the national economy from its predicament. The economic difficulties facing us today have accumulated over the past few years. Taking full account of the difficulties will give us more initiative than underestimating them. At the same time, we should also perceive the favorable conditions for surmounting these difficulties. On the heels of construction in the previous thirty years and as a result of reform, opening to the outside, and development in the past ten years, our country's economic strength has greatly increased. Since we made efforts to improve the economic environment and rectify the economic order in the past year, we have reached a greater common understanding. The prospects for our development are bright. All comrades must fully develop the spirit of arduous struggle and diligence and thrift, set an example, and live frugally for a few years with the people of the country as a whole. . . . If the party Central Committee does not control necessary resources, construction of key projects cannot be guaranteed and the task of improving the economic environment and rectifying the economic order cannot be fulfilled. It is necessary to strengthen the party Central Committee's authority and oppose decentralism so the national economy, under stronger leadership, can develop in a sustained, stable, and coordinated way. Our efforts to improve the economic environment and rectify the economic order do not mean retrogression or scrapping reform.[4] Our efforts in this regard create conditions for deepening reform and guaranteeing the healthy development of reform, and benefit the coordination of reform. Any view or action that separates our efforts against reform is incorrect. Taking a negative attitude toward improving the economic environment and rectifying the economic order means taking a negative attitude toward reform.

3. Regarding the integration between planned economy and market regulation:

China's socialist economy is a planned commodity economy based on public ownership. There is an essential difference between this type

---

[4]In 1988, the Chinese government inaugurated an economic contraction to cool down China's excessive economic growth and high inflation. Many people in China took these measures as the first step in reversing the economic reforms. See Part II

of economy and the capitalist commodity economy, subject primarily to spontaneous regulation through the market based on private ownership. In an overall sense, the ability to purposefully develop the national economy in a planned and proportionate way is a sign of the superiority of the socialist system and a basic feature of the socialist economy. The planned system China formerly practiced, which was overcentralized and too rigidly controlled, should be reformed. Over the past ten years, while implementing guidance through planning, we have used the positive functions of regulation through the market and achieved marked success in promoting economic development, enlivening the market, and improving the people's standard of living. Certainly, blindly weakening or totally negating the planned economy and trying to create a completely market-oriented economy would not work in China and would throw the economy and society into confusion. At present, in the course of improving the economic environment and overcoming economic disorder, more stress should be laid on the guiding role of state plans. At the same time, it is necessary to further consolidate market order. Efforts must be made to create a socialist commodity economy mechanism suited to China's conditions and capable of organically combining economic plans with market regulation. The extent, style, and scope of combining economic plans with market regulation should be readjusted and improved from time to time in line with actual conditions. This is a major question of theory and practice. It is hoped that all comrades of the party, economic workers in particular, will make arduous efforts to solve this problem step by step.

4. Regarding the question of giving prominence to the system of public ownership and developing an economy with multiple economic elements:

In developing China's economy, we must continue to persist in giving prominence to the system of public ownership and developing an economy with multiple economic elements, thus bringing into play the beneficial and necessary supplementary roles of the individual economy, the private economy, Sino-foreign joint ventures, cooperative enterprises, and foreign-owned enterprises.

Persisting in this policy means better bringing into play the superiority of the socialist system and speeding up China's economic development. It does not mean in any way weakening or eliminating the position of public ownership, much less privatizing the economy. The proportion occupied by the nonpublic sector in China's national economy, as well as its scope of development, should be decided on the basis of the actual level of China's productive forces and objective requirements. This proportion should not simply be regarded as a measure of the accomplishment of the reform.

The state should support the development of the public sector in terms of funds, credit, and energy and raw materials supply. At the same time, we should thoroughly reform the management mechanism of publicly owned enterprises. Large and medium state-owned enterprises are the main pillar of China's socialist modernization and the main source of state revenue. To bring into full play their role as the mainstay is especially significant for China's economic development. We must comprehensively create the necessary conditions for them while encouraging them to strengthen their foundation, improve operations and management, carry out technical transformation and innovation, and fully tap internal potential to enhance their capacity to assume responsibility for profits and losses, to accumulate funds, to transform and regulate themselves, and to bring into better play the superiority and leading role of public ownership.

In supporting the development of large and medium state enterprises, the state should proceed in a planned manner by taking into consideration the production policy and actual possibilities, then prioritizing them. The state should refrain from allocating its resources equally to all enterprises without discrimination. In China at present, the development of the individual economy and the private economy, which are subordinate to the socialist economy, is important and indispensable to developing social production, providing conveniences for the people's livelihood, and increasing job opportunities. . . .

5. Regarding the question of upholding the multiple forms of distribution focused on distribution according to one's work and the prevention and correction of unfair social distribution:

Developing multiple economic elements while giving prominence to the system of public ownership will certainly require multiple forms in the distribution system focused on distribution according to one's work. Through reform, we have made progress in establishing and perfecting this distribution system. For the sake of achieving the goal of common prosperity, we believe in letting some people get rich first through their honest labor and legal business operations. This policy is correct and should be further implemented.

We should realize that in China there are many problems in the area of distribution, some of which are rather serious. On the one hand, in enterprises, establishments, and party and state organs, the problem of an egalitarian trend in the distribution of income among workers, who mainly rely on their wages for income, has not been completely solved. In some localities, departments, and sectors, this problem has become more serious. On the other hand, excessive disparity among income has led to new, unfair social distribution. This is mainly manifested in the excessive differences among the income of workers, cadres, and intellectuals who rely mainly on their wages for income on the one hand, and, on the other hand, working personnel of many companies in the nonproductive fields and some people who have taken a second profession, especially owners of private enterprises and some self-employed workers. This has aroused extensive concern in society and strong complaints from the working people. Unfair social distribution is an economic, social, and political problem. It has dampened the enthusiasm of workers, cadres, and intellectuals and has inflated consumption funds. Of particular note is the fact that speculation, profiteering, bribing, bribe-taking, embezzlement, theft, and other methods of reaping staggering profits have upset the economic order, disrupted the social atmosphere and stability, and caused serious consequences. Therefore, we should pay close attention to and seriously solve this problem. Legal income should be protected, while excessive income should be subject to necessary regulation through taxation. Illegal income should be resolutely banned. It is also necessary to gradually improve the material treatment of mental and manual workers whose income is too low.

Now a considerable amount of funds for investment in fixed assets and circulating funds are inappropriately turned into consumption funds, seriously affecting the development of the economy and its staying power. This must be resolutely corrected. At the same time, we must also uphold the principle of combining material incentives with moral encouragement, and rectify the erroneous trend of considering everything in terms of money in order to give full play to and protect the initiative of the broad masses of workers.

6. Regarding the question of strengthening agriculture and other aspects of primary production and readjusting the economic structure:

To ensure a steady, sustained, and coordinated development of the national economy, we must proceed from our country's long-term strategy for modernization and from the actual conditions in which the present structure of production is irrational to a serious extent, to strengthen the basic industries and to readjust the structure of production. We must strive to strengthen the staying power of our country in economic and social development and refrain from taking short-term action to achieve superficial prosperity. We must make vigorous efforts to strengthen agriculture, energy, transportation, communications, important raw and semifinished materials, and other basic industries as well as infrastructures. We must ensure the development of science, technology, and education, and strictly control the scale and systems of the processing industry and nonproductive construction. To this end, we must continue to reduce the scale of investment in fixed assets, strictly control the growth rate of consumption funds, vigorously carry out the campaign to increase production and practice economy, and gradually strike a balance in finance, credit, foreign exchange, and major materials. We should concentrate our financial and material resources on the development of agriculture and other basic industries, and increase the production capability of society as a whole. This concerns the interests of the whole country, the fundamental interests of people of all nationalities, and the future of socialist modernization. Therefore, we must advocate that the immediate interests be subordinated to the long-term ones, the interests of the part subordinated to those of the whole, and the interests of the individual and the collective subordinated to those of the state. The steady development of agriculture, especially grain production, is the foundation for the development of the national economy as a whole. We ourselves must solve the problem of feeding 1.1 billion people by adopting correct principles and making persistent efforts in this regard; we just cannot rely on anyone else to solve this problem for us. At no time must we forget this basic condition of our country. . . .

7. Regarding the question of the development of socialist democracy and the legal system:

Development of a high degree of socialist democracy and a perfect socialist legal system is a major goal and task of China's socialist modernization program. It is also a common aspiration shared by the party and the masses. Since the founding of the People's Republic, especially during the last decade, our country has scored remarkable achievements in developing democracy and the legal system. Basically, there are laws to follow in the main aspects of state affairs and social life. At the same time, it should be noted that the development of democracy and the legal system in our country remains a very arduous task. Without democracy, there could be no socialism. The socialist legal system is the manifestation of and guarantee for socialist democracy. Disruption of the socialist legal system is bound to jeopardize socialist democracy. It is necessary to strictly abide by the constitution and other laws and to continue to perfect China's People's Congress system and the systems of multiparty cooperation and political consultation under the leadership of the Communist Party. It is also necessary to establish and perfect the procedures and systems of democratic policy decision making and democratic supervision, expand the channels for dialogue and contacts with the masses, raise citizens' consciousness to enable them to participate in the administration of government, and ensure that the will and interests of the broad masses are truly embodied in state affairs and social life. Like the development of the economy, this is a vital guarantee for China's long-term order and stability and for its prosperity. Our development of democracy and the legal system must proceed from China's reality and along the socialist direction and proceed step by step in a guided and orderly way. In this process, we may use for reference certain practices of capitalist countries, but we definitely cannot copy them mechanically. We must draw a clear line of demarcation between socialist democracy and capitalist democracy and between socialist democracy on the one hand and extreme democracy and anarchism on the other hand. A very few people have advocated so-called administration by elitists, political pluralism, and the multiparty system. The essence of this is to exclude the broad masses from democracy, negate the leading position of the Communist Party, and replace the socialist People's Republic with a bourgeois republic.

The trend of extreme democracy and anarchism has a fairly broad social foundation in China and constitutes serious disruptive forces to our cause and is easily used by an extremely few reactionaries. We must be highly vigilant against and resolutely resist the spread of this trend. To do so is aimed at guaranteeing the democratic rights of the majority and ensuring the healthy development of socialist democracy and the legal system.

People's democracy and the dictatorship over hostile elements and antisocialist elements are closely linked and in unity with each other. As long as class struggle remains within a certain scope, the function of this dictatorship cannot be weakened.

8. Regarding the question of development of socialist spiritual civilization:[5]

The purpose of socialism is not only to realize economic prosperity, but also to achieve all-around social progress. Our fundamental policy is to persist in grasping socialist material civilization and socialist spiritual civilization at the same time. The building of spiritual civilization, in the final analysis, is to raise the quality of the entire nation and cultivate new socialist people with ideals, morality, culture, and discipline. We cannot imagine a nation without strong spiritual support being able to stand on its own feet among nations in the world. We must draw deep lessons from stressing the building of material civilization on the one hand and slackening the building of spiritual civilization on the other in the past several years. We must effectively grasp the building of spiritual civilization while promoting the development of material civilization. The development of education and science is a project of vital and lasting importance, and has an important and profound meaning in raising the socialist productive forces and the quality of the nation. Our education and science are still quite backward, so it is all the more necessary for us to adopt effective measures and consciously grasp this work well. We should vigorously strengthen and improve our work in the ideological sphere in light of people's actual thinking, in close combination with the building of modernization and the actual situation in carrying out the reform and open policy. We should strengthen and improve ideological and political work. We should unremittingly conduct education on patriotism, collectivism, socialism, the thinking of self-reliance and hard struggle, and revolutionary tradition for the people of the whole country, especially youth and teenagers. We should also continually conduct education on communism for members of the Communist Party, the Communist Youth League, and advanced elements. We should use Marxism and socialist ideology to guide theoretical, propaganda, educational, journalist, publication, literary, and art fields, and occupy the cultural front and press circles. We should enrich the spiritual life of the masses. We should actively lead the broad masses to consciously resist the influences of various erroneous ideologies and corrupt thinking. We should cultivate

---

[5]The term concocted by the CCP for filling the ideological void in China since the end of the Cultural Revolution (1966–76) and the national loss of faith in Maoism. See Document #73.

a scientific, healthy, and civilized living environment, and enable the masses to become genuine socialist workers and builders possessing consciousness and initiative. Public schools at various levels should not only strive to improve their teaching of culture and knowledge, but also prioritize moral education and establish correct political orientation of serving the people and socialism, and adhere to the policy of letting a hundred flowers blossom and a hundred schools of thought contend,[6] so as to allow the scientific and cultural fields to prosper and develop. We should actively absorb our own historical culture and all outstanding achievements of foreign culture. We should resolutely eliminate all feudal and bourgeois cultural dregs and spiritual garbage. At present, on this issue, we must pay particular attention to opposing national nihilism, which totally negates Chinese traditional culture, and the ideology of worshiping and having blind faith in things foreign.

9. Regarding the question of strengthening leadership by the working class, consolidating the worker-peasant alliance, and promoting the great unity of people of all nationalities throughout the country:

The workers, peasants, and intellectuals are the basic force for achieving socialist modernization. Wholehearted reliance on the working class is determined by the nature of our party and state. The working class people, particularly industrial workers, are closely linked to modernized large-scale production. They are the representatives of advanced productive forces and production relations. They have a high degree of organization and discipline. During the long revolutionary struggle and practical construction, they have shown a firm political stand and the spirit of self-sacrifice, a hard-working enterprising spirit, and initiative. They are worthy of being called the leading class and the backbone of the socialist cause of our country. Any view that belittles the role and awareness of the working class is totally wrong. A handful of people are attempting to create a so-called middle class in China and to rely on this class to subvert our socialist system. This negative example has proved even more that we must wholeheartedly rely on the working class.

---

[6]This phrase refers to the short-lived policy of the CCP promoted in 1957 to allow intellectuals and artists relative freedom of expression. This so-called Hundred Flowers Campaign was quickly terminated and followed by the Draconian Anti-Rightist Struggle in which critics of the regime who had been outspoken in the Hundred Flowers Campaign were persecuted.

The vast number of peasants in China have always been a natural ally of the working class. They are the firm supporters of the socialist system and the leadership of the party. We should take further steps to strengthen the assistance of industry to agriculture, strengthen the assistance of urban areas to rural areas, and constantly adopt practical measures to consolidate the worker-peasant alliance on a fresh basis politically and economically as well as in education, science, and culture. This is the basic condition for stability in our state and our society.

The intellectuals in our country are a part of the working class. Without knowledge and intellectuals, it is impossible to build socialism. This basic view of our party and the policies concerning intellectuals laid down since the [December 1978] Third Plenary Session of the Eleventh CCP Central Committee[7] have not changed and will not change due to recent political disturbances. We already have a very good contingent of intellectuals who persist in taking the socialist road. Party committees and governments at all levels should continue to carry out the principle of respecting knowledge and respecting intellectuals, and should strive to create and provide good working conditions and living conditions for them.

The party and the government have always considered youth, including young intellectuals, the future and hope of our motherland, and have consistently treated them with warm love and set strict demands on them in the sincere hope that they will grow up healthy and become qualified personnel quickly. We also sincerely hope that the broad masses of intellectuals, particularly young intellectuals, will seriously study Marxism-Leninism-Mao Zedong Thought, integrate themselves with social practice and with workers and peasants, constantly draw nutrition from the people's history-making activities, and give full play to their wisdom and talents in the course of the motherland's socialist construction. We should, on the basis of consolidating the worker-peasant alliance, further develop the most comprehensive united front of all socialist workers, the patriots who support socialism, and the patriots who support the reunification of the motherland, thus strengthening unity among the people of all nationalities throughout the country.

Ours is a unified, multinational country. All our achievements of

---

[7]The watershed party meeting at which Deng Xiaoping shifted government policy to economic reform soon after the death of Mao Zedong in 1976. See Chronology.

revolution, construction, and reform are scored with the common efforts of people from all our country's nationalities. Under the leadership of the CCP and the government, the various nationalities have not only established and developed the new type of relations of equality, unity, and mutual aid but, through the introduction of regional autonomy, the minority nationalities are ensured the right of being their own masters and managing their own internal affairs. Political, economic, educational, cultural, and other undertakings have also developed apace in the national minority areas; we must continue to firmly carry out the principles of national equality, national unity, and the common prosperity of all nationalities. We must fully trust and rely on the cadres and masses of all nationalities and take a clear-cut stand and carry on a resolute struggle against all conspiracies to split our motherland. We must improve the legal system aimed at strengthening the regional autonomy of minority nationalities. We must make great efforts to train cadres and professionals of all kinds of the national minorities and ensure that the national autonomous areas can fully exercise their right of autonomy. Necessary measures should be adopted to continue to help and support the minority areas in developing their economic, educational, cultural, and other undertakings, and prolonged, unremitting efforts must be made to gradually eliminate the gaps that exist to different extents between different nationalities for reasons of history.

10. Regarding the question of strengthening party building:

Ours is a great Marxist political party, the decisive force for maintaining the political stability of China for a long time to come, and a strong core for leading people of all nationalities to build socialism with Chinese characteristics. The struggle to check the turmoil and quell the rebellion has once again tested our party, and proved that, viewed as a whole, the party is both good and strong [applause].

Our party was born, developed, and grew in close contact with the masses. Without the support of the masses of people, the party cannot survive even for a single day. After we became the party in power, some phenomena of bureaucratism, commandism, abuse of power for personal gain, corruption, and degeneration emerged, which resulted in alienation from the masses of the people. In the last few years, because party building and ideological and political work have been weakened, problems of ideology, style of work, discipline, and organization within the party have been further aggravated. We must adhere unwaveringly to the aim of serving the people wholeheartedly and persist in the fine style of work characterized by a close combination of theory with practice, maintenance of close ties with the people, criticism, and self-criticism. We must run the party strictly in accordance with the party constitution. We must make firm decisions and take resolute and effective measures to eliminate all obstacles and overcome various corrupt phenomena so as to restore and develop the flesh-and-blood ties between the party and the people [applause].

Organizations at all levels in the whole party, primarily the party Central Committee, must strictly carry out the democratic system. Leading organs at all levels must uphold the system of combining collective leadership and division of labor with individual responsibility, improve the democratic activities within the party, strengthen democratic supervision, and guard against the practice of a few people having the final say; still less should we allow certain individuals to make arbitrary decisions. Moreover, we should attach great importance to the improvement of grass-roots party organizations and change their weak and lax state.

All Communist Party members and party cadres, leading cadres in particular, must strictly abide by party discipline and self-consciously maintain unity with the party's line, principles, and resolutions in word and deed. In no way should we allow the practice of each going his own way.

The improvement made by the party in terms of theory is the basic guarantee for the correctness and scientific nature of party leadership. In view of the many new circumstances and issues in the world and in China, the important responsibility our party shoulders in China's socialist construction, and its significant position in the international communist movement, it is necessary to view learning and studying basic Marxist theories as an urgent task and to emphasize this task to the whole party. We must study and probe major theoretical questions on contemporary politics, economics, and society under the guidance of Marxism. Within the party, primarily among high-level party cadres, it is necessary to promote the practice of earnestly learning and studying the basic theories of Marxism-Leninism-Mao Zedong Thought, especially learning and studying Marxist philosophy and grasping the scientific world outlook and methodology. A Communist Party member, who lacks Marxist theoretical accomplishments and who is not good at using the correct stand, viewpoints, and methods to analyze and solve questions can in no way play his dual role. Still less is it possible for him to become a qualified leading cadre of the party. It is imperative to resolutely correct the state of affairs whereby many leading cadres are buried in routine work, relax their study of theories, and pay no attention to ideological and political trends. We should conscientiously raise the theoretical level and the political sensitivity of our comrades in the whole party.

Comrades and friends, the current international situation is developing from tension to relaxation and changing from confrontation to dialogue. There has been a great change in the situation where superpowers manipulate international affairs. Hegemonism is running into snags and is foiled everywhere. The Third World countries are playing an ever-increasing role in international affairs. It is possible to maintain lasting peace in the world and avoid a world war by relying on the concerted efforts of all peace-loving countries and peoples in the world. Peace and development are two main themes in today's world. There has been no change in this general trend and pattern of the international situation. It is possible for us to achieve a fairly long-term peaceful international environment for the socialist modernization program of our country. It should be noted, however, that the world is not peaceful and tranquil. Many contradictions, struggles, and factors for instability remain.

It should be stressed that international reactionary forces have never given up their basic stand of being hostile to and subverting the socialist system. Since the late 1950s, they have shifted the focus of their policy to peaceful evolution after the failure of their armed intervention trick. Applying political, economic, and cultural means and taking advantage of the temporary difficulties of socialist countries and the opportunity of reforms being carried out by these countries, they have carried out infiltration, exerted influence, supported and bought out so-called political dissidents, cultivated the blind worship of the West, and disseminated Western capitalist political and economic modes, values, and decadent thinking and lifestyle. When they think there is an opportunity to take, they fabricate rumors to provoke incidents, plot turmoil, and conduct subversive activities. Class struggle is no longer a major contradiction in our society, but it still exists to a certain degree and may become acute under given conditions. This is exactly where international hostile forces have found a basis for carrying out the peaceful evolution strategy. The struggle between infiltration and non-infiltration, subversion and antisubversion, peaceful evolution and non–peaceful evolution is a protracted one. The people of all nationalities in our country and comrades in the whole party, especially leading cadres, must maintain high vigilance against this [applause]. . . .

Socialist China has one-fifth of the world's population [approximately 1.2 billion] as well as tremendous actual and potential economic strength. This is an objective reality that no one can overlook. Internationally, more and more well-informed people have realized that any attempts to discriminate against or isolate China are unwise as well as utterly futile. No economic sanctions whatsoever can shake our determination to revitalize China and uphold the socialist road in the slightest, nor our confidence in living in friendship with people all over the world.

The People's Armed Forces, composed mainly of the People's Liberation Army, and led by the Communist Party of China, are the solid pillar of the people's democratic dictatorship and form the powerful backing of our socialist cause. History in the past forty years, especially the struggle to put down the counterrevolutionary rebellion, proves again that without the People's Army, the people would have nothing [applause].

The People's Liberation Army will forever be the defenders of our country, socialism, and the people's interests, as well as the wall of steel of the republic. Our socialist construction is being carried out in a situation in which hostile forces, international as well as internal, are still engaged in activities of sabotage and subversion against us. All party members and people across the country, in amassing forces to achieve economic development, must place great stress on strengthening national defense, education in national defense, and the whole nation's consciousness of defense, and strive to promote the revolutionization, modernization, and regularization of the Army.

Comrades and friends:

Over the past forty years, our party and government have been making constant efforts to end the division of China and to realize reunification as early as possible. After the [1978] Third Plenary Session, the principle of peaceful reunification of the motherland and the concept of one country, two systems were put forward, and have become basic policies of our country. The Chinese government has reached agreements respectively with the British and Portuguese governments on the solution of the Hong Kong and Macao issues. We will not change the capitalist system of Hong Kong and Macao, nor will we allow Hong Kong to be used as a base to overthrow the central government. With the motherland growing stronger and more prosperous, Hong Kong and Macao will have greater stability and prosperity.

The common efforts of the people on both sides of the Taiwan Strait have brought about gratifying changes in the relations between the mainland and Taiwan. However, the Taiwan authorities still maintain their stand of opposing the CCP, and refuse to make peace. They persist in following the three no's policy,[8] and put man-made obstacles to the normal development of relations and friendly contacts between the two sides of the strait. They pursue a so-called elastic diplomacy in an attempt to create two Chinas or one China, one Taiwan, and keep China in a lasting state of division. This means, in effect, connivance with and help to the growth of the forces that demand Taiwan independence. It runs counter to the basic interests of the Chinese nation and the common wishes of all Chinese compatriots on both sides of the strait. To realize the reunification of our motherland, we pin our hopes on the people of Taiwan and on the Taiwan authorities. We firmly oppose any words or deeds that may lead to the separation of Taiwan from the motherland. The Taiwan authorities should adapt themselves to the historical trend and, as early as possible, make enlightened decisions that will help to unify the country. We believe that as long as all Chinese compatriots aware of the supreme interests of the nation as a whole join together and work in unison, the great prospect of the nation's reunification will surely be realized at an early date [applause].

Comrades and friends: When Marx and Engels, the great teachers of the proletariat throughout the world, successively passed away about one century ago, not many people then believed in the theories of scientific socialism that they conceived. Today, socialism has become a living reality in the world, and is being practiced by hundreds of millions of people. In the course of development, new socialist elements have experienced twists and turns. However, history has proved, and will continue to prove, that the socialist system has a strong historical vitality and is full of life. Seeing only the whirlpools and countercurrent, but not the progression of the long river of history, only reveals the viewer's political shortsightedness. The replacement

---

[8]The Taiwan government's policy of "no contact, no negotiation, and no compromise" with the Chinese Communist government. See Documents #42 and 43.

of socialism by capitalism is truly the major historical trend, as well as a decisive stage in which mankind enters the realm of freedom from the realm of necessity [applause].

While celebrating the fortieth anniversary of the founding of the People's Republic of China, we are recalling the past, looking forward to the future, and keeping China in mind and the whole world in view, and are full of confidence in the socialist cause and in the future of the communism of mankind [applause].

6

Beijing Political Situation: Qiao Shi Criticizes Nonorganizational Activities within the CCP

Jen Hui-wen

Source: Hong Kong, *Hsin Pao*, October 15, 1993, p. 31, *FBIS*, October 15, 1993.

Since last October when the Fourteenth CCP National Congress reconfirmed the third generation of the leading collective, with Jiang Zemin at the core, the CCP Central Committee Political Bureau Standing Committee,[1] consisting of Jiang Zemin, Li Peng, Qiao Shi, Li Ruihuan, Zhu Rongji, Liu Huaqing, and Hu Jintao, has gradually tended to wield power independently. The "financial brake" that started in July and the anticorruption struggle that followed are the two important practical examples of this.

Nevertheless, as Deng Xiaoping has repeatedly pointed out since his [February 1992] tour of southern China, "if any problem does occur in China, it will occur from within the CCP." Recently, several retired CCP elders and senior cadres who have retired from the CCP Political Bureau to the National People's Congress [NPC] and the Chinese People's Political Consultative Conference [CPPCC],[2] and those who

---

[1] The top executive organ of the CCP.

[2] The CPPCC is a "united front" organization set up in China in 1949 consisting of representatives from the CCP and the eight democratic parties. Its annual meetings are largely ceremonial, and it wields no real political power.

still retain positions in the State Council, have either sent signed letters criticizing the "financial brake" as a policy mistake or seized the opportunity of marking Mao Zedong's 100th birthday (which falls on December 26) to insinuate to Deng Xiaoping by repeating the two whatevers (short for the political slogan that "we should resolutely support whatever policy decisions Chairman Mao made and unswervingly follow whatever instructions Chairman Mao gave," chanted by Hua Guofeng, Mao Zedong's designated successor [in 1976]) and to interfere with the rule of the third generation. This situation has received the great attention of the CCP senior echelons.

According to informed sources in Beijing, in response to the above-mentioned phenomenon, Wei Jianxing, member of the CCP Central Committee Political Bureau and secretary of the Central Commission for Discipline Inspection,[3] stated seriously for the first time, at a Standing Committee meeting of the Commission, that behavior that goes against the party's discipline must be criticized, helped, and coped with. CCP General Secretary Jiang Zemin and Political Bureau Standing Committee members Qiao Shi and Hu Jintao attended the meeting, at which Qiao Shi spoke on behalf of the Political Bureau.

Yao Yilin and Others Criticize Zhu Rongji

The informed source said: Since July, several former members of the Central Advisory Commission,[4] the CCP Political Bureau, and the State Council have been active. The most active of these were: Song Renqiong, former [vice] director of the Central Advisory Commission; Yao Yilin, former member of the CCP Political Bureau and vice premier of the State Council; Li Ximing, member of the CCP Political Bureau and currently NPC vice chairman; Wang Bingqian, former state councillor and currently NPC vice chairman; Yang Rudai, former CCP Political Bureau member and currently CPPCC vice chairman; and Deng Liqun, former vice head of the Central Propaganda Department.

In July, Yao Yilin, Li Ximing, Wang Bingqian, and Li Guixian (state councillor) prepared a report entitled "Existing Problems in Cur-

---

[3]The main internal disciplinary organization of the CCP.

[4]The Central Advisory Commission was established in the 1980s to serve as a transitional body to ease the retirement of elder CCP leaders. It has since been dissolved.

rent Economic Development and the Monetary Market" and wrote a letter to the State Council, alleging that the current overheated economy and monetary chaos were not the result of whether or not reform has been adequate but of the mistakes in central policies and some leaders' fondness for greatness and success. They said the fact that regionalism and sectarianism have become much more serious in recent years has been caused by deviations in central policies and by the incorrect guiding ideas of some leaders. Moreover, they asked that individual central leaders bear the responsibility.

This criticism obviously shows dissatisfaction with State Council Vice Premier Zhu Rongji over his economic work. But today, when a "preliminary success" has been scored after three months of rectifying the monetary order and strengthening the central authorities' macro-regulation and control of economic activities all over China, the criticism has failed. An economic work conference of the ten provinces and autonomous regions of central, southern, and southwestern China was called under the chairmanship of Jiang Zemin in Canton in late September. Jiang Zemin praised the new relationship between the center and localities, which had formed in the course of reform and opening up and which became more mature in the drive of macroeconomic regulation and control. This was a response to the criticisms of Yao Yilin and others.

Song Renqiong Launches an Attack amid "Mao Zedong Fever"

The informed sources added: Song Renqiong was only nominally resting in the hospital, but in fact he has been active.[5]

In early July, he called a forum on the "Reasons for Today's Overheated Economy" and coordinated with Yao Yilin and others. In early August, he put forward the suggestion that "veteran cadres should study Mao Zedong Thought seriously" and signed a letter together with more than forty others, including Song Ping, former member of the CCP Central Political Bureau Standing Committee, and Deng Liqun, asking the CCP Central Committee to launch a "Marxism-Leninism-Mao Zedong Thought Propaganda and Education Campaign" for the

---

[5]Feigning "illness" and retiring to a hospital to prepare a political comeback is a common tactic in China's Byzantine political process.

entire party on Mao Zedong's 100th birthday. In early September, Deng Liqun also called the forum "Review Mao Zedong Thought and Qualify as a Follower of Marxism-Leninism" with over thirty participants. The participants' speeches virtually changed the forum into a criticism of Deng Xiaoping's theory of building Chinese-style socialism or into a reminiscence about the "two whatevers."

Concerning the launching of activities commemorating Mao Zedong's 100th birthday, as early as April, CCP elders Deng Xiaoping, Peng Zhen, and Wan Li all gave instructions saying that "they must be moderate and not excessive." In September, when commenting on the "Mao fever" in society, Wan Li pointed out that attention must be paid to the party members who cling to the "two whateverism," for they have always opposed the central task of economic construction and the reform and opening up, while trying their best to create "Mao Zedong fever."[6] Their purpose is nothing more than grasping the problems currently existing in the party, but which are being solved, to negate Deng Xiaoping's theory of running the country. Whereas the people from the democratic parties told the CCP at the New Year tea party that if "Mao Zedong fever" was created again, it was surely to enhance the might of the "leftists" inside the party and of the "whatever clique," which had restarted activities recently. Here we can see that Song Renqiong and others advocated "Mao fever" but failed to win support inside and outside the party.

The informed source said that because the third-generation leaders were interfered with by the de-organizational activities of Song Renqiong and others, Wei Jianxing pointed out at a meeting of the Central Commission for Discipline Inspection Standing Committee that the duty of the Central Commission for Discipline Inspection is to supervise the party organizations at various levels, from the central to the local authorities, according to the party constitution and party discipline and that the Central Commission for Discipline Inspection has the power to criticize, handle, and correct de-organizational words and deeds that violate the party constitution and party discipline and harm the central task of the party.

Qiao Shi said at the meeting: "The CCP is for seeking interests for the people and the party members are the people's servants, so they must voluntarily strictly observe the party's discipline and organiza-

---

[6]See Documents #32 and 33.

PART I. POLITICS 43

tional principle; no matter how senior their positions, how great their seniority, and no matter how big the contributions they have made to the party and the people in the past, they should not be involved in liberalism nor carry out de-organizational activities that violate the party's discipline and organizational principle, because this is not permitted by the party. The criticisms and assistance given to some comrades by the CCP Central Committee Political Bureau Standing Committee and the secretaries of the Central Commission for Discipline Inspection are necessary."

The informed source also said that Jiang Zemin, Qiao Shi, Liu Huaqing, and Wei Jianxing have talked to Song Renqiong, Yao Yilin, Li Ximing, Yang Rudai, Wang Bingqian, and Deng Liqun, respectively. The Central Commission for Discipline Inspection is considering whether it should take disciplinary action against Song Renqiong and others.

At the same time, Liu Huaqing relayed a message to the retired military cadres who cling to the "two whatevers." In the name of the CCP Central Committee and Central Military Commission, he said: "For the whole party and the whole Army there is only one central leadership and one core; the senior military cadres must maintain their integrity in their later years, avoid words and deeds that transgress the organizational principle, and refrain from making the mistakes we made in the past."

The CCP Should Rebuild Supervisory Organ

When asked about his views on the illegal organizational activities pursued by Song Renqiong and others, a senior cadre from the Central Party School[7] told this author: "The phenomenon of Song Renqiong reflects the fact that some people in the party never want to give up the ultra-leftist viewpoint, they cannot forget the 'two whatevers,' they have always doubted or even opposed Deng Xiaoping's theory of building socialism with Chinese characteristics, and they think that Deng Xiaoping is a 'revisionist' who is pursuing capitalism and self-evolution. They hold that only by reestablishing the authoritativeness of Mao Zedong Thought can they save the CCP and China. This

---

[7]The training center that prepares lower-level CCP personnel for primary positions in the CCP hierarchy.

kind of interference from ultra-leftist thinking inside the party will exist for a long time, but, so long as the reform and opening up can deepen continuously, it will be more difficult for them to stir up big waves."

7
Learn from Mao Zedong, Be a Staunch Revolutionary—Text of Deng Liqun Address at a December 7, 1991 Forum . . .

Deng Liqun

Source: Beijing, *Guangming ribao (Enlightenment Daily),*[1] January 12, 1992, p. 3, *FBIS,* January 4, 1992.

The old comrades now seated here were about the same age as you students when they were undergraduates of Peking University and joined the [revolution]—all were in the prime of life. Fifty-six years have passed, and we are now all men in our seventies and eighties. We were born in an eventful era; so many events have we gone through that there is no end to telling them. In this land of China, we have witnessed how [KMT leader] Chiang Kai-shek betrayed the revolution, how he schemed his way to power and fell after losing the people's hearts; how heroic CCP members [in 1927] were massacred; how the CCP won the people's mandate and help, relied on and led them, and finally won the victory of the democratic revolution and [in 1949] founded the PRC; and how the imperialists mercilessly burnt and killed China and Chinese people and insanely plundered it, and how they were swept away by the iron broom of the Chinese people. . . . For the last fifty to seventy years we have witnessed many big and small and domestic and foreign events. It has been very kaleidoscopic. There have been worries and excitement and weal and woe. With the experience of so many stormy historical events, we can say we indeed

---

[1]The CCP-run newspaper aimed at Chinese intellectuals.

have had an eventful life, and we feel we have had a full and happy life. None of us has ever regretted that we threw ourselves into the revolutionary movement and so many revolutionary struggles. Instead, we all feel as Comrade Mao Zedong said: It has been a boundless joy!

Summing up past historical experiences, we can conclude that, whatever the changes, as long as we rely on the masses, we will be able to remain composed amid changes, win every battle we fight, and conquer all that we set out to conquer, and that it will be dangerous once we are divorced from the masses. Stalin quoted a Greek myth in his prologue to the *History of the Communist Party of the Soviet Union (Bolshevik)*, saying that Antaeus was an invincible hero. The secret of his success was that every time he fought, he would press his body to mother earth to gain unlimited power to beat his opponent. Later, new enemies emerged and, having found out his trick, held Antaeus high in the air with a masterful stroke, thus preventing him from touching the earth, and finally strangled him. This story is very philosophical and a graphic abstraction of human experiences in historical, natural, and social struggle. Stalin expanded on this story: "I believe that Bolshe-viks are like the Greek mythological hero Antaeus. Like Antaeus, they are strong because they keep in touch with the masses, the mother that gave birth to, raised, and taught them until maturity. So long as they remain in touch with the masses—their mother—they will be on top of everything and unconquerable." Stalin's remark is irrefutable truth and always carries significance in reality.

Contrary to the wishes of domestic and foreign hostile forces, so-cialist China is still standing tall in the East and the socialist cause is thriving and moving forward. A decade or so of reform and opening up has scored world-renowned achievements; combined national power has increased, and the people's living standards have improved. In sum, we are in a good and encouraging situation. All socialist countries are engaged in reform, and only China has scored notable success. This does not mean that there are no shortcomings or mistakes in our work. There are many difficulties for intellectuals, especially for teach-ers. But compared with over a decade ago, the general level has been raised. We could achieve this, in the final analysis, because of the correct line and policies and effective work following the [1978] Third Plenary Session; we have based ourselves on people's interests, main-tained close ties with them, and received their support. That is why we have been able to "sit tight in the fishing boat despite the rising winds and waves," and hold our ground and march forward. There were many causes for the violent change in the Soviet Union and East Europe, but the basic one was that they had been seriously divorced from the masses. Therefore, "the national flag changes without one shot or any shelling." Why were we able to hold our ground when the Soviet Union and East Europe were washed away by the violent change? Much can be studied here. We should do some serious thinking and probing, and gain fruitful consensus on what is good and should be preserved and enhanced. I believe that we have done well in all the basics, but there are things that are not quite satisfactory; in some places we are divorced from the masses. So we should study well lessons in this aspect. With which issues are the masses discontented? Which issues must we improve? Summing up earnestly both the positive and negative sides will help us improve our work and raise it to a new level.

That is why we say that the masses of people are the source of our strength in vanquishing the enemy. Provided we rely on the masses, we will surely conquer everything. This is absolutely true. Of course, there are also times when we may encounter difficulties and serious setbacks and fail. An expression of the revolutionaries' firmness is that their confidence is never shaken in the face of temporary difficulties, setbacks, or failures. Instead, they always rely on the masses and endeavor to find strength from the masses until they achieve the final victory. Comrade Wang Zhen put it very vividly by saying: On the battlefield, it often happened that when we encountered difficulties, the other side had also encountered difficulties. Under such circumstances, persistence meant victory. Especially when the two armies matched each other in strength, the side that persisted for a longer time would surely win. This is certain. Victory usually falls to the side that persists.

Mao Zedong's career proved that he was able to think of more methods and give fuller play to his wisdom when [early CCP leaders] joined the revolution. They had fully reckoned the great difficulties and risks they would encounter. That is why they were able to follow Chairman Mao and carried out the revolution persistently. At present, the international situation is turbulent, and there are also many problems in our country. Some people are anxious about this. I think this is unnecessary. We must realize that our party Central Committee is mature enough to control the situation and the masses of people have unlimited strength. Facts over the past two years prove that under the leadership of the party Central Committee with Comrade Jiang Zemin as the nucleus, we can overcome one difficulty after another and advance from victory to victory. The existence and development of socialism reflect its great vitality. It represents the orientation of the development of human history. However, it is unrealistic to think that we can sit back and relax now. In this world, we cannot do so on many questions. . . .

8
To Emancipate the Mind, It Is Necessary to Eliminate "Leftism"

Shi Guanping

Source: Beijing, *Ban yue tan (Bimonthly Commentary),* #14, July 25, 1992, *FBIS,* August 25, 1992.

"Emancipating the mind" is possibly the most frequently used phrase in China today.[1] It is indeed inspiring to note such a popular sentiment and trend.

The issue of emancipating the mind is no longer a question of how to verbalize it but how to implement it. In general, most localities have done solid work in tackling the elimination of "leftism." However, a worrisome situation has emerged: Carrying out endless idle discussions while hardly touching on things "left."

As we all know, the new wave of emancipation of the mind brought about by Comrade Deng Xiaoping's important southern tour speech [in February 1992][2] is directed against the deep-rooted "leftist" concept. Because of the influence of such concepts, some comrades were troubled by the question of whether a move is "socialist" or "capitalist." As a result of their rigid way of thinking and overcautiousness, they hesitate to take the steps toward implementing the policy of reform and opening up as well as economic construction, leaving the fate of China's socialism and the future of the Chinese nationality to face yet another round of severe

---

[1]The phrase employed in the 1980s by party reformers led by then CCP General Secretary Hu Yaobang to attack leftist ideology in China.

[2]See Document #46.

challenges. This calls for relentless efforts to practically break the chain of "leftism"; it will be futile to just idly talk about emancipating the mind.

It is obvious that a small number of localities are not paying attention to this problem, for much has been said but little has been done. Leading comrades in these localities merely shoved the phrase "emancipating the mind" into the text of speeches and documents, but hardly ever got close to the harms of "leftism"; when asked about the manifestation of "leftism," they were either vague or unable to provide an answer. Such superficiality will certainly do nothing to promote emancipation of the mind, and thus no actual results can be expected.

The existence of such phenomena is not without reason. Other than ignorance arising from a lack of sufficient alertness toward things "left," it seems the "three fears" would have to be eliminated as well:

1. The fear of negating themselves. Some comrades said or did something wrong during the time when "leftist" thoughts ran rampant, and are afraid that eliminating "leftism" would involve them and negate some of the work they have done.[3] This is not unusual, and there is no reason for holding back in fear because whatever is wrong must be corrected. Those who take early actions to correct mistakes will be in an active position, while those who delay action will be in a passive position. Mistakes must be replaced with what is right. If this is also termed as negation, then it is nothing more than the need to negate the old in order to create something new to perfect oneself. Moreover, this concerns not only the question of personal honor but also the interests of the party and the state. We should never recoil in fear out of personal selfishness.

2. The fear of undermining unity. There is no denying that the process of eliminating "leftism" usually involves the rights and wrongs of the comrades on certain important issues. However, this is not intended to ascribe personal responsibility but to right the wrongs so as to advance our common cause. As long as we can avoid disputes and work with a forward-looking principle, then we will not undermine unity. In contrast, instead of not being able to tell wrong from right, unifying understanding and emancipating the mind through the elimination of "leftism" is more conducive to the implementation of the policy of reform and opening up and economic development.

---

[3] A rather oblique reference to the possibility that party leaders and cadres who had ordered killings during the Cultural Revolution (1966–76) thereafter would be brought to justice under a regime led by reformers.

3. The fear of numerous changes in trends. Some comrades adopt a wait-and-see attitude and are hesitant about flushing out "leftism" because they are worried about another Anti-Rightist movement. This fear can easily be overcome. We need not be afraid if we do not promote rightism in the course of flushing out "leftism." It should be noted that both "leftism" and rightism have betrayed the party's basic line, and they will ruin socialism. Although we should guard against rightism, the principal danger comes from "leftism." Therefore, we may justifiably and forcefully flush out "leftism." It is inevitable that a few people have taken the opportunity to promote rightism and bourgeois liberalization. As such, we must not lower our guard. . . . If we cleanse away "leftism" and guard against rightism, there is no reason why we should not feel at ease and move forward boldly.

In reviewing the past, we note that everyone has had the experience of shaking off the restrictions of "leftism" as they continue to emancipate their mind. While still on the topic of "socialists" and "capitalists," the leftists tenaciously defended nonsocialists as if they were socialists and criticized noncapitalists as if they were capitalists. They also rejected, without exception, those who did not belong to either of the two groups. Many comrades had such "leftist" thoughts or committed such actions in the past. It looks rather childish now, but actually it is not. There was no existing model for socialist construction to follow. Thus, it was very natural that these thoughts and actions developed during the course of groping and moving from the realm of necessity to the realm of freedom. We did not, and should not, stop advancing because of these fears.

9
The CCP and China's Modernization:
Interview with He Xin

Wu Yuehui and Zhang Yijun

Source: Beijing, *Renmin ribao,* July 15, 1991, p. 5, *FBIS,* July 23, 1991.

On the occasion of the seventieth anniversary of the CCP founding [in July 1921], a middle-aged scholar said that the mass foundation on which the CCP depends for existence will be more extensive in the next ten years and it will maintain closer ties with the masses. In this sense, he believed that new developments will be attained in democracy within and outside the party. "But I do not believe that the CCP will make the democratic changes expected by the West," he insisted.

These remarks were made by He Xin, forty-two, a member of the National Committee of the Chinese People's Political Consultative Conference, in response to predictions by some Western analysts that the CCP will make "democratic changes" in the next decade. He said that most Western prophets do not have an adequate understanding of the conditions in China. Therefore, their predictions about China's future have always been off the mark.

Drastic and profound changes have taken place in China and the rest of the world over the past seventy years since the CCP founding, He Xin said. As a political party in the forefront of the trend of China's modern history, the CCP must make political, ideological, and organizational adjustments in the face of the changing trends worldwide. This calls for reform. In the past decade of reform and opening up, profound changes have taken place in the party.

When we mentioned the West's prediction of "peaceful evolution" in the CCP in the next decade, he said that the last ten years of this century will be very important for China. He said: "I also believe that the CCP will make profound changes in the next decade. Making no change would be strange. The problem is how to change and in what direction. There are many differences between my understanding of this question and those who predict 'peaceful evolution' in the CCP."

He Xin said that he has made painstaking efforts in studying CCP history. He believes that the party has created a brand new political tradition in Chinese history. The outstanding political characteristic of the party is that it has persisted in maintaining independence and following its own road based on China's specific conditions over the decades. This was the greatness of Mao Zedong Thought. The thesis of "building socialism with Chinese characteristics" advanced by Deng Xiaoping is a continuation of Mao Zedong Thought. Those who think that the CCP will blindly imitate others sooner or later have underestimated the political power of the party. A party like the CCP, which has tempered itself in internal and external political storms, will not collapse easily.

True, He Xin said, the party has made many mistakes during the past seventy years, but the party has always, in keeping with the new changes in history, taken the initiative to correct them while broadening its social base or the united front. The party is good at drawing both positive and negative lessons from history, making public its own mistakes, and even criticizing its own leadership, including Mao Zedong.[1]

It is undeniable that the development of currency and a commodity economy has brought about complications in both society and the party, such as the problem of corruption. However, he said, "according to my observations, most of the high-ranking Chinese leaders are statesmen who are honest in performing their duties, are law abiding, and wholeheartedly serve the people. They are not corrupt pursuers of privileges. Moreover, the problem of corruption cannot be resolved by mere wrath. The solution lies in the perfection of institutions, the rule of law, and reforms."

On the so-called question of "privileges," He Xin insisted: First, it is a universal practice to provide certain conveniences for state leaders in the performance of their official duties and their everyday lives. Second, the conveniences enjoyed by the high-ranking Chinese officials are quite limited and the gap between them and the ordinary citizens as far as living standards are concerned is comparatively narrow. He said that overseas media played up the problem. He Xin thinks that some of these stories were just political rumors and exaggerations. One of the reasons Mao Zedong launched the "Cultural Revolution" was to solve the problem of privileges of socialism (that is, "restricting the bourgeois rights"), but he did it by improper means and therefore it was not successful. . . . "Theoretically," he said, "officials in socialist countries, as servants of the people, should not pursue privileges. In reality, there are officials who abuse their power. But the abuse of power is restrained by our system and denounced as immoral." There were mistakes in this regard over the past few years and some leaders neglected to check the political morality of officials, he said, and this led to the money-oriented attitude of some officials, arousing strong public resentment. But, he said: "These officials actually accepted capitalist

---

[1]A reference to the *Resolution on CCP History* issued in 1981 that provided the official party line on Mao Zedong's mistakes and contributions to the communist movement in China.

values and violated socialist principles." He continued: "If you want to know about real privileges, let us take a look at the West. The privileges enjoyed by the U.S. presidency and the British royal family are unimaginable to ordinary people, not to mention those enjoyed by billionaires. All these privileges are regarded as being only right and proper under private ownership."

He Xin noticed strong public resentment toward the corrosion of politics by money and commodities, but he said that this is not a political phenomenon unique to China. Similar phenomena are frequently observed in other developing countries and are not rare in developed countries. Why has this aroused such strong social criticism in China? He Xin said that the criticism serves as a foil to show the honest and clean style upheld by the political tradition of the CCP.

10
There Is No Harm in Taking Over

Source: Chengdu, Sichuan Province, *Changzhang jingli ribao (Factory Director Management Daily),* April 24, 1993, p. 3, *FBIS,* May 19, 1993.

What should we learn from the West? This is an old and difficult question.

Of the world's civilizations, that of the Chinese nation once took the lead. Surprisingly, this was exaggerated by state administrators of the older generation, who said: Chinese civilization "benefits the barbarians" and all quarters of the world are coming "sincerely to be subjected to it" and "appeal for the heavenly grace." . . . We have dreamed the dream of superiority for several thousand years, but on how many occasions have we awakened and humbled ourselves to learn something from other countries?

Finally, a more powerful civilization finally came from the West to the East. In the first comparison, we found that ours had nearly become a fossil. It is understandable how puzzled we were, and yet our countermeasures were infuriating. Perhaps it is good for us to look up the old accounts.

Four hundred years ago, Matteo Ricci came to China with a map of the world. Since China was not placed in the center of the map and was far smaller than the Chinese had imagined, he was angrily condemned by orthodox mandarins.

Three hundred years ago, China's intellectuals compared traditional calendar mathematics with Western astronomical mathematics. And the Chinese lost at on-the-spot competitions and a typical figure, Yang Guangxian, made this "sensible remark": "In China, we would rather not have a good calendar than have Westerners!" Since then, Western science has been labeled a "devil."

Two hundred years ago, King George III of England sent an envoy, Lord Macartney, to negotiate trade with China. Upon his arrival, Chinese officials considered him an envoy who had come to pay tribute. Macartney repeatedly explained that Britain was not a vassal state of China and refused to kowtow to the Emperor Qianlong. This greatly infuriated the Chinese side.

The closed-door culture collapsed. The Westernization movement, which aimed to use the barbarians' strengths to keep the barbarians in check, failed. Consequently, on the afternoon of June 25, 1901, Chinese government troops burned the embassies of various Western countries in Beijing. They used this odd "declaration of war" to fan a xenophobic frenzy among the people to "help the Qing Dynasty [1644–1911] wipe out Westerners." As a result, it led to invasion and looting by the eight-power allied force. . . .

Fortunately, over the past fifty years, Western imperialism has not succeeded in its sinister omen of "saving itself from its approaching doom," and the newborn red regime has had no need to always say: "Prepare for war." Fortunately, we have come to a time of reform and opening up and the question of whether the economy should be capitalist or socialist has been emphatically settled. However, the question of what we should learn from the West has not been settled yet.

It is easy to say that we should filter out useless things, use things with judgment, absorb the strong points, and supplement weaknesses for our use. . . . But this does not have practical significance because it reflects the psychology of the former heavenly empire. Values and standards are our own, and the question of what to take and what to give up depends entirely on subjectivity. With one hand holding a pair of scissors and the other a sieve, one is ready to judge anything one does not see clearly. Although it is called importation, it has, in fact, labels affixed to it. If this continues it could end up in a bad way if importation does not go well.

Let us learn first how Westerners would ask the question. For example: Why should we learn from the West? Because developed industrial societies are models of modernization. Their current achievements with respect to civilization are the goal we want to achieve. Can we not learn from the West? No. So far, no other civilization has been worth learning from. So how and what should we learn?

The Japanese would answer the last question this way: Learn it all! They have done so without any doubt. Japan's success at least furnishes two pieces of historical evidence: It was guided by Western civilization first and modernized gradually, and then it changed to modernization supported by its own civilization. This is the practical way. Second, so-called wholesale Westernization did not cause the Japanese to lose their national character. Rather, their cultural traditions have been strengthened. So where did the Japanese get such courage at the beginning of their modernization? Because they came to understand that Western civilization is an inseparable whole, and that if they had to reject it, they had to reject it all. The tangible things are not important, but the intangible things are the very quintessence. . . . If we cannot find the proof directly, how then can we compare? In modern China, there was a giant thinker called Lu Xun. He left us with a famous plan, eclecticism. Ancient sages also left us a colorful methodological teaching: Aim high or you will fall below average.

What should we learn from the West? After all these thoughts, will we finally sum it up with the word—all?

C. Political Structure—Central

11
Democracy, Factions within the Party

Xi Guangqing

Source: Beijing, *Qiushi (Seeking Truth),*[1] #11, June 2, 1991, pp. 12–15, *FBIS,* July 23, 1991.

Making an earnest effort to implement democratic centralism[2] and to further extend and develop democracy within the party constitutes an important task of party-building during the new period. However, several years ago, when bourgeois liberalization spread unchecked, some people took over the slogan of developing democracy within the party and brazenly attacked our party's democratic centralism as "autocracy," asserting that only by allowing the presence of different factions and lines within the party, and enabling these factions to make known their position clearly and openly, will there be true democracy within the party. This view negates the democratic nature of the Marxist party, distorts the basic principle of democracy within the party, and sets the development of democracy within the party and the improvement of democratic centralism against each other. It has resulted in ideological confusion and interfered with the normal development of democracy within the party. Thus, we must clear up this erroneous and harmful viewpoint on the theoretical level.

Democracy within the party refers to the system that gives party members the right to partake in the management of party affairs and voice their opinions. It is a basic organizational system within the Marxist party. That the Marxist party must adhere to this system and

---

[1]The major theoretical organ of the CCP.

[2]A Leninist concept guiding the organization and activities of the Communist Party in which the minority is subordinate to the majority and the decisions of higher bodies are obligatory for lower-level party organs.

principle is something determined by its own nature and mission. The Marxist party is the vanguard of the working class, which is truly opposed to autocracy and oppression, and favors democracy, equality, and freedom. Thus, the Marxist party is, by nature, democratic rather than autocratic. . . . Marxism-Leninism is the theoretical basis of our party. It is an important ideological condition that enables our party to preserve its advanced nature and accomplish its mission. A basic trait of Marxism-Leninism is that it is not an ossified dogma, but is a scientific doctrine that develops with temporal changes and social progress. Its essence lies in the fact that it proceeds from reality and seeks truth from facts. Without democracy within the party, with its lively and free discussion and contention, and without a democratic atmosphere favorable to development and innovation, it will be impossible to closely combine Marxism with objective reality and develop Marxism. . . .

Another reason why a Marxist party must practice the system of inner-party democracy is that democracy within the party is an important component of the party's organizational principle, namely, democratic centralism, and is the basis of centralism within the party. As the organic combination of democracy and centralism, democratic centralism represents both centralism and democracy. In order to safeguard the party's unified fighting power, it is impossible not to have centralism within the party. However, this kind of centralism within the party must have democracy as its basis. The reason is that only democratically elected leading organs and leading members can truly represent the aspirations and wishes of the working class and the masses of the people, win the support of the whole party, and have true revolutionary authority. It is only by formulating and implementing the party's line, principle, and policies through collective and democratic discussion in specific organs that it is possible to truly pool the wisdom and experience of all people and enhance the scientific quality of the party's policy decisions. Only when the higher authorities of the party regularly listen to the views of the lower bodies and the party rank, exchange information, and discuss issues with them that the lower bodies and party members will be able to profoundly understand and conscientiously implement the resolutions of the higher authorities in the light of reality, thereby achieving true unity within the whole party. Only when the democratic rights of party members are respected and protected in real earnest, and when party members can make criticisms and suggestions to and exercise supervision over the party's leadership and work, will it be possible to truly enhance the sense of responsibility of the vast numbers of party members, arouse their enthusiasm, form a huge rallying force, and enhance the scientific quality of the party's policy decisions, thereby laying a solid foundation for the unity of will and action in the whole party. In short, only when democracy is fully developed will there be correct centralism, and it is only on the basis of a high degree of democracy that a high level of centralism can be truly achieved. It is particularly easy for party members and cadres in power to develop arrogance, conceit, and bureaucratic styles and divorce [themselves] from the masses and from reality. A few of them may even violate law and discipline, abuse their power for personal gain, practice graft, accept bribes, and become degenerate. This makes it all the more necessary for us to develop democracy within the party, strengthen criticism and supervision by the masses inside and outside the party from the bottom up, and make this a regular practice. . . .

As the party in power, our party is in a very good position to develop democracy within the party, and has done a lot in this connection. However, because of deviations in ideological consciousness, this question has not been resolved to our satisfaction for some time. Democratic life within the party was full of life in the first few years following the founding of the People's Republic [in 1949]. Later, because the development of democracy within the party was neglected, the personality cult began to grow.[3] As a result, power became over-concentrated, centralism was stressed at the expense of democracy, and inner-party democratic life became abnormal. During the Cultural Revolution [1966–76], in particular, democracy within the party was trampled underfoot, and this produced harmful consequences. At the [1978] Third Plenary Session, the party profoundly summed up the above historical lessons, made an earnest effort to put right the over-concentration of power and abnormalities in inner-party democratic life, and unequivocally took the extension and development of democracy within the party as an important task in improving democratic centralism in the new historical period. Through unremitting efforts, democracy was further developed within the party. However, because the development and strengthening of democracy within the party is a historical process, it is impossible to eliminate undemocratic practices

---

[3]A reference to Mao Zedong's increasingly autocratic leadership from 1949 onward, which generally mimicked the Stalin cult in Soviet Russia.

within the party overnight, and such practices may still be very serious in some localities and units. Thus, the development of democracy within the party is still an arduous task before us.

How can we extend and develop democracy within the party? Advocates of "the multifactional party system" suggested that the party should allow the presence of different factions and lines, and enable these factions to make known their stance clearly and openly. The Marxist party-building theory and practice tell us that the multifactional party system within the party not only cannot develop democracy within the party but will distort and undermine democracy within the party, and even fundamentally change the nature of the party as the vanguard of the working class.

First, because the practice of the multifactional party system will fundamentally change the nature of democracy within the party, it will also change the nature of the party. All forms of democracy have their distinct class nature. As the Marxist party is the vanguard of the working class, naturally democracy within the party cannot be anything but the democracy of the working class. This class nature means that democracy within the party must have the guiding line and unified organizational discipline of Marxism and the proletariat as its prerequisite. On the other hand, factions within the party invariably stick to their own program and principle and refuse to accept the party's unified theory, line, and organizational discipline. Inner-party democracy without a common prerequisite means different factions pursuing their own propositions and remolding party "democracy" in their own image. The history of the international communist movement has proved time and again that the Marxist party that pursued this kind of inner-party democracy would degenerate into an opportunistic party and would even go along with the bourgeois party in its evil deeds.

Second, the practice of the multifactional party system is bound to undermine normal democratic life within the party and sound the death bell for genuine democracy within the party. Applying the Marxist party-building theory, the proletarian party has developed its own scientific criteria for inner-party democracy on the basis of summing up its own practical experience and assimilating the fruits of modern democracy. These include: the party's leadership organs and leading members should be democratically elected on the whole; major party issues should be collectively and democratically discussed and decided on by specific organs; there should be collective leadership in leading organs of the party;[4] the democratic rights of party members must be respected and protected. The practice of democracy within the party shows that only by truly adhering to these criteria and continuously improving them in the course of practice can we develop and protect normal democratic life within the party. If the multifactional party system is practiced and opposition factions are allowed within the party, not only party members but also party organizations will be subject to the restrictions and control of factional principles. When everything revolves around factional principles and factional interests, it will be very difficult to correctly adhere to the scientific criteria of inner-party democracy, and normal democratic life within the party will suffer.

Third, the practice of the multifactional party system not only cannot achieve the true goal of developing democracy within the party, but may turn it into a means of destroying inner-party democracy. The development of democracy within the party has never been the goal. It is just the means to an end. Its starting point and foothold is to fully arouse the enthusiasm and creativeness of party organizations at various levels as well as the entire party rank, pool their correct opinions, and achieve a high degree of party unity. This has always been an important criterion for measuring the development of democracy within the Marxist party. When the multifactional party system is practiced and different factions are allowed within the party, the solid and unified party is bound to split into many parallel and opposing organizations. There will be several leadership cores instead of a unified leadership, and the whole party will be caught up in meaningless factional squabbles or irreconcilable struggles. Under the circumstances, it is futile to talk about giving full scope to the enthusiasm and creativeness of the whole party, strengthening its political, ideological, and organizational unity, and enhancing its fighting power and rallying force. Not only that. Practice has proved that under the attack of enemies both from within and from without, the party is bound to fall apart and head toward destruction. Thus, when Lenin criticized factional activities inside the Russian Communist Party in 1921, he sharply pointed out: "All factional activities are harmful and cannot be tolerated because even if the representative persons of particular fac-

---

[4]The notion that no one single leader should rule the Communist Party autocratically.

tions really desire to maintain the unity of the party, factional activities will still undermine concerted efforts and enable enemies who have sneaked into the party to step up activities aimed at further splitting the party and, through these splits, to realize their counterrevolutionary aims" (*Selected Works of Lenin*, vol. 4, p. 478). In short, theory and practice both prove that the so-called multifactional party system not only is not a theory for the development of democracy within the party, but is a theory that directly harms and undermines inner-party democracy.

It must also be pointed out that agitating for the multifactional party system under the signboards of developing democracy within the party is tantamount to transplanting the multifactional party system of the bourgeois party into our party and turning our party into a bourgeois party. The Marxist party-building theory tells us that in modern society, all parties are political representatives of particular classes, and they structure their organization and launch activities according to the interests and wishes of their respective classes. As the political representative of the bourgeoisie, the bourgeois party shoulders the mission of protecting the rule of the minority capitalist class. The very nature of the bourgeoisie as a class that goes after superprofit, however, means that inside this class there are inevitably different strata, cliques, and factions with conflicting interests. This determines the existence of several political parties within the bourgeoisie, and that there are several rival factions within each political party. Meanwhile, the bourgeois party must also make use of such disguises as the multiparty system and the multifactional system to hide the essence of its monopoly rule. The objective position of the working class in modern society means that it has unified interests, common ideals, collectivism, a high degree of organizational discipline, and other special qualities. Other than fighting for the interests of the working class and the masses of the people, the communist party, which has struck deep roots in this class, does not have any interests of its own. Thus, it can become a consolidated, strong, and great party with ideological, political, and organizational unity. Any attempt to obliterate the essential distinction between the party of the working class and the party of the bourgeoisie and advocate introducing the multifactional party system of the bourgeois party into our party, whatever the subjective motive, will only turn our party into a bourgeois party and make it lose its nature as the vanguard of the working class. . . .

In order to further develop democracy within the party, we must find out the real causes of our mistakes. What is the cause, then? Some people think that the cause lies in democratic centralism. Hence they want to abolish democratic centralism. We cannot subscribe to this view. To begin with, this does not tally with facts. Seen from the history of our party over the past seventy years, the development of democracy within the party has been normal and fine most of the time. The reason is that we have correctly implemented democratic centralism. It is also through reliance on democratic centralism that our party has been able to put right various mistakes, even the grave mistake of the Cultural Revolution [1966–1976], and once again embark on the correct road. Second, the reason why democracy within our party is underdeveloped, even seriously undermined, is manifold and complicated. Still, the main reason is that the party's democratic centralism has not been implemented in real earnest and has sometimes been undermined. The development of democracy within the party and the improvement of democratic centralism are not antagonistic, but unified. Thus, democratic centralism does not pose any obstacle to democracy within the party, it protects democracy within the party. . . .

12
Consciously Maintain the Party's Authority

Chen Yeping

Source: Beijing, *Qiushi,* #20, October 16, 1991, pp. 11–16, *FBIS,* December 10, 1991.

Comrade Li Peng [State Premier] said in a meeting with foreign guests: "The central collective leadership, with Comrade Jiang Zemin as the nucleus, has smoothly accomplished the transition of power in China. This is a strong and authoritative leadership that ensures long-term stability. Under this leadership, the basic political line and the policy of reform and opening to the outside world formulated by Deng Xiaoping will be carried through into the future." Under the new situation at home and abroad, we must earnestly study the Marxist view of authority and consciously maintain the party's authority, particularly the authority of the central collective leadership. This will be of immense significance in strengthening party building, enhancing the party's fighting capacity in an all-around way, strengthening and improving the party's leadership, and successfully building socialism with Chinese characteristics.

In his 1873 article entitled "On Authority," Engels gave a detailed exposition of the Marxist view of authority with Bakunin's anarchism in mind. He pointed out: "Here, authority refers to the imposition of other people's views on us. On the other hand, authority also presupposes subordination" (*Selected Works of Marx and Engels,* vol. 2, p. 551). In different historical periods, authority is exercised by different classes. At a time when the exploiting class is in a ruling position, the interests represented by the authority are the interests of the ruling class, which stand fundamentally opposed to the interests of the exploited and oppressed peoples. This kind of authority can only be maintained through coercive measures. After the seizure of state power by the proletariat, the interests represented by the authority are the interests of the proletariat and all laboring people. The maintenance of this authority means the maintenance of its fundamental interests. Thus, among the people this authority is established on the basis of conscious subordination. Only hostile forces or people without any awareness would resort to coercion. The meaning and function of the authority of the proletariat find expression in political and economic management and in certain spheres and aspects of social management and ideological theories.

In the political sphere, authority is primarily something indispensable to the party system of the proletariat. Engels pointed out: "Without compelling certain people to accept the will of others, that is, without authority, there will not be any concerted action. Be they the wishes of the majority of voters, the wishes of committees that function as leading organs, or the wishes of individuals, they are wishes imposed on people who hold differing opinions. However, without these wishes, which are unified and are of guiding significance, it is impossible to achieve any kind of cooperation" (*Selected Works of Marx and Engels,* vol. 4, p. 397). There must be unified wishes within a proletarian organization, and a proletarian party must practice democratic centralism and strict discipline. These are the basis for the party to improve its organizational system and political life. Our party is the core of leadership of all Chinese people. In order to unite the entire working class and the people of all nationalities in waging a guided and organized struggle, we must first of all build our party into a strong core of leadership that is highly centralized and unified both ideologically and politically while being highly unified in action. This means that we must establish, in our organizational system and political life, a kind of authority that requires every party organization and party member to submit to the party Central Committee. Thus, the Party Constitution stipulates that individual party members are subordinate to the party organization, the minority is subordinate to the majority, the lower party organizations are subordinate to the higher party organizations, and all the constituent organizations and members of the party are subordinate to the National Congress and the Central Committee of the party. Unlike bourgeois parties, which encompass factions that represent the interests of different groups of capitalists, all the constituent organizations and members of our party fight for the fundamental interests of the proletariat and the entire populace. There are no inevitable conditions for the birth of factions, and factional activities will not be tolerated. Our party has all along opposed the mountain-stronghold mentality,[1] sectarianism, liberalism, and other undesirable tendencies that may weaken the central authority, and has waged resolute struggles against splittism of every description, thereby ensuring the authority of the Central Committee in leading the revolutionary wars, so that the cause of the Chinese revolution can develop, both in scope and in intensity, from defeat to final victory. If, contrary to this, we allowed the development of tendencies that might weaken the central authority, the revolutionary ranks would most certainly disintegrate, with each doing things his own way. This way, we would not only be unable to join forces to defeat the enemy, but would be crushed by the enemy one by one.

In the political sphere, authority also finds expression as an important means with which the proletariat seizes political power and maintains its political rule. Engels pointed out: "Revolution is no doubt the most authoritative thing on earth. Revolution means that some people use guns, bayonets, and cannons, in other words, extremely authoritative means, to force others to accept their wishes. If the winning party does not want to lose the achievements it fought so hard for, it must

---

[1] Party leaders who create insular organizational and political bailiwicks independent of central control.

maintain its rule by capitalizing on the fear produced by weapons among the reactionaries. Had the [1871] Paris Commune not relied on the authority of the armed people who fought the bourgeoisie, could it have lasted more than one day? Conversely, do we not have reasons to blame the Commune for not making sufficient use of this authority?" (*Selected Works of Marx and Engels,* vol. 2, p. 554). This is the case with the seizure of political power, and the same is true with the consolidation of political power. This is a scientific conclusion drawn from the summing up of experience in the proletarian revolution. As a state under the people's democratic dictatorship, China must maintain the authority of democracy and the legal system. It must not allow the unchecked spread of anarchism, or the presence of the "liberty" to oppose the CCP leadership or socialism. Around the spring and summer of 1989, people who stubbornly clung to the stand of bourgeois liberalization ignored this authority in engineering turmoil and counterrevolutionary rebellion in their vain attempt to disrupt the political order of socialism, overthrow the government, and seize power. At this critical juncture, the party Central Committee and State Council resolved to quell the counterrevolutionary rebellion in a single move. At that time, some well-intentioned people failed to see the necessity of checking the turmoil and quelling the counterrevolutionary rebellion. However, following the development of events at home and abroad, more and more people have come to see that although exploiting classes have been wiped out as classes following the basic completion of the socialist transformation of the means of production, class struggle will continue to exist within given limits for a long time to come and may even intensify under given conditions. Thus, "revolution" as "the most authoritative thing on earth" not only cannot be weakened or done away with, but must be maintained and strengthened. It is precisely the authority of revolution that has enabled us to win a victory in checking and quelling the turmoil and counterrevolutionary rebellion and save the people's republic.

The Marxist View of Authority and the Personality Cult

There is an essential difference between the Marxist view of authority and the personality cult. Consciously maintaining the authority of the collective leadership of the party Central Committee has theories of historical materialism on the relations between the masses, classes, political parties, and their leaders as its basis. Lenin pointed out: "The masses are divided into classes. . . . Classes are usually led by political parties; political parties are usually run by fairly stable groups made up of the most authoritative, influential, and experienced people called leaders who are elected to the most important offices" (*Selected Works of Lenin,* vol. 4, p. 197). The historical mission of the proletariat can be realized only through highly conscious revolutionary movements, and this task has a lot to do with the party of the proletariat and its leaders. Without leaders, the struggle of the proletariat will slip into a state of spontaneity, fumbling around, and laxness. Thus, no class in history could have achieved dominance unless it was able to choose political leaders and advanced representatives who were good at organizing and leading movements. This is particularly true with the proletariat, which shoulders a great historical mission.

Our party's first, second, and third generations of central collective leadership with Mao Zedong, Deng Xiaoping, and Jiang Zemin as the nuclei are political leaders chosen by the Chinese proletariat to organize and lead revolution and construction. The victory of the Chinese revolution and the tremendous successes of construction have been achieved under their leadership. Thus, consciously maintaining the authority of the central collective leadership is where the fundamental interests of the whole party and the whole nation lie. In order to draw a clear line of demarcation between the Marxist view of authority and the personality cult, we must prevent problems in two respects.

First, we must maintain the authority of the party's central collective leadership, maintain the authority of the leaders (the individual leaders), and oppose anarchist tendencies to negate all authorities. Historical materialism maintains that the masses create history. This basic viewpoint not only does not deny the role of individuals in historical development, but intrinsically embodies affirmation of the individual role of historical figures and proletarian leaders. The historical mission of the proletariat can be accomplished only through highly conscious revolutionary movements, and this task has a lot to do with the leadership of the party and its leaders. Without leaders, mass struggle will slip into a state of spontaneity, fumbling around and laxness. . . . After the [1978] Third Plenary Session, our party conscientiously summed up its experience since the founding of the PRC and adopted a series of major measures to eliminate the personality cult. "The party forbids all forms of personality cult" was written into the party constitution adopted by the [September 1981] Twelfth CCP National Congress as one of the basic principles of democratic centralism. Confused and poisoned by anarchist ideas, some people distorted this stipulation made in the party constitution and denied all authorities. After the "Cultural Revolution" [1966–76], some people with ulterior motives stirred up trouble by availing themselves of the opportunity afforded by the call to rectify mistakes of the personality cult to fan the anarchist trend of thought and negate the Four Cardinal Principles. . . . To historical materialists, maintaining the authority of leaders is in complete agreement with opposition to the personality cult. We must value the role of leaders without exaggerating it. We must respect leaders and maintain their authority while opposing the personality cult and the deification of individuals.

Second, we must see through theoretical propositions that peddle personal dictatorship under all sorts of signboards. A few years ago, a trend of thought that called itself "neo-authoritarianism" created an uproar for some time. Its basic stand was: In the process of modernization, the liberalization of the economy can be realized only through the centralization of political power. For this reason, reform in the political sphere should mainly be realized through necessary centralization and monopoly of political power, rather than through the further promotion of socialist democracy. Its essence lay in stressing the authority of decisions made by the elites. The power of conducting, regulating, controlling, and adjudicating cases in political life was vested in a handful of "political elites," particularly Comrade Zhao Ziyang, who was in charge of the Central Committee at that time. "Neo-authoritarianism" has nothing in common with the Marxist view of authority. Its fundamental objective is to establish a bourgeois dictatorship in the name of democratic politics to suit the needs of the capitalist economy of the West. It rejects true democracy, establishes the "authority" of a handful of "political elites," and advocates doing things according to their desire to develop capitalism.[2] . . . The fact that the backbone force that advocated "neo-authoritarianism" turned out to be the backbone force that incited anarchism during the turmoil and rebellion of 1989 was convincing proof. . . . We must oppose the unbridled fostering of the absolute authority and personality cult of individual leaders while opposing anarchism, which denies all authority.

---

[2] "Neo-authoritarianism" was advocated by many democratic elites who believe tough measures are necessary to remove politcal and cultural obstacles to democracy in China.

13

Take Insistence on Reform and Opening Up as Main Criterion for Political Integrity

Zhu Zilin

Source: Beijing, *Gongren ribao (Worker's Daily),* July 3, 1992, p. 3, *FBIS,* July 23, 1992.

Comrade Deng Xiaoping's speeches during his [February 1992] southern inspection tour point out: "A correct organizational line must be relied on to guarantee a correct political line," "the key, in a sense, lies in man." "It is necessary to foster man and to select people with both ability and political integrity for leadership groups in accordance with the criterion of 'being more revolutionary, younger, better educated, and more professionally competent.' We say that our party's basic line must operate for 100 years to ensure long-term good order and peace, and we must rely on this." Enterprise cadre quality has a bearing on the enterprises' future and destiny; in the course of reforming the cadre system and the enterprises, the enterprises should and must build a force of cadres that will adhere to the party's basic line, make the party rest assured, enjoy the masses' trust, and rejuvenate the enterprises.

In his speeches, Comrade Deng Xiaoping reiterated his remarks made at the end of May 1989: "We must now select those who people generally recognize as adhering to the line of reform and opening up and have made achievements in their official careers, and we must boldly place them in the new leadership organs to enable the people to feel that we are genuinely and sincerely embarking on reform and opening up." Here, Comrade Deng Xiaoping stressed the criterion for cadres, the mass line, and the necessity to emancipate the mind. This ought to be a guiding principle for doing a good job in reforming the cadre system and implementing the cadre line of "appointing people on their merits."

The cadres must have both ability and political integrity. Political integrity is "adhering to the line of reform and opening up." Reform and opening up are ways to make the country powerful and enrich the people, a hope of invigorating the nation, and our party's only choice.

Only by being determined to carry out reform and insisting on opening up can we perfect and develop socialism. Therefore, the attitude adopted toward reform and opening up now is an important criterion for measuring whether a cadre has political integrity or not. Ability means having achievements in one's official career. Achievements in one's official career are the comprehensive embodiment of the quality in the aspects of knowledge, wisdom, ability, and work style. Ability must be measured by achievements in one's official career. Whether or not the criterion for measuring a cadre with both ability and political integrity can be insisted on is the key to success or failure in reforming the cadre system. Everything will be spoiled if one's individual tastes are taken as a criterion; if people are appointed by favoritism; if we indulge in the practice that when one becomes an official, one's people, whoever they may be, will benefit; if we form a faction, a clique, or get a few people to band together; or if one is promoted because of seniority in disregard of talented people. The formula: 10 minus 1 equals 0 of Yu Zhian, director of Wuhan Steamship Generator Plant, is applicable here. If one has 10 parts of power in one's hand and uses one part to pursue private ends, all one's power will be forfeited before long and reform certainly will also be ruined.

The mass line is the basic line of all the party's work; to reform the cadre system, it is also essential to take the mass line. Whether or not a cadre has both ability and political integrity must be "generally recognized by the people" and "the people must be enabled to feel that we genuinely and sincerely embark on reform and opening up." Reforming the cadre system is an extremely important reform as well as an important policy matter, and the workers are very sensitive to this. We must change the previous method of making a mystery of personnel work, trust the masses, rely on them, ask them to supervise our work, and allow them to examine our work. Some enterprises that carry out a pilot project of selecting and appointing cadres must adopt the measures and methods of making the selection and appointment conditions known to the public, offering equal opportunity, carrying on fair competition, developing the practice of self-recommendation and democratic election, conducting public opinion polls, and discussion and decision by a party and government joint meeting so that people can draw from their successful experiences in reforming the cadre system.

Difficulties in reforming the cadre system are very great, and obstacles mainly come from outmoded concepts that shackle people's minds. Therefore, it is imperative to emancipate the mind and to be "bold" and resolute. People's political integrity and ability are relative, and there is no "perfect" and "versatile person." It is necessary to establish a correct view of talented people. Comrade Mao Zedong said: A person has both strong and weak points and merits and demerits in his disposition and habits. We must not pay attention to one in disregard of the other. Only by knowing the strong and weak points of people, being good at appointing them, and not being skeptical about them can we ensure that "the brave devote their energy, the wise do their best to offer advice, the reporters spread the benefits, and those with political integrity pledge loyalty."

When the cadre system is reformed well and those the people generally recognize as adhering to the line of reform and opening up and having scored achievements in their official career are boldly placed in the leadership organs, the enterprises stand a very good chance of take-off and our country will be full of promise.

14
Leadership Should Be Put Firmly in Hands of Loyal Marxists

Zhao Ziping

Source: Beijing, *Qiushi,* #15, August 1, 1992, *FBIS,* September 16, 1992.

Ensuring that leadership is held in the hands of people faithful to Marxism is a major issue that ensures that our country will always advance along the road of building socialism with Chinese characteristics. At present, ensuring that the leadership is held by people faithful to Marxism is mainly an issue of ensuring that leading cadres at all levels conscientiously, faithfully, and resolutely carry out the party's basic line of "one center, two basic points."[1]

Since the [1978] Third Plenary Session, our party has formulated a basic line, which is "taking economic construction as the central task, adhering to the Four Cardinal Principles, and persistently carrying out reform and opening up." This basic line represents Comrade Deng Xiaoping's theory about building socialism with Chinese characteristics. It is the ideological achievement in the combination of Marxism with our country's actual conditions and the brilliant fruit of our efforts to emancipate our minds and to seek truth from facts. The practice of reform and opening in the past more than ten years has shown that the basic line is suited to our national conditions and complies with the people's wishes.

After the political line is established, cadres form a decisive factor. A person loyal to Marxism must rather deeply understand and master the party's basic line and, in particular, should more profoundly and comprehensively understand the viewpoint that reform is also the emancipation of productive forces recently put forward by the party central leadership. Only thus can he or she have higher political consciousness and stronger organizational ability to implement the basic line. We should develop productive forces under the socialist conditions and should also emancipate productive forces through reform. That is, the two sides of developing and emancipating productive forces should be properly integrated. People constitute the most active factor in productive forces, so it is necessary to fully arouse people's work enthusiasm and initiative and reasonably bring them into play. This requires that leading cadres follow the basic principles of Marxism and do creative work to mobilize and organize the masses, conduct propaganda among them, and lead them in working hard to carry out the party's basic line. The leading cadres should also coordinate people's relations; solve problems in people's minds; resolve various contradictions; and encourage the broad masses of people to boost their spirit, emancipate their minds, unburden their minds, take the initiative in putting the party's line,

---

[1]Enunciated at the 1987 Thirteenth Party Congress by the then CCP General Secretary Zhao Ziyang, this policy line called for taking economic construction as the primary goal (the "one center"), while adhering to reform and opening up to the outside world and maintaining the Four Cardinal Principles and opposition to bourgeois liberalization (the "two basic points").

principles, and policies consciously into practice, and devote themselves to the great practice of deepening reform and expanding openness.

The party's basic line is of across-the-board and long-term guiding significance. The so-called across-the-board guiding significance means that the concrete principles and policies in the economic, political, ideological, and cultural fields should all be based on it and should take it as the general guiding principle. The so-called long-term guiding significance means that the party's basic line will be in force throughout the whole initial stage of socialism, for as long as 100 years. In this historical stage, some of the concrete principles and policies in some fields may be revised, replenished, and improved according to developments in the situation; some may have to be rescinded as they are no longer suited to the changing new situation. However, the basic line is relatively stable and will remain invariable for at least 100 years. The long-term guiding significance of the basic line reflects the prolonged nature of the initial stage of socialism and the arduousness of the tasks in this period. A leading cadre faithful to Marxism should now master the revolutionary theory of dialectics, closely link theory with practice, faithfully perform his own duties, keep the overall situation and interests in his mind, have foresight, and follow the across-the-board and long-term guidance of the basic line. Only thus can he always adhere to the foothold of "one center, two basic points" in his work practice of leading reform and construction, always grasp the central link of economic construction, and orient the work in all fields to the central link and make it serve the central link. Only thus can he have an integrated and congruent understanding of various concrete principles and policies and grasp their intrinsic relations and be more conscious and less blind in his work. In the course of implementing the party's basic line, disruption may come from both "leftist" and rightist ideologies. Leaving the party and state leadership at all levels in the hands of people faithful to Marxism and conscious in adhering to the party's basic line is the organizational guarantee for preventing and overcoming the erroneous deviations.

In order to ensure that the party and state leadership is held in the hands of people faithful to Marxism, it is necessary to properly effect the following points in our work.

• Under the prerequisite of putting cadres under the party's management, through the reform of the cadre and personnel system, selecting cadres with a firm political position and with the determination to break fresh ground in their work and appointing them to leading posts at all levels. The principle of putting cadres under the party's management means that under the unified leadership of the Central Committee and party committees at various levels, cadres are managed in different ways and at different levels according to a whole set of principles, policies, standards, and methods for training, assessing, and appointing cadres. This system took form in the prolonged revolutionary struggle and nurtured a large number of leaders for the party, the government, and the army. Its correctness has been proved in history and must be maintained. Under the new historical conditions, the party set out the "four requirements" for the cadre contingent. Useful explorations and reforms were carried out in some concrete aspects of the cadre and personnel system. For example, the authority of cadre management was devolved to an appropriate degree; the overall management of the cadre and personnel work was strengthened; major cadres were recommended to the government and other departments; the election system and appointment system were reformed; the system of openly inviting applications for some leading posts was adopted on a trial basis; the post responsibility and assessment system for cadres was established; the system of lifetime office tenure for cadres was abolished; the cadre exchange and evasion system was established; leading cadres were nominated and assessed in a democratic way; and the structure of leading bodies and the quality of leading cadres were improved. All this represents the achievements of such explorations and reforms. Reforming and improving the cadre and personnel system is aimed at better selecting and appointing cadres who are faithful to Marxism, fully and accurately carry out the party's basic line, and pursue reform and openness to the leading bodies of the party and the state at various levels. For this purpose, we should continue to adhere to the "four requirements" for the cadre contingent and adhere to the standard of having both political integrity and work ability. There exists organic congruence between political integrity and work ability and between the revolutionary character on the one hand and being young in average age, well educated, and professionally competent on the other. Neither side can be neglected. The leadership of the party and the state at various levels cannot be held by people without political integrity and revolutionary character. At the same time, if one only has the desire to serve the people but lacks the ability to serve, one is still an incompetent cadre. If the locality or the department being governed by a leading cadre cannot create a new situation in its work and cannot improve its work over a long time, and if the masses there are unsatisfied, then he must not be a qualified leading cadre. At present, it is necessary to quicken reform of the cadre and personnel system and to select and promote more cadres with both political integrity and work ability, being both red and expert[2] with courage and insight, being regarded by common consent as persisting in reform and opening up, and having made solid achievements in their work at the leading posts at all levels.

• Strengthening the work of giving training and education to the cadre contingent and improving the ideological style of the leading bodies. At present, the level of mastering Marxist theory by many leading cadres is still far from meeting the requirements laid down by the central leadership and is still not commensurate with the leadership responsibilities they are shouldering. Some young cadres who were promoted to leading positions at various levels in recent years have not yet received systematic theoretical training on Marxism. How can a cadre who does not earnestly study Marxist theory master the basic principles of Marxism and become a person faithful to Marxism, and how can they properly exercise the leadership of the party and the government? Therefore, raising the cadres' Marxist theoretical level is a pressing task that brooks no delay for the time being. Systematic education in ideological theory should be conducted among leading cadres at all levels so that they can be prompted to conscientiously study the basic principles of Marxism and the works by Comrade Mao Zedong and Comrade Deng Xiaoping; can better understand the theory about building socialism with Chinese characteristics and the basic line of "one center, two basic points"; and can adhere to the principle of combining theory with practice and apply Marxism to analyze and resolve problems appearing in the course of economic construction, reform, and opening up. . . .

---

[2]The ideal enunciated during the Maoist period of striking a balance between technical competence and political loyalty.

15
Deng Xiaoping Orders "Fusion" of Party, Government

Willy Wo-lap Lam

Source: Hong Kong, *South China Morning Post*, April 1, 1993, p. 13, *FBIS*, April 1, 1993.

Patriarch Mr. Deng Xiaoping has laid down new edicts for consolidating the Communist Party leadership, most of which have been endorsed by the National People's Congress.

Chinese sources said that Mr. Deng had given instructions on the "fusion of party and government," or senior party leaders playing significant roles in the government and in the legislature.

Moreover, the patriarch had again warned that if corruption could not be stemmed, the Communist Party might be "adulterated."

The sources said that while up to the party congress in 1987 Mr. Deng had agreed to the principle of "the separation of party and government,"[1] the patriarch now thought it advisable for top party leaders to concurrently hold government and legislative positions.

"Deng thinks that one reason for the atrophy of the Communist Party of the former Soviet Union was that Soviet apparatchiks were cut off from day-to-day administration and economic policy making," a source said.

"The patriarch thinks that for the party to thrive, it must take an active part in government and in the market economy."

For example, it was Mr. Deng who decided late last year to confer upon party chief Mr. Jiang Zemin the position of state president as well as head of the military commission.

Upon Mr. Jiang's election as head of state last weekend, the Chinese media pointed out that it would now be more convenient for the party chief to take part in government decision making and to represent China on overseas visits.

---

[1] A central plank in the reform program, "separation of party and government" called for ending direct CCP control of the various ministries and state organs by abolishing the ubiquitous system of "party groups" in the state bureaucracy and allowing nonparty government officials greater leeway in decision making.

In the middle of last year, the patriarch also decided that party units and senior cadres could run businesses on the side.

According to the China-watching journal *The Mirror* [published in Hong Kong], Mr. Deng has asked the new congress and judicial organs to pay special attention to fighting corruption.

"If the working style (of the party) continues to deteriorate, what good will it do even if economic construction is successful?" he asked.

Mr. Deng added that if corruption among cadres persisted, "the nature of the entire economy would be adulterated, and a world marked by corruption, theft, and influence peddling would come into being."

Interviews given by congress deputies to the official media, however, show that not all legislators share Mr. Deng's conservative political ideas.

The semiofficial Hong Kong China News Agency has reported that many deputies are worried about the prospects of reform.

16
1941 Deng Speech on One-Party Rule Suppressed

Willy Wo-lap Lam

Source: Hong Kong, *South China Morning Post*, February 17, 1990, p. 12, *FBIS*, February 18, 1990.

Chinese authorities are suppressing an old Deng Xiaoping speech that attacks one-party dictatorship.

In a speech entitled "The Party and the Anti-Japanese Democratic Regime," which was delivered in April 1941, Mr. Deng criticized the practice of "the (Chinese Communist) Party running the country."

Excerpts from the speech, which has been held under lock and key in the Central Committee's Party History Research Office, have been carried in the just-published issue of *Contemporary*, a Hong Kong–based China-watching weekly.

According to *Contemporary*, Mr. Deng's old speech formed the major theoretical basis for ousted party chief Zhao Ziyang's efforts in 1987 and 1988 to introduce political reform.

"After Zhao fell out of favor, (Beijing) has forbidden the speech to be disseminated, in order to avoid its being put in a passive position," the weekly said.

In the speech, which was given to a group of senior party cadres, Mr. Deng argued for the separation of party and government and for a higher degree of "participation by the masses."

"The mentality among some comrades of using the party to run the country is a concrete manifestation of the rotten tradition of the Kuomintang [the Nationalist Party] being reflected in our party," Mr. Deng said.

Mr. Deng, then a thirty-six-year-old political commissar of a major People's Liberation Army unit, said that the concept of "party supremacy" had led to the CCP being isolated from the people.

"Some comrades have developed the concept of 'the party above all else' into 'party members above all else,'" he said. This had led to party members committing all sorts of misdemeanors.

Mr. Deng also pointed out that the practice of party cadres "making decisions on complex policies behind closed doors" and "regarding noncommunist cadres and the masses as puppets" would "necessarily" result in errors.

He pointed out that the CCP's role should be confined to the formulation of "political principles" and that it should not interfere in the work of the government.

The 1941 speech constituted one of the earliest pleas for democracy made by CCP elders.

"The benefits of democratic politics reside in the fact that it can reflect the opinions of various classes in good time, and that it enables us to consider correctly and carefully how to solve problems," he said.

Many of the points made by Mr. Deng in 1941 were enshrined in Mr. Zhao Ziyang's Political Report to the Thirteenth Party Congress of late 1987, which analysts consider as the high-water mark of political reform in China.

After the June 4 Tiananmen Square crackdown, the CCP reissued old works by Mr. Deng as well as his unpublished writings.

Most of these works, however, deal with the importance of "combating bourgeois liberalization."

Chinese sources say that, aside from the 1941 speech, Mr. Deng has also spoken out in favor of democratization and the separation of party and government in internal addresses throughout the years.

The sources say that after Mr. Deng has condemned reforms made by the Soviet President, Mr. Mikhail Gorbachev, it is most unlikely that the patriarch will allow his "liberal" articles and speeches to be published.

17
Commenting on the Fallacy of "Depoliticizing the Army"

Zheng Nianqun

Source: Beijing, *Jiefangjun bao (Liberation Army Daily)*, August 14, 1990, p. 3, *FBIS*, September 17, 1990.

Bourgeois liberalization "elitists" regarded the Chinese People's Liberation Army [PLA] as their biggest obstacle in the pursuit of capitalism in China, and before and after they provoked that counterrevolutionary rebellion in Beijing last year, they tried in every possible way to vilify and attack the army, forward a reactionary proposition on "depoliticizing the army," and advocate that the party should be separated from the army, the army should remain "neutral" in political struggle, the army should not deal with internal affairs, and so on. We must expose and criticize these fallacies.

The Crucial Point Is to Oppose and Negate the Party's Absolute Leadership over the Army

While preaching "multipartism," those who adhere to bourgeois liberalization say that a crucial question of the Communist Party's reform is the "separation of the party from the Army"; in the course of the turmoil and rebellion, their prominent figures publicly proposed to "abolish the Central Military Commission" and to "abolish the party branches of all organizations and the Army" and said that the

"Army is the state's army and the people's army but not the army of your Communist Party alone." They set the party against the state and set the party against the Army in a vain attempt to use the "nationalization of the Army" to negate the party's absolute leadership over the Army. This is their motive for preaching the "depoliticization of the Army."

It is an important principle of Army building to persist in the party's absolute leadership over the Army. Comrade Mao Zedong clearly and definitely pointed out: Our principle is that the party commands the gun and the gun must never be allowed to command the party. Since our Army was founded, it has been under the party's absolute leadership and has struggled hard to implement the party's programs and line. Prior to liberation, our Army fought a protracted bloody battle to implement the party's minimum program—overthrowing domination by imperialism, feudalism, and bureaucratic capitalism; after the seizure of state power [in 1949], our Army combated foreign aggression, consolidated state power at home, struggled hard to carry out the party's maximum program—pursuing socialism and communism—and guaranteed the smooth progress of the socialist revolution and construction. Our party's nature and historical mission and the nature of our Army as a people's army have determined that our Army must be unconditionally placed under the CCP's absolute leadership. In the course of our Army's development—centered on the issue of party leadership over the Army—the party Central Committee waged a protracted and unremitting struggle against all erroneous acts of weakening party leadership and all plots in an attempt to abolish party leadership over the Army, upheld the party's absolute leadership over the Army, and guaranteed our Army's proletarian quality. Recently the party Central Committee and Central Military Commission have repeatedly emphasized the party's absolute leadership over the Army; this has been proposed in light of the revolutionary tradition of our party leadership over the people and on the basis of the new characteristics of the international and domestic class struggles and the special mission entrusted to the Army in the new historical period. At present, our party's ability to unswervingly exercise absolute leadership over the Army has a bearing on the important issues of whether or not our Army can be forever politically qualified and of whether or not our country can be in good order and secure permanently. . . .

The Army's Function of Consolidating
State Power at Home Brooks No Negation

Another important argument for the "depoliticization of the Army" is that the Army's function is "merely resisting foreign aggression." During last year's turmoil, some prominent bourgeois liberalization figures did their utmost to oppose the troops entering the city and enforcing martial law and said: "Why do the troops come to Beijing instead of going to the Laoshan front [near Vietnam] to fight?" and "The Army is meant to resist foreign aggression and Beijing is not a frontier." They set the Army's function of resisting foreign aggression against its function of consolidating state power at home.

As is known to all, the Army is the product of class struggle. As an important component of the state machine, the Army has had the function of dealing with internal affairs since it came into being. Before the seizure of state power, the Army's task was to defeat the hostile class through armed struggle; after the seizure of state power, it must be prepared to smash the reactionary class's counterattacks at all times and consolidate state power. Engels pointed out: "If a political party is unwilling to lose the fruits for which it has striven, after winning victory, it must rely on its weapons to cause fear in the reactionaries in order to maintain its domination" (*Selected Works of Marx and Engels*, vol. 2, p. 554). Lenin pointed out: "Whoever does not expect to realize socialism through the social revolution and the dictatorship of the proletariat is not a socialist. Dictatorship is state power that directly relies on violence. In the twentieth century (and the whole civilized era), violence is not a fist nor a club but an army" (*Complete Works of Lenin*, vol. 23, p. 93). These statements of Engels and Lenin clearly expound the Army's function in consolidating state power. The fact that it checked the turmoil and put down the counterrevolutionary rebellion last year explains once again that the gun is relied on to seize state power, and likewise, state power cannot be consolidated without the gun. When our country is at a crucial moment, when its fate hangs in the balance, the People's Army led by the party is relied on to vigorously turn the tide and control the situation. The lesson paid for with blood tells us that the Army is the pillar of the socialist republic, and on the one hand, it shoulders the sacred mission of resisting foreign enemy invasions and safeguarding the country's independence and territorial sovereignty and integrity, while on the other hand, it assumes the tasks of preventing the enemy's subversion, suppressing counterrevolutionary riots and rebellions, and protecting the people's peaceful labor at home. Those who deny the Army's domestic functions either harbor an ulterior motive or are extremely childish and ridiculous.

In fact, when social order encounters serious sabotage, political rule faces serious threats, and an incident cannot be suppressed by any other means, either a capitalist or a socialist country will usually use its army to control the situation. After the Second World War, Britain used its Army to interfere in workers' strikes on thirty-five occasions. What happened to the United States, which flagrantly censured our country for putting down the rebellion? Putting aside what happened long ago, since the 1960s, the United States has used its Army for this purpose on dozens of occasions. In 1963, due to continuous black people's and students' demonstrations in Cambridge in the state of [Massachusetts], a U.S. national defense unit was stationed in the school for as long as a year; in the spring of 1968, to cope with black people's riots, the federal army sent a force of over 88,700 soldiers to cities, including Chicago. It can be seen that in the world, there is no country whose army functions only to deal with external affairs.

The Army Has Always Been a Tool for Class Struggle

With half-baked knowledge and an ulterior motive, the bourgeois liberalization "elitists" attacked our Army with the so-called functions of a Western bourgeois country's army, that it does not intervene in party struggle, and babbled that the army should remain "neutral" in political struggle. Their intention was obvious and easily seen; they wanted our Army to look on with arms folded when our country was at a critical juncture so that their criminal plot to overthrow the people's regime could succeed.

A state is the product and manifestation of uncompromising class contradictions. As an important component of the state's political superstructure, the Army is a violent tool of class struggle. In history, the army of any country serves the ruling class's interests. The army of ancient slave society served the interests of the slave-owning class and its freemen; the army of a feudal country serves the interests of the landlord class and its literati and officialdom; the army of a bourgeois country serves the interests of the bourgeoisie; likewise, the army of a socialist country serves the interests of the working class and laboring people. There is and cannot be any supra-class or "neutral" army in the world. The Chinese PLA is the Chinese People's Army and fights thoroughly in the people's interests. When the people's interests face a serious threat, as the People's Army the PLA can by no means look on with folded arms, be absolutely "neutral," and it will naturally carry out the party and state's orders and stand up to defend the people's interests. The liberalization "elitists'" attempt to allow the Army to be "neutral" and not "interfere in" their criminal antiparty and antisocialist activities is a daydream.

Indeed, some Western countries' constitutions provide certain articles and the U.S. Constitution provides that the Army does not belong to any political party, the president is the Armed Forces' commander-in-chief, and Army servicemen "are not allowed to participate in any party activities"; many bourgeois countries stipulate that soldiers cannot take part in an election and cannot concurrently be a congressman or government official. However, this does not show that a Western army is "neutral." U.S. law provides that the army "shall not participate in" party struggle, and it seems that the U.S. Army has not participated in the struggle between the Republican and Democratic parties. However, as long as we analyze from a class viewpoint, the problem is clear. Over the past 100-some years since the American War of Independence, there have been dozens of presidents, the Democratic and Republican parties have been the banker by rotation, and have merely struggled within the monopoly capitalist class; the regime's class substance has not changed. Their Army surely did not intervene in the parties' internal struggles, which did not touch the capitalist system and the bourgeoisie's basic interests. Nevertheless, once their class interests and political domination face a threat and the situation cannot be controlled by any other measures, they will use the Army for suppression without hesitation. A Paris reporter asked the governor of the State of California why troops were sent to the University of California to suppress students in 1969. The governor spoke without reservation, saying that it was to suppress the left; reliable information proved that the Communist Party manipulated the students from behind the scenes. The fact mercilessly laid bare their lies. Their so-called allegation that the Army does not participate in politics and remains "neutral" in party struggle is completely made to conceal the reactionary class substance of their Army. . . .

The "depoliticization of the Army" preached by the bourgeois liber-alization "elitists" not only is deceptive talk but also further exposes their sinister intention to vainly attempt to alter our Army's nature. The aim of their so-called "depoliticization of the Army" is substantially that they want our Army to abandon proletarian politics, go for their bourgeois politics, and serve their criminal political aim. After the suppression of the counterrevolutionary rebellion in Beijing, when those "elitists" were summing up the lessons in failure, they said bit-terly: "It was an unwise move" not to grasp the Army. At that time, if "a division had been grasped, the situation would have been quite different." In the future it is necessary to "do PLA work in a big way." Some U.S. bourgeois politicians also said that a very unwise move of China's "democratic movement" was not grasping the Army. These remarks show that their so-called allegation of the "depoliticization of the Army" is a completely false and deceptive trick, and its aim is to draw the Army over to their side. In fact, hostile forces at home and abroad have regarded the Army as an important target by which to carry out peaceful evolution, and as evolutionary and anti-revolutionary developments unfold, they will further intensify their sabotage of the Army. In view of this, we must maintain sharp vigilance.

Comrade Deng Xiaoping said: "However it is updated, our Army is forever the Army led by the party, forever the guard of the state, forever the guard of socialism, and forever the guard of the people's interests." We must resolutely get rid of the interference of the "depo-liticization of the Army," strengthen political building, and forever maintain our Army's clear-cut political nature. Under absolute party leadership, we must build our Army into a great wall of steel forever loyal to the party, people, and socialist motherland so that it will be in an invincible position in the struggle between infiltration and anti-infil-tration, between subversion and antisubversion, and between peaceful evolution and anti–peaceful evolution.

18
Army Sets Up Committee to Prevent Coup Attempts

Willy Wo-lap Lam

Source: Hong Kong, *South China Morning Post*, August 14, 1992, p. 1, *FBIS*, August 14, 1992.

The People's Liberation Army (PLA) has set up a committee to prevent coup d'etats from taking place.

The committee, which operates under the guise of a research institute on Asian security matters, is involved in research on how the Army can bolster Communist Party dictatorship without posing a threat to its ruling elite.

Chinese sources said yesterday that the committee reported directly to the Central Military Commission (CMC), which is the Army's highest authority.

The vice-chairman of the CMC, General Liu Huaqing, a long-time protege of patriarch Mr. Deng Xiaoping, oversees the committee and its operations.

General Liu, who will likely succeed President Mr. Yang Shangkun as the CMC's first vice-chairman later this year, is believed to make periodic reports to Mr. Deng on the committee's findings.

Aside from senior officers and researchers in military think tanks, the committee draws on the expertise of diplomats, academics, and journalists.

Senior Colonel Liu Yazhou, who is the son-in-law of the late president Mr. Li Xiannian, is a leading member of the committee. . . . Sources said the CMC, which is still controlled by Mr. Deng, its immediate past chairman, became interested in coup research after the ignominious fall of the Ceausescu regime in Romania in late 1989.

The sources added that in spite of Mr. Deng's praise for the PLA for crushing the 1989 "turmoil" and for offering "escort" for his latest round of reform, the patriarch had qualms about loyalties—especially of the younger and better-educated officers.

"Deng knows that the Communist Party has to go on relying on the PLA to maintain its monopoly on power," a military source said.

"However, he does not want a maverick faction within it to be strong enough to stage a coup."

The source said that the "coup committee" had studied in detail every major coup in Third World countries in the past decade.

Committee experts are especially interested in the coups that took place in Thailand in recent years.

It is understood Mr. Deng is fascinated by the Thai experience because at least until the recent bloodshed, the heavy involvement of the army in Thai politics has not affected the economic development of the country.

Working closely with the PLA's intelligence units, the committee's key task is to identify potential "dissident rings" within the Army and the secret police that might pose a challenge to the administration.

Dissension within the ranks was amply demonstrated in the run-up to the Tiananmen Square crackdown, when senior generals as well as mid-echelon officers openly displayed reluctance to use force to crush the democracy movement.

And while the democracy movement has apparently petered out, Mr. Deng was worried about the existence of underground political organizations, and that such units might find adherents within the PLA.

Political analysts in Beijing said that since launching his "second wave of reform" in Shenzhen early this year [1992], Mr. Deng had been obsessed with PLA loyalty. . . . Military sources said that aside from holding meetings with party elders and Politburo members in the Beidaihe seaside resort last month, Mr. Deng also conferred with members of the top brass.

A major theme of these informal sessions was to ensure that the younger officers not be corrupted by "Westernized values."

D. Political Structure—
Regional and Local

19
Beijing Military Region to Improve Party Committee

Yi Jianru

Source: Beijing, Xinhua (New China News Agency), November 4, 1991, *FBIS*, November 15, 1991.

Recently the Beijing Military Region[1] held a meeting of secretaries of the party committees at the three levels of military region, Army, and division to expose contradictions, discover inadequacies, and conduct face-to-face criticism and self-criticism by using the method of holding a heart-to-heart talk, thereby enhancing their consciousness to set high demands on themselves to do a good job of building the party committee groups.

The party committees at all levels of the Beijing Military Region conscientiously attached importance to improving themselves in accordance with the requirements of strengthening party building and, as a result, achieved noticeable progress. The party committee of the military region maintains that it is all the more necessary to attach importance to building good party committee groups when the situation for making such an endeavor is favorable and further promote unity when the situation of unity is good. It maintains that it won't do for the military region to attach importance to this endeavor only after a number of problems have cropped up. Based on this understanding, the Standing Committee of the Military Region led its cadres to inspect, guide, and help the party committee groups at the levels of Army and

[1]China is divided into seven military regions, of which Beijing's is the most important.

division, one by one. They conducted numerous investigations and research, held group consultations to analyze the condition of every party committee, and discovered the strong points as well as the weak links of each and every one of them.

At the meeting attended by secretaries of the party committees at the three levels, the party committee groups at all levels realistically analyzed efforts made to build and improve themselves while the Standing Committee of the Military Region collectively heard their briefings and made comments on them. They calmly exchanged views and opinions and pointed out shortcomings and problems. Full understanding was achieved between the higher and the lower levels, and their exchanges were conducted on an equal footing. The atmosphere was serious, conscientious, and lively. The party committee of a certain Army group gained an experience of "honestly laying a foundation and paying close attention to implementation in a down-to-earth manner" from its efforts to promote development of party committee groups at the grass-roots units, thereby achieving progress in the work to promote building of the Army units. While fully encouraging their achievements, the Standing Committee of the Military Region pertinently pointed out that their work in certain areas had not been carried out and exhorted them to spend more time and effort to make progress while exposing contradictions. . . .

20
Step Up Building of Armed Police Forces, Be Loyal Sentinels of the Party

Xu Shouzeng

Source: Beijing, *Renmin ribao*, October 11, 1991, p. 3, *FBIS*, October 23, 1991.

At present, our country is at a critical period in the development of its history. Our party shoulders the historic mission of uniting and leading the people of all nationalities in the country to engage in self-reliance and hard struggle in order to build our country into a prosperous, democratic, and civilized modern power. In the struggle to defend the political power of the state and safeguard social stability, our Armed Police Forces are constantly in the "front line," assuming a difficult but glorious mission. In order not to disappoint the party's and the people's earnest expectations of us, party organizations and party members at all levels of the Armed Police Forces should give full play to the role of the party committees as core leaders, the role of party branch committees as fighting fortresses, and the role of party members as exemplary models, and lead the entire body of officers and men in a relentless effort to uphold the party's absolute leadership over the forces, abide voluntarily by the command of the party, and serve as the loyal sentinels of the party and the people.

To step up the building of the Armed Police Forces, it is necessary to strengthen the party's leadership over them in terms of politics, ideology, and organization. This concerns the fundamental question of the direction of the Armed Police Forces' building and the preservation of its proletarian character. To uphold the party's absolute leadership over the Armed Police Forces, it is necessary to integrate their tasks and grasp the building of party committees and party branch committees at all levels and of the ranks of party members.

The party branch committee is the grass-roots organization of the party in the Army and is also the basic link needed to realize the party's leadership over the Armed Police Forces. Vigorous efforts to step up building party grass-roots branch committees and give full play to their role as fighting fortresses represent the basic guarantee for the implementation of the party's guidelines, policies, and principles at grass-roots level and the maintenance of the Armed Police Forces' centralization and its obedience to the party's command. Right now, it is necessary to further realize the instructions of the party Central Committee and the Central Military Commission on stepping up party building in order to bolster the building of the forces' grass-roots party branch committees. In line with the principle of "keeping an eye on construction, promoting education, stressing assistance, and fostering popular advances," it is imperative to deal effectively with the existing weak links in the building of the forces' party branch committees, upgrade the party branch committees' ability to resolve their own problems as well as the ability of the leading grass-roots units to carry out overall construction, and strive to build the party branch committees into fighting fortresses that have sound organization, a tough system, and strong leadership to ensure the completion of all tasks by the forces and raise their overall fighting capacity.

21
On Party Building in Colleges

Source: Guangzhou (Canton), *Guangdong People's Radio Network*, October 18, 1991, *FBIS*, October 24, 1991.

A five-day provincial work meeting on party building in universities and colleges ended in Zhongshan City yesterday. Xie Fei, provincial party secretary, and Zhu Senlin, provincial party deputy secretary and acting provincial governor, attended the meeting and spoke.

Fang Bao, member of the provincial CCP Committee Standing Committee and head of the provincial Educational Leading Group, delivered a speech at the meeting entitled: Vigorously Strengthen Party Building to Build Universities and Colleges into a Powerful Front for Guarding against Peaceful Evolution, and Training Builders and Successors of Socialist Construction. Du Lianjian, secretary of the Working Committee for Higher Education, relayed the spirit of the national work meeting on party building in universities and colleges.

Meeting participants maintained that universities and colleges are shouldering a strenuous task of training the builders and successors of our socialist construction. Universities and colleges are places where various ideological trends converge, and an important front for which socialist and capitalist ideological trends scramble. With regard to the building of party organizations in universities and colleges, we should pay more attention to ideological development. We should regard as a long-term strategic task the work of profoundly carrying out socialist ideological education and criticizing the influence of bourgeois ideological trends. This has been demanded by the purpose of universities and colleges of providing teaching and training. This is also a question for study as far as the building of the party itself is concerned.

22
Improve Large, Medium State-Owned Enterprises: Investigation of How Capital Iron and Steel Corporation Conscientiously Strengthens Party Leadership in Course of Reform

Source: Beijing, Joint Investigation Team Report, *Renmin ribao*, December 11, 1991, p. 5, *FBIS*, January 3, 1992.

In our efforts to activate state-owned large and medium enterprises, we should by no means ignore the key issue of earnestly strengthening and improving the party's leadership in enterprises. A host of facts have showed clearly that in all successful enterprises, party organizations have played a strong and effective role as a political nucleus. Capital Iron and Steel Corporation [outside Beijing] is a typical example. People who have visited Capital Iron and Steel Corporation all gasp with admiration at the fact that the contracted system reform has given full rein to the magic strength of the socialist public ownership. In addition, they have also had a deep impression of the Capital Iron and Steel Corporation party organizations' strong role as a political nucleus.

In what ways does Capital Iron and Steel Corporation strengthen and improve the party's leadership? An investigation report by a Beijing Municipal CCP Committee joint investigation team . . . holds the view that over the past twelve years, under the leadership of the central authorities and the municipal party committee, Capital Iron and Steel Corporation has persistently integrated the Four Cardinal Principles with reform and opening up, given full play to the socialist public ownership's superiority, and carried forward the traditions of "the Anshan Iron and Steel Company Charter" and the Daqing spirit.[1] In addition, it has also made new innovations, vigorously introduced from abroad advanced technologies and management experience, and

---

[1] The Anshan Steel Corporation and the Daqing Oilfield (located in China's northeastern provinces of Liaoning and Heilongjiang, respectively) were lauded during the Cultural Revolution (1966–76) for mobilizing workers for production along political and ideological lines.

achieved preliminary results in exploring new ways to build socialist large enterprises with Chinese characteristics. In light of its own special features, Capital Iron and Steel Corporation has carried out reform of the enterprise's leadership and management systems, and gained successful experience in many fields, such as mobilizing the enthusiasm of workers and staff members as masters of the country, strengthening the party's building, and paying attention to ideological and political work. The following is our report:

Uphold the Party Committee's Political Leadership and Reform and Gradually Perfect the Leadership System in Large Enterprises under the Socialist Ownership by the Whole People

Capital Iron and Steel Corporation's Leadership System.

After it adopted the contracted system, proceeding from the reality of extraordinarily large enterprises under the ownership of the whole people, Capital Iron and Steel Corporation started to reform its leadership system to meet the needs of the all-personnel contract system, which mainly relies on the vast numbers of workers and staff members. The new leadership system can be summarized as follows: The Workers and Staff Members' Representative Assembly [WSMRA] (which is named the Working Personnel's Representative Assembly in the Capital Iron and Steel Corporation) is the enterprise's supreme power institution; under the Factory Committee's leadership, the system under which the general manager assumes full responsibility is adopted; and the party committee is responsible for practicing political leadership in the enterprise.

The WSMRA is the enterprise's supreme power institution. The major functions of the representative assembly are to hold discussions and make decisions on major reform plans and measures concerning the enterprise; on annual plans and long-term development programs guiding the enterprise's production, operation, technological exploration, major renovation projects, personnel training, distribution, and livelihood; and on the contracted methods and "contract, guarantee, and assessment" plans drawn up by the enterprise's various units and departments. The WSMRA will also be responsible for holding democratic elections for leading members of the Factory Committee and all subordinate work committees, as well as for the corporation's general manager and his deputies.

The Factory Committee is a permanent WSMRA institution. When the WSMRA is not in session, the Factory Committee, representing the interests of the state, enterprise, and staff, will be responsible for making major policy decisions concerning the enterprise in accordance with the party's principles and policies and with the law of the state.

The general manager is a commander with full powers. He is mainly responsible for organizing and conducting production and operation according to the policy decisions made by the WSMRA and the Factory Committee. The general manager has full power to organize, control, command, and coordinate the enterprise's day-to-day production and operation.

The party committee is responsible for practicing political leadership in the enterprise. Such political leadership will mainly be reflected in upholding Marxist and socialist principles; and supervising and ensuring the implementation of the party's line, principles, and policies, as well as the state's laws and systems. The party committee is the enterprise's policy-making center, and problems that are submitted to the WSMRA should first be discussed by the party committee. In addition, the party committee should strengthen self-building, carry out ideological and political work, provide guidance to trade unions and youth league organizations, and uphold the principle that the party has control over cadres.

1. The formulation of major policy decisions has been appropriately separated from routine command. As an extraordinarily large enterprise [of over 200,000 workers], Capital Iron and Steel Corporation usually makes policy decisions on major issues in three steps. The party committee discusses issues of principle concerning the enterprise and determines the enterprise's correct development orientation. The WSMRA and the Factory Committee are responsible for making policy decisions on major issues concerning the enterprise's production and operation. During his implementation of policy decisions made by the WSMRA and the Factory Committee, the general manager has the right to make decisions on how to solve concrete problems cropping up during production and operation. By so doing, the enterprise's formulation and implementation of major policy decisions are separated, and the work of both levels strengthened. As a result, the enterprise's leadership system can fulfill the demands of the new situation in production and operation.

2. Through guiding and supporting workers and staff members to

exercise their democratic rights, the party committee can translate its own ideas into the will and actions of the vast numbers of workers and staff members. Take the formulation of annual plans, for example. The party committee will first hold discussions to determine general guiding principles and policies. Then, in accordance with the principles and policies fixed by the party committee, the Factory Committee will work out and pass down a concrete work plan to all workers and staff members for discussion and revision, and then submit the plan to the WSMRA for examination and approval. In such a way, the party committee's propositions can be perfected and implemented, thus becoming acceptable to the vast numbers of workers and staff members . . . .

**Persistently Strengthen the Party's Building,
Give Full Rein to the Working Class's Vanguard Role**

*Take Root among the Grass-Roots Units, Comprehensively
Reinforce the Party's Strength on the Forefront of Production*

The Capital Iron and Steel Corporation party committee has realized that to ensure a thoroughgoing implementation of the party's line, principles, policies, and tasks, it is imperative to rely on the performance of grass-roots party organizations and every party member and to ensure that there are communists in every corner who have taken responsibility for earnestly uniting the masses in all fields of endeavor. Therefore, they attach great importance to reinforcing party organizations on the forefront of production, expanding the party's forces, and giving play to the party's role. There are 48,066 party members in Capital Iron and Steel Corporation, accounting for 26 percent of the total number of workers and staff members. From 1979 to the first half of 1990, Capital Iron and Steel Corporation recruited 19,743 party members, 14,260 of whom are working on the forefront of production, making up 52.13 percent of the total. On the forefront of production, 22.3 percent of the total number of workers and staff members are party members . . . .

23
Strengthening Village-Level Organizations with the Party Branch as the Core

Source: Beijing, Commentator, *Renmin ribao*, September 13, 1990, p. 1, *FBIS*, September 20, 1990.

On August 9, *Renmin ribao* published an article on how Shandong Province's Laixi County village-level organizations were developed and strengthened: Develop village-level organizations with the party branch as the core, and strengthen the overall functions; with villagers' self-government as the basis, democratic politics are to be properly developed, thus motivating internal vitality; with the collective economy as the foundation, socialized services are to be properly developed. . . . Since rural reform was initiated, the original organizational pattern of the people's commune has been changed. When the contract system of responsibility linked to production is extensively practiced,[1] the question as to what sort of new organizational leadership and new operational and management structure rural areas should institute is being explored through practice in all localities. . . .

At the recent National Work Conference on Strengthening Village-Level Organizations in Rural Areas, Comrade Song Ping said: Peasants' problems are always the fundamental problems of China's revolution and construction. The success or failure of our undertaking depends on whether or not our party is able to attract large numbers of peasants and rally them around it so that it can bring into full play their initiative and creativity for the struggle to realize the party's political line and to safeguard the peasants' immediate interests. . . .

Why is the party branch the core of village-level organizations? Because the major task of the party branch is to carry out the party's line, principles, and policies and the decisions passed by the higher authorities. It sticks to the socialist orientation, leads the masses in the development of the rural economy, and takes the path to obtaining common wealth. Socialism cannot be born spontaneously. In rural areas, with party organizations stabilizing the contract system of re-

---

[1]Throughout the 1980s, a contract system leasing land to China's farmers was instituted as the large-scale people's communes established in 1958 were dismantled.

sponsibilities linked to production as the basis, all villages should take into account their actual situations, and seek new economic and cultural patterns that peasants are willing to accept and that develop their socialist nature. If party organizations give up their own responsibilities and give a free hand to the self-development of rural areas, it will end very badly. The reason Chinese peasants unswervingly follow the party is that the socialist cause led by the party is in keeping with their fundamental interests. The fact that the party branch plays the role of the core of village-level organizations is exactly the wish of the vast numbers of peasants.

The party branch's role as the core is always shown in the decision making on major matters. A village is a "small society." In developing the "two civilizations" [material and "spiritual"] there are many important things to do, such as the development of economy, education, and culture; the amendment of village rules and civil agreements; etc. The party branch will win the masses' confidence and support only if it makes appropriate policy decisions.

As for economic work, the party branch should attach importance to the development of the collective economy. Without a definite collective economic basis, there will be no economic strength to support agriculture, nor will there be strength to develop the village's public welfare and educational undertakings. Without a definite collective economic basis, many tasks of the party branch can hardly be accomplished, and it will be difficult for its position as the core to stay firm. However, since the level of rural productive forces of our country is extremely unbalanced, we should pay attention to stratification and classification and should be careful and stress steadiness when developing the collective economy. We should stabilize the system of contracted responsibilities on the household basis with remuneration linked to output. And with this as the basis, we should vigorously develop and improve the two-tier management structure, integrating the initiative of household management and the superiority of collective management.

What sort of men should we choose for cadres? Do cadres seek the interests of the masses wholeheartedly? These are the matters peasants are most concerned about. The party branch should be responsible for the education, training, selection, recommendation, and supervision of cadres of collective enterprises and other mass organizations. It should select for various leading positions those who are full of enthusiasm for making contributions, who possess leadership ability, and who are young and energetic. Moreover, it should frequently educate and supervise them in their enthusiasm to do things for the masses and in their integrity and abiding by the law so that they can be the good "civil servants" of villagers.

Following the [1978] Third Plenary Session of the Eleventh CCP Central Committee, the success in rural reform could be attributed to the important experience that peasants' autonomy in rural production and management [achieved]. As for village matters, it is necessary to mobilize villagers to discuss and handle them, and it is necessary to respect the democratic rights of peasants and bring into full play the roles of the villagers' committee and cooperative and management organizations. The party branch must act according to law when leading people in accomplishing tasks. It should strengthen its leadership of the work of the villagers' committee in accordance with the "Regulations on Villagers' Committees (Provisional)," and support and help in the work done by the villagers' committee set up by those people trusted by villagers. It is necessary to strengthen the party branches of villages and the Communist Youth League and the women's representative associations so as to bring into full play their roles in the development of the two civilizations in rural areas.

In order to do the above-mentioned things properly, the party branch must strengthen itself. First, it should select a good party branch secretary. Then, it should strengthen the education and management of party members so as to build up the ranks of qualified party members. In this way, village-level organizations will have a sufficient supply of cadres or "souls of the village." Village-level organizations are the basis of socialist grass-roots-level state power. If the party branch plays the role of the core in village organizations, the socialist rural strongholds will be strengthened daily, the economy will develop, and the living standards of peasants will continuously improve.

24
Rich Farmers Run for Political Leadership

Source: Hangzhou (Zhejiang Province), Xinhua, September 17, 1991, *FBIS*, September 17, 1991.

An increasing number of farmers who became rich by developing private rural industries under the tide of economic reform and opening to the outside world have now turned their attention to running for political leadership positions in the villages.

The villagers' committee is the grass-roots executive organization in rural China.

In Eastern China's Zhejiang Province, which boasts the most developed rural industrial enterprises, 74,000 of the province's 90,000 villages conducted reelections of villagers' committees last year. Some 40 percent of the more than 70,000 chief leaders of these committees are those farmers who had got rich by developing private industries or by contracting certain enterprises and factories. Among the total 300,000 members of these committees, the percentage of such farmers is as high as 70 percent.

Jiang Linyou is a farmer from Yajiang village of the province's Jinyun County. By contracting a rural enterprise in a neighboring village several years ago, Jiang has quickly turned rich.

Last year, Jiang returned to his own village to run for the chief leader of the villagers' committee and succeeded. Since then, Jiang has led his villagers to work hard, constructing reservoirs, building electricity transmission lines, and opening up 26.6 hectares of land for planting mulberry trees to raise silkworms. Jiang also managed to bring about 200,000 yuan [$35,080] for his village by signing a contract on labor export through his former business relations. In doing so, however, Jiang's own annual income was decreased by at least 10,000 yuan [$1,754] compared with that at the time when he was contracting the enterprises at the neighboring village.

Asked why he gave up his former profitable job to get a job with less income, Jiang said, "In the past I was poor. It is the policies of the party and government that have made me rich. Now it is my duty to help others to become wealthy. I would not have been able to assume the duty if I had no power in my hands." The enthusiasm of these rich farmers for the posts of village leaders worries some people but pleases others.

A former head of a village in the province's Dongyang City, who lost the election last year, complained that these rich farmers were pounding too much at the old village leaders.

However, an official from the provincial government commented that most of these newly elected village leaders are young people who are energetic and have organizing and management abilities. In contrast, he added, most of the former village leaders were too old, incapable, and conservative. . . .

25
CCP Stresses Western Political System Does Not Conform to National Condition

Shu Si

Source: Hong Kong, *Chengming (Contending)*, #192, October 1, 1993, pp. 20–22, *FBIS*, October 15, 1993.

A document demanding control of deputies to people's congresses by "upholding the Four Cardinal Principles" is circulating within the CCP, and its purpose is to enable party organizations at various levels to have behavioral norms when they try to control people's congresses at various levels and to restrain deputies in order to prevent actions that are not helpful to the CCP's totalitarian rule.

In light of the "loss of control over the elections" of local people's congresses at various levels in May and June of this year,[1] the CCP Organization Department[2] has sent investigation teams to various localities to investigate conditions, and submitted a general report to the senior level of the CCP. After reading the report, the first response of

---

[1] Such elections to local people's congresses over the years have often been an outlet for popular political protest.

[2] The central party organization responsible for appointments throughout the vast CCP apparatus.

CCP leaders such as Jiang Zemin was: "The perfection of the socialist democratic system can be carried out only under the leadership of the CCP." The response of political elders such as Peng Zhen was: "Some deputies to people's congresses have become increasingly reluctant to listen to calls."

The Sound of Guns during "June 4" Was Also a Warning to the Deputies of People's Congresses

Before the June 4 Incident, because the macropolitical climate was relatively mild, some deputies to the National People's Congress [NPC] and some deputies to local people's congresses at various levels began to become "not that obedient." The sound of guns during the June 4 Incident in 1989 played a role to mute demands for democracy in intellectual circles on the one hand, and, on the other hand, scared "disobedient" deputies to the people's congresses. Some deputies to people's congresses who were "reckless" and "not repentant," like [the journalist] Hu Jiwei, were dumped by the standing committees of people's congresses at various levels through a voting process forced by party organization departments at various levels. However, "not even a prairie fire can destroy the grass; it grows again when the spring breeze blows." Along with the rise of a new round of economic reform, the "liberalization" trend of thought among deputies to people's congresses has swelled again. . . .

At present, after learning from experiences and lessons in relation to people such as Hu Jiwei, deputies to people's congresses of various levels are not willing to continue to appeal for democracy openly; they use the voting rights they can get hold of in the voting process to silently resist attempts by party organizations at various levels to control the people's congresses. The phenomenon of "loss of control over elections" last year in Zhejiang and Guangxi Provinces was the best example.

Some deputies to people's congresses are even cleverer. They establish secret ties at people's congresses and have derived a method of dealing with party organization departments: they vote completely according to a "suggested list of candidates" handed to them by party organization departments in the preliminary voting process, or they express "unconditional support for the party's decision" when the leaders of party committees at various levels come to their houses to "solicit opinions," but then take them by surprise during the formal election process by crossing out those names supplied by the party organizations and adding their own favorite names, or just randomly writing down several names to show their silent protest against this kind of "democratic" style.

After seeing the emergence of this kind of phenomenon in various localities, the senior level of the CCP had a terrible headache. In particular, after Li Peng lost many votes at the NPC this spring, the senior level of the CCP had a strong sense of danger coming from the "out of control" condition. Therefore, it instructed the CCP Central Committee Organization Department to send some capable personnel to several provinces where elections were seriously out of control to carry out month-long investigations.

After investigations, the relevant personnel thought that if measures were still not taken, this kind of situation would become more serious in the period to come. The more serious consequences of the development would inevitably be that loss of control over county-level elections would have an impact on provincial people's congresses, where some deputies who claim that they "dare to speak the truth" would be elected NPC deputies. Eventually this group of deputies, who seek nothing other than the expression of their "individual wishes" and blindly pursue the "independence of deputies to people's congresses," would launch a sudden attack at the next round of the NPC. By then, a list of candidates for leading NPC posts and for leading State Council posts during the change of administration would probably meet a strong rejection. There is no way to tell how serious this situation could become, but precautionary measures must be taken to minimize the possibility of political incidents during the election process at the next round of the NPC.

26
Internal Report: China Risks Breakup Like Yugoslavia

Source: Hong Kong, AFP (Agence France-Presse), September 20, 1993, *FBIS*, September 20, 1993.

China will break apart like Yugoslavia soon after paramount leader Deng Xiaoping dies unless the central government takes drastic steps to halt mounting regionalism, an internal report here warned.

The eighty-six-page report also proposed adopting a U.S.-style federalist system that would reshape China's rubber-stamp parliament into a more democratic institution and create a legal framework for handling conflicts of interest between Beijing and the provinces. It has caused a commotion here by predicting for the first time, with Deng pushing ninety years old, what has long been whispered in private—economic warlordism by the provinces is driving the country toward major upheaval.

"If a 'political strongman' dies, it is possible that a situation like post-Tito Yugoslavia will emerge," said the report titled "Strengthening Central Government's Leading Role Amid the Shift to a Market Economy." "In years, at the soonest a few and at the latest between ten and twenty, the country will move from economic collapse to political breakup, ending with its disintegration."

It argued that Beijing gave up too much power to the provinces after Deng launched market reforms in 1978, especially since the sudden shift to a market economy last year, which resulted in an economic free-for-all by provinces used to four decades of rigid state planning.

The report, written by two influential Yale University–educated scholars and printed by the Chinese Academy of Sciences, foresaw a power struggle between Beijing and the provinces as well as interprovincial clashes. It was distributed to government leaders and senior lawmakers, who have drawn heavily on its analysis and borrowed many of its suggestions, knowledgeable Chinese sources said.

E. Corruption and Political Responsibility

27
Resolutely Wage Struggle against Corruption: Speech by State Premier Li Peng

Source: Beijing, *Renmin ribao*, September 27, 1993, *FBIS*, September 30, 1993.

Over the past few months, the CCP Central Committee and the State Council have grasped three important issues: First, a decision was made to deepen reform and strengthen and improve macro regulation and control of the national economy in order to solve conspicuous contradictions and problems that have surfaced in economic development, mainly through economic means. Initial achievements have been made in implementing this decision. Second, systematic and comprehensive research has been done on how to accelerate the building of a socialist market economy system, focusing on reform in the areas of banking, finance, taxation, management of state assets, the investment system, and the foreign trade system. Important reforms in these sectors will be implemented in the near future. Third, the anticorruption drive has been launched in order to foster an honest work style. These three issues are very important, and success in these areas will have great practical importance and profound historic significance for building the socialist market economy system, for guaranteeing the sustained, healthy, rapid, and sound development of the national economy, and for promoting the building of socialist spiritual civilization.

Various Departments of the State Council Must
Resolutely Implement the CCP Central Committee's
Decision on the Struggle Against Corruption.

Since Comrade Jiang Zemin made the important speech at the second plenary session of the Central Commission for Discipline Inspection [the party's internal disciplinary body], various departments of the

State Council have seriously learned from it and implemented it and have begun to take action. Many of the departments have worked out or promulgated detailed arrangements for promoting the anticorruption struggle in accordance with their real situations, and the masses have responded well. This is a good start. It must be understood, however, that to genuinely implement the CCP Central Committee's decision properly and to achieve results in the near future, resolute and persistent efforts must be made. Leaders at various levels, especially cadres at the senior and middle levels, must study once again Comrade Deng Xiaoping's expositions on correcting the party's work style, strengthening the building of clean government, and combating corruption. They must grasp the spirit of Comrade Jiang Zemin's important speech and profoundly understand that launching the anticorruption struggle is a significant matter that has a bearing on the fate of the party and the country and is an important guarantee for implementing the party's basic line and enabling reform, opening up, and economic construction to proceed smoothly. We must unify our understanding and firmly carry out the CCP Central Committee's decision on the anticorruption struggle.

What I want to stress here is that the departments of the State Council have an important responsibility in this struggle and are in a very important position. The most acute problem of corruption at present is the exchange of power for money and the abuse of power for private gain. The State Council is the country's highest administrative organ, and all its departments hold governing power; corruption will develop if the supervision and restriction mechanism is not enhanced. Regarding the anticorruption issue, the State Council and all its departments have done a great deal of work over the past few years; for example, through the supervision system, they handled a number of serious cases, corrected the unhealthy trend in trade, and checked the "three kinds of random appropriations," achieving certain results. The achievements of the anticorruption struggle should not be overestimated, however. It must be understood that, in some government departments and among some personnel working in those departments, as well as among some leading cadres, the phenomenon of corruption exists and is rather serious in some cases. Some people have neglected or failed to fulfill their duties, have perverted justice for bribes, have offered and accepted bribes, have resorted to blackmail and extortion, have become corrupt and decadent, and have already committed crimes. This situation can be found not only in economic departments, but in law enforcement departments as well. The unhealthy trend in trade has reemerged time and again after repeated efforts to ban it—and sometimes it has become even more acute. We must pay earnest attention to these problems and take resolute measures to tackle them. We may say that the key to achieving the desired results in the anticorruption struggle lies in the successful efforts of government departments. The masses of the people are looking to us, as are local governments and lower-level departments; they have pinned high hopes on the anticorruption struggle in all departments of the State Council. The leading comrades in various departments and commissions of the State Council, and in the units directly under it, must play an exemplary role in abiding by discipline and law and being honest in performing their official duties. . . .

Earnestly Strengthen Leadership and Carry Out Thorough Investigations and Surveys, Using Reform to Promote the Anticorruption Struggle

To implement the CCP Central Committee's decision on the anticorruption struggle in the near future, a great deal of hard and careful work must be done. In order to strengthen guidance, the State Council has decided to hold a joint meeting of ministry and commission leaders to organize and push forward the anticorruption drive. The leading comrades of these departments should personally assume leadership and establish a responsibility system at all levels, with one level grasping and guiding the next lower level, with a view to earnestly strengthening leadership, inspection, and supervision over the anticorruption struggle in their departments. Attention and support must be given to the Ministry of Supervision and administrative supervision departments at all levels, enabling them to play their role fully in the anticorruption struggle.

In the anticorruption struggle, leading organs and leading cadres must play an exemplary role. The State Council departments must first do what they ask the local authorities to do; senior-level departments must first do what they ask lower-level units to do; and the State Council personnel, ministers, and vice ministers must first do what they ask lower-level personnel to do.

The leadership work style must be improved, and in-depth investigation and study must be carried out. To enable the anticorruption struggle to score actual results, holding meetings and issuing documents is not enough; it is necessary to carry out in-depth investigation and study, understand the real situation, take effective measures, and carry out supervision and inspection. The leaders of every department should go to the grass-roots level, dissect one or two sparrows, sum up experience, and give overall guidance for the anticorruption struggle in their own department. Concerning the units and links that have serious problems and that have caused strong grievances among the people, leaders should visit them personally or send someone to help handle the cases. . . .

The anticorruption struggle must be combined with the drive to deepen reform. Deepening reform is the key to solving deep structural problems in the anticorruption struggle. The government's functions must be further restructured. At the same time, sound supervisory and restraining mechanisms must be developed to standardize the activities of the government. Legislation must be stepped up so that government departments can really operate according to the law, so that they must operate according to the law and must strictly enforce the law. Lawbreakers must be pursued responsibly in order to close the loopholes in the system and stop the use of administrative power at will.

The crackdown on corruption must be combined with encouraging justice. The majority of our cadres are good, honest, and dedicated to their duties. In the process of the anticorruption struggle, the advanced units and individuals who are efficient, honest, hard-working, dedicated, selfless, and courageous in fighting corruption in various localities and departments should be publicized; at the same time, we must report the situation of investigations into those major and serious cases that have a substantial impact so as to enhance confidence in fighting corruption among people throughout the country. . . .

28
Take Vigorous Measures to Restrain Several Unhealthy Tendencies

Source: Hong Kong, Zhongguo tongxun she (China News Agency), October 4, 1993, *FBIS*, October 4, 1993.

The CCP instructed party and government departments in various localities to "take vigorous measures to restrain several unhealthy tendencies that have whipped up strong resentment among the masses," including the tendency of "banqueting at public expense."

According to a source in Guangdong, where banqueting at public expense is the most popular, the provincial party committee has warned high-ranking party and government cadres not to drink imported wine and eat abalone, shark's fin, and edible bird's nests at public expense.[1] In Shenzhen [a special economic zone in southern China], which sees the highest rate of consumption on the mainland, party and government cadres were also warned against wining and dining and sending gifts at public expense or attending dinner parties at enterprises' invitation, as the Mid-Autumn Festival was drawing near. It is learned that business in restaurants, night clubs, sauna parlors, and karaoke bars in Guangzhou and Shenzhen is decreasing and that the consumption of social groups has declined by 20 to 30 percent. But many people are concerned that this situation only appears when the anticorruption campaign is being launched with the force of a thunderbolt. As soon as the "storm" blows over, they said, everything will slip back into its old way or even go from bad to worse.

Indeed, this is not a groundless worry. In the past, the central, provincial, and municipal governments have issued many documents trying to stop banqueting at public expense, which had run rampant, but the tendency persisted, rising and subsiding. Taking advantage of the opening up, many mainland officials banqueted at public expense in a big way. It is reported that banqueting at public expense made up 60 percent of the turnover of large and medium restaurants and guest houses. Such banquets were often given to mark the opening or the anniversary of a business, as well as the laying of a foundation stone or

---

[1] Very expensive delicacies in Chinese cuisine.

the completion of a project. They were also given at press briefings, meetings to select advanced units or individuals, or a business fair as well as for signing contracts, celebrating festivals, establishing favorable human relationships, and "gaining the favor of important officials. . . ."

The catering culture of an ancient country developed to a surprising extent once it was "grafted" on public money: Every night saw some people sitting at rows of tables enjoying food of every kind, including fish, bears' paws, and even food of which one ingredient was gold, and drinking famous imported wine while playing and singing. Such a catering culture, I think, has nothing to do with our 5,000-year-old culture. With "culture" gone, what is left is "sumptuous dining and wining."

In such a big country as China, too many places want money while the government's budget does not provide an ample surplus every year. So far, the food and clothing problems have not been solved in some areas, and more than 30 million people still lead a poor life. Again, a large number of primary school buildings are in a state of decay, and many peasants cannot afford to send their children to school. However, extravagance and money worshipping have become the order of the day in official circles, and tens of billions of yuan of public money have been spent on sumptuous wining and dining and overseas trips. Such a sharp contrast makes us feel acute distress.

Banqueting or traveling at public expense is found in every country, but on the mainland it has become a puzzling and long-standing problem with economic management and the style of the CCP. The main causes are: 1) On the mainland, public ownership is the main form of ownership, so public money is spent in a wide area and on a large scale. 2) The management authority has no authority, so it cannot exercise effective control when public spending inflates drastically. In the meantime, the government budget is not subject to control and rigid examination, and cadres who abuse public money for personal purposes are not punished. 3) There is a lack of media supervision and of channels by which the masses can exercise supervision. . . .

29
Political Jokes Mock Chinese Leadership

Marlowe Hood

Source: Hong Kong, *South China Morning Post*, December 7, 1991, p. 5, *FBIS*, December 9, 1991.

A young man on the Beijing-bound No. 252 train casts a wary glance front and back before leaning toward the woman seated next to him.

"Have you heard the one about God and Deng Xiaoping?" he asks in a hushed voice. She nods yes, suppressing a giggle with her hand. "Well then," he says, "how about the two protesters arrested for cursing Li Peng?" This time she shakes her head.

When political jokes flourish in China—as they do now—it is no laughing matter.

Not since the denouncement of that violent absurdity known as the Cultural Revolution [1966–76] have so many ordinary Chinese lampooned, in private conversation, the powers that be.

As early as the Han Dynasty, 2,000 years ago, emperors isolated by their own pomp and power sent agents into wine parlors to collect the ancient equivalent of political jokes in order to gauge the mood of the masses.

If Deng were to harvest this year's bumper crop of antigovernment zingers, he wouldn't find them funny at all.

Take the one told by the young man on the train, overhead earlier this month. Two protesters arrested after the brutal crackdown of June 4 are about to be sentenced for marching in the streets while carrying placards attacking China's despised Prime Minister.

The first one, whose sign read "Overthrow Li Peng!," winces as the judge condemns him to five years in a labor camp. The other protester, who had scrawled "Li Peng is a fool!," hopes to fare better, and so is utterly shocked when he receives a sentence of fifteen years. "But why the difference?" he blurts out. "You are both guilty of counterrevolutionary agitation," intones the judge. "But you," he continues, pointing at the second protester, "have revealed a state secret."

Jokes with a punch line, which have appeared only recently, are but one form of Chinese political humor. Even more common are rhymed couplets, doggerel, and mock edicts, which often make wicked use of ambiguities in the language.

One little ditty, for example, expresses popular indignation at the fact that China's leaders—at all levels—are doing everything except running the country:

> The Central Committee is busy with factional warfare.
> Provincial leaders are hunting for overseas airfare.
> Urban officials are eating and drinking up a storm.
> In the villages and townships gambling is the norm.

Another limerick-like verse summarizes the follies of forty years of "socialism with Chinese characteristics":

> In the fifties, we were eating steel,
> In the sixties, we lived on the brink,
> In the seventies, we "grasped the key link,"
> In the eighties, we learned to make a deal.

(Mao Zedong ordered millions of useless backyard furnaces built in 1958 during the Great Leap Forward, an economic experiment that left millions dead from starvation. The Cultural Revolution erupted in 1966, and was followed by a decade in which the concept of "class struggle" was enshrined as the "key link." The era of reform during the 1980s was the Chinese equivalent of the "me decade.")

Special privileges for the children of high-level officials, as the following verse suggests, are a real sore point among most Chinese, especially when compared to an idealized past in which communist leaders were less corrupt:

> Mao Zedong's son went to the "front line,"
> Liu Shaoqi's[1] son is into rocket design.
> Deng Xiaoping's son is accepting "charity,"
> Wang Zhen's son is studying overseas.

(Mao's oldest son was killed in action during the Korean War. Liu's

---

[1]Liu Shaoqi, Mao's first heir apparent in the 1950s and 1960s, was purged in the Cultural Revolution.

son is a rocket engineer. Deng Pufang, head of the China Handicapped Association, has been criticized for siphoning contributions into personal business ventures. Octogenarian Wang Zhen's animus against "bourgeois liberalization" has not prevented him from sending his children to the United States for schooling.)

Of all the oblique indicators of the current government's health and prospects, the sudden proliferation of political humor should be among the most troubling to the handful of old men who rule China. It bespeaks an utter disdain for not only senior leaders, but the regime they are trying to prop up.

Which brings us back to the one about Deng and God. One day God decides to visit the world's great nations and their leaders. First he drops in on President Bush, who gives him a guided tour of the United States. "So what do you think, God," Bush asks eagerly. "How long before we create a heaven on earth?" God shakes his head slowly. "At least a century," he replies.

Upon hearing this prognosis, a crushed Bush nearly breaks into tears. After God inspects the Soviet Union, Gorbachev asks him the same question. "Five hundred years, maybe a millennium," God replies. Gorbachev is so devastated to think that even his great-great-great-grandchildren won't see the new era that he begins to sob.

Finally, God visits China. "Tell me, God, when will we reach utopia?" Deng Xiaoping asks after showing him around. God starts to cry.

30
State Draft Law Aims to Compensate Victims

Ma Chenguang

Source: Beijing, *China Daily,*[1] November 19, 1993, p. 4, *FBIS*, November 19, 1993.

The draft State Compensation Law aims to help those who have suffered from government errors and improve supervision of State organs.

It was reviewed at the Fourth Session of the Standing Committee of

---

[1] An English-language daily published in China.

the National People's Congress (NPC) late last month and is expected to be ratified at the Fifth Session in December.

With six chapters and thirty-nine articles, the draft law is the country's first bill compensating citizens and organizations for losses caused by government indiscretion.

It also increases supervision of government organs. This signals a shift from past policies, which emphasized supervision of citizens.

The bill, which took legal experts six years to draft, has undergone careful legislative study and is almost finished, said lawmaker Sun Lihai in an interview.

Sun, Vice-Director of the Civil Laws Department of the Legislative Affairs Commission of the NPC Standing Committee, said the draft law has four key points.

First, it will protect the rights of all Chinese.

Second, it provides compensation for citizens who suffer losses at the hands of State organs.

Third, it will further the country's ongoing anticorruption campaign. It calls for government organs to collect money from those responsible to compensate victims.

Finally, it will help promote social stability.

Under the bill, citizens and organizations whose legal rights are violated during administrative and criminal proceedings can claim compensation from administrative and judicial government institutions.

Administrative institutions include the State Council, its ministries, commissions, and offices, and regional administrative bodies.

Judicial institutions include departments in charge of public and State security, procuratorial organs, and people's courts and their functionaries.

Government departments found guilty of infringements are responsible for paying compensation fees.

The bill further stipulates that government organs should thoroughly investigate cases and are entitled to collect compensation fees from guilty parties.

Sun said the draft law shows China's willingness to be responsible for mistakes.

Before 1976, China provided living allowances or assigned jobs to the children of citizens who were wrongfully persecuted.

Later on, the country compensated people for losses caused by misapplication of the Customs Law and the Administrative Procedure Law.

Sun said compensation cases are on the rise in 1991 and 1992. Court rulings ordered government organs to pay more than 40 million yuan ($7.01 million) in compensation fees to citizens and organizations, he said.

The draft bill states that citizens can claim redress if they are illegally detained, put into custody, arrested without being charged, beaten, or illegally injured during the process of arrest and detainment.

Those found guilty of a crime but later proven innocent can also file damage claims. Citizens may also bring suit if their property is illegally detained, if their assets are illegally frozen, or if they are wrongfully accused of a crime.

31
Peasants Win Lawsuit against Town Government

Source: Harbin City, Heilongjiang [Black Dragon River] Province, *Heilongjiang Provincial Radio Service*, December 19, 1990, *FBIS*, December 21, 1990.

The Daoli District People's Court in Harbin today made a first-time judgment on our province's first large-scale lawsuit lodged by peasants as a group. According to the judgment, the Taiping Town Government of the Daoli District in Harbin and the seed company of the Xiangfang experimental farm of the Dongbei Agricultural Institute should pay 134,916.38 yuan [$23,664] for the economic losses of 709 peasant households.

Early this year, on the recommendation of others, the seed station of the Taiping Town Government purchased more than 26,000 kg of corn seeds of the 4-Dan–8 variety from the seed company of the Xiangfang experimental farm of the Dongbei Agricultural Institute. The seeds were old ones from 1988. The seed station sold the seeds retail to peasants as seeds with a 90 percent sprouting rate. However, the actual sprouting rate was only 65 percent; thus the interests of peasants were seriously damaged.

After more than two months of efforts to hear the case, the Daoli District People's Court held that the Taiping Town Government and the seed company of the experimental farm of the Dongbei Agricultural Institute, by raising the sprouting rate without authorization, did not enforce relevant state laws and regulations on businesses, and therefore they should be held liable for compensation. It also made the judgment that the Taiping Town Government pay 74,204.01 yuan [$13,015] and the seed company of the Xiangfang experimental farm of the Dongbei Agricultural Institute pay 60,712.37 yuan [$10,649] to peasants for their economic losses, thus safeguarding the legal rights and interests of the 709 peasant households.

32
Deng Liqun Comments on Youth, Mao "Craze"

Source: Hong Kong, Zhongguo tongxun she, September 6, 1991, *FBIS*, September 9, 1991.

In a recent speech, Deng Liqun, member of the Central Advisory Commission, called on departments responsible for ideological work to study a number of matters concerning the "Mao Zedong craze," which occurred over the last few years, to guide young people to learn from Mao Zedong.

Deng Liqun said: The "Mao Zedong craze" has lasted one to two years. The research in this phenomenon amounts to making a social investigation and holding a public opinion poll because such a phenomenon is not man-made; rather, it came into being in the ordinary course of events and historical development. When we have witnessed many events in China and a sharp change in the international situation, it will benefit our writing to understand and study the "Mao Zedong craze," which is a social phenomenon.

Deng Liqun continued: Some people have studied and analyzed the "craze," believing it has something to do with young people cherishing the past. This is not correct because the reason for young people developing intense interest in Mao Zedong in a bid to find spiritual sustenance in the past was that they could do nothing to check the prevailing malpractices of corruption, bribe taking, and abusing power for personal gain. Mao Zedong was resolute in launching the movements against "three evils" and "five evils," while he led a simple life.

How fine it would be if our cadres could follow his example! The thinking of the young is not without some truth. We are duty-bound to guide and educate them. If our party failed to check corruption, overhaul and consolidate party organizations, and prevent cadres from abusing power for personal gain—or even allowed it to spread unchecked—how could the people be satisfied and how could we prevent the people from thinking of the past?

33
"Mao Zedong Fever" in China Continues to Heat Up

Zhao Shenyu

Source: Beijing, Zhongguo xinwen she, August 29, 1993, *FBIS*, August 30, 1993.

As the 100th anniversary of Mao Zedong's birth draws near, the "Mao Zedong fever" that has existed for many years has recently shown signs of heating up.

Over the past few years, the "Mao Zedong craze" appeared in China, during which Mao Zedong was brought down from the shrine and entered the minds of millions of Chinese people as a mortal man with human feelings and sincerity.

The "Mao Zedong craze" has recently started to heat up, the most obvious sign being that various businesses are using the Mao craze to promote their special products.

In June of this year, China Leasing Co., Ltd. launched an original project involving the unique production of "valued souvenirs to mark the 100th anniversary of Mao Zedong's birth." The souvenirs were made of gold and inlaid with natural diamonds from South Africa. They all bear sequence numbers and the personal signatures of Mao Zedong's relatives, such as Shao Hua, Mao Anqing, and Mao Xinyu. The souvenirs sold very well as soon as they were put on the market.

According to another original idea of Shenzhen's Xianke Recreational and Communications Corporation, which cooperated with the

Central Archives and the Central Document Research Office, a set of compact disks entitled "Voice of the Giant—Mao Zedong" will be produced, and they will reproduce seven recorded speeches given by Mao Zedong on seven occasions in different historical periods. This will be a very special project.

Another characteristic of the current Mao Zedong fever is that various symposiums on Mao have been held.

In early July this year, a symposium on Mao Zedong's life and thought was held in Shaoshan, Mao's birthplace. The meeting received 350 papers. It has been said that the symposium made a new breakthrough in the study of Mao's thought in his early years. . . . Various art performances and various television programs may also push the Mao craze to new heights.

Deng Zaijun, a famous television director, has been assigned to direct a twenty-one-episode television series called "Mao Zedong's Poems." The series will reproduce Mao Zedong's noble character and broad vision as a leader of the people and a national hero as well as a great poet.

Reportedly, various shows will be put on that will involve singing Mao's poems as well as other songs eulogizing Mao.

F. Policy Making in China:
A Case Study of the Three Gorges Dam

34
Please Attend to the Opposing Opinions on the Three Gorges Project: A Letter to the Leadership of the CCP

Li Rui[1]

Source: March 12, 1993, translated in Dai Qing, *Yangtze! Yangtze!: Debate over the Three Gorges Project,* edited by Patricia Adams and John Thibodeau (Toronto: Earthscan Publications, Ltd., 1994), pp. 66–71.

To: Comrade Jiang Zemin and other Chinese Communist Party Politburo Standing Committee members:

According to press reports, the State Council has set up the Three Gorges Project Development Corporation. Preparatory work for the construction of the Three Gorges Project has officially begun. Lu Youmei, the general manager of the development corporation, has indicated that the company will strive to push the project ahead, so that the damming of the Yangtze River will coincide with the reunification of Hong Kong and China [in 1997]. Lu has also said: "I hope that the comrades in the preparation office will not be afraid and just do it [i.e., build the dam]. If they make some mistakes, I will take responsibility for them."

I wrote a letter to the communist leadership on January 1, 1992, in which I illustrated the many advantages and disadvantages of the Three Gorges Project in great detail and explained why the project should not be started right away. This letter reiterates many of those points.

---

[1] Li Rui, previously Mao Zedong's secretary on industrial affairs, was also vice-minister of the Ministry of Water Resources and Electric Power. He is currently an adviser with the Energy and Resources Research Institute of China.

The last paragraph of the "Resolution on the Construction of the Three Gorges Project on the Yangtze River" passed by the National People's Congress (NPC) in April 1992 states:

> With regard to future work on the Three Gorges Project, research shall continue towards the proper solution of the potential problems that have been identified. We must be cautious, treat problems very seriously, and welcome the opinions of all interested parties. In so doing, the construction of the Three Gorges Project will be made safer and more reliable.

Unfortunately, these words appear to be only lip service. When the motion to pass the resolution was discussed in group meetings of the NPC, many delegates voiced opposing opinions. Delegates from Sichuan Province, in particular, made impassioned speeches, expressing their grave concern about the project.

Several months before the March–April 1992 NPC meeting, the Chinese media launched a massive campaign to publicize the view that the project had to be started right away. The campaign pointed out that the Central Committee of the Communist Party had already approved the project, and that the approval of the resolution by the congress was a mere formality. Despite such a massive media campaign, one-third of the delegates still did not vote in favor of the project. Such opposition was unprecedented in communist China. It should make the people in charge think carefully.

Since the resolution was passed, I have been exposed to many different ideas and viewpoints concerning various aspects of the project. The most important issue, for which there are many opposition opinions, is sedimentation. It is feared that the current plan for a 175-meter-high dam would cause significant sedimentation, adversely affecting the port at Chongqing [Sichuan] and blocking navigation. In the 1970s, when we discussed the sedimentation problem at the Gezhouba Dam project [also on the Yangtze], Premier Zhou Enlai clearly stated that navigation should be the number one consideration in the development of the Yangtze River. Premier Zhou said harshly, "the dam should be destroyed if it blocks the waterway." . . .

The assessment report, which endorsed the current 175-meter dam, does not provide guaranteed and reliable solutions to the problem of sedimentation. In fact, many of the consultants and specialists argued against the project for this reason. . . . Instead of a 175-meter dam, these specialists proposed the construction of a 160-meter or lower dam, so that navigation on the Yangtze River would not be so adversely affected, and the number of people displaced by dam construction could be reduced. What I wish to emphasize here is that the sedimentation that will result from the 175-meter dam will create serious problems for navigation on the Yangtze. It is still not too late to "be cautious, treat problems very seriously, and welcome the opinions of all interested parties."

In short, there are many disadvantages to the Three Gorges Project. Its capacity to control floods is limited and, worse yet, it passes the problem on to neighboring Sichuan Province. It will necessitate massive population relocation, and its resettlement plan is ridiculous. The dam is not the best option for generating electricity, as there are numerous alternatives that would produce greater benefits.[2] It would unnecessarily obstruct navigation, and, finally, it goes against current wisdom, which states that large hydroelectric projects do not work and are often abandoned.

One must also remember that the environmental effects of such a large dam cannot be predicted accurately. At this time, there remain many unknown elements that make it difficult to give any definite answers and conclusions.

Once again I would like to make my opinion known to the Central Committee of the Party—postpone construction of the Three Gorges Project and bring all preparation work to a halt. This would reassure the public and prevent future troubles. In the past several years, I have attended many group discussions of the Central Advisory Commission of the Communist Party. Whenever the Three Gorges Project was discussed, many veteran comrades expressed opposition opinions. However, they had no place to present these views. For example, last year a group of specialists with the Chinese Academy of Sciences undertook a field trip to the Three Gorges. Upon completing their study, they submitted a report with opposition opinions, but no one paid attention to it.

The leading group's assessment that chose the plan for a 175-meter dam was completely under the control of the ex-leaders of the former Ministry of Water Resources and Electric Power, and of Qian Zhengying in particular. The discussions were not founded on democratic or

---

[2]See Document #51 for a discussion of the electrical energy "bottleneck" in China's economy.

scientific principles. Briefly, there were two major problems with the assessment report:

First, the study did not follow recognized river planning procedures. Normally, river planning should take into account the characteristics of the entire river valley, and, through comparison with alternative plans, draw its conclusions. The Yangtze planners, however, had already decided that the Three Gorges Dam was the only option even before they started to collect data and formulate arguments to support their decision. In this way, the discussions on the Three Gorges Project can be compared to an election with a single candidate. This is all the more disturbing as we have had a very successful case of alternative planning in the Yellow River Valley. Why should we not follow that example in the case of the Three Gorges?

Second, all of the discussions were controlled by a single organization. They were originally to be led by the State Planning Commission and the State Science and Technology Commission. But it is argued that Qian Zhengying later persuaded the State Science and Technology Commission to let the Ministry of Water Resources and Electric Power lead the study. The leadership of the assessment group (including the members of the leading group and the heads of the experts' groups) was composed completely of pro-dam individuals. The director and deputy directors of the leading group were ex-ministers, ex–vice ministers, and leaders in charge of the Three Gorges Project in the Ministry of Water Resources and Electric Power, while the fourteen experts' groups were composed mostly of ex–department directors of the ministry.

The leading group approved and invited 412 specialists to be part of the experts' groups, but very few of them had different opinions from those of the Ministry of Water Resources and Electric Power. Many dissident scientists and specialists were excluded, and the participation of specialists was limited to the subject matter for which their experts' group was responsible. The experts were permitted to approve or disapprove of only the section they were studying. None of them participated in discussions of the project as a whole, and, as a result, many were unable to air their opposing opinions on the project overall. For these reasons, it is misleading to say that the plan for a 175-meter-high dam was approved by 403 of 412 specialists and opposed by only nine.

It is clear that the protracted nature of the assessment report was a result of an exclusive focus on the issue of dam height. The study concentrated on the comparative study of 185-, 180-, 175-, 160-, and 150-meter-high dams, but no comprehensive studies to compare the Three Gorges Project with alternatives for achieving flood control, electricity generation, navigation, and so on, were ever undertaken. In other words, the study was the verification of one option—the election of a single candidate. Can such approaches be considered democratic and scientific? This is simply a disguised form of the old tradition where the person with power lays down the law.

The January 1993 issue of the periodical *Party Documents* published a number of instructions or directives concerning the Three Gorges Project by Chairman Mao and Premier Zhou. One of the instructions was Mao's written reply of April 10, 1966, to a letter by Wang Renzhong, in which Wang asked Mao's direction on a report on the Three Gorges Project by Lin Yishan. In his letter Mao wrote: "We need an opposition opinion."

More than twenty-seven years have passed since that letter was written; however, Mao's instructions are not out of date. I request that the Central Committee invite a number of specialists who represent different points of view and oppose the immediate construction of the Three Gorges Project (or the 175-meter-high dam plan) to a special meeting. Please pay careful attention to their opinions, and excuse me for using an old saying, "Listen to both sides and you will be enlightened."

35
Li Peng Sends Letter to Three Gorges Experts' Meeting

Source: Beijing, Xinhua, May 25, 1993, *FBIS,* May 25, 1993.

This afternoon, seventeen experts of the core group for examining the initial design signed their names on the conclusion report of examining the initial design for the Three Gorges Key Water Conservancy Project. Thus the seventeen-day examination meeting by experts for the initial design of the Three Gorges Project was successfully concluded. During the course of the meeting, Premier of the State Council Li Peng wrote a greeting letter to the meeting.

Premier Li Peng said in his letter: In April last year, the Fifth Session of the Seventh National People's Congress adopted a "Resolution on the Construction of the Three Gorges Project," approved the inclusion of the Three Gorges Project in the Ten-Year Program for National Economic and Social Development, and decided to let the State Council select an appropriate time for the implementation of the construction project. At present, the project is in a preparatory period for its initial construction work. Taking a firm grip on and doing a good job in the examination of the initial design for the Three Gorges Project is an important link in ensuring the smooth construction of the project. It is hoped that all experts taking part in the meeting will, in the spirit of being responsible to the state, to science, and to history, fully express their views, make suggestions and proposals, do a good job in examining the initial design, and revise, supplement, and further improve the initial design.

The current meeting of experts to examine the initial design for the Three Gorges Key Water Conservancy Project was held in accordance with a decision made at the first conference of the Committee for the Construction of the Three Gorges Project of the State Council. According to the guidelines of the conference, the initial design was first examined by experts and then by the committee. Therefore, the General Office of the State Council's Committee for the Construction of the Three Gorges Project invited 126 experts to form a core expert group and ten expert groups on specific fields. The eleven chapters of the initial design were to be examined first by the ten expert groups on specific fields, and the core expert group would then put forward its conclusion in its overall examination of the initial design.

At the examination meeting, those experts gave full play to democracy in the field of technology, sought truth from facts in a serious manner, held enthusiastic discussions, approved the initial design in principle, and put forward many good opinions and suggestions. . . .

G. Foreign Policy

36
On the Resurgence of Communism:
The Goddess Restores the Crack in the Sky

Wei Wei

Source: Beijing, *Dangdai sichao* (*Contemporary Ideological Trends*), #6, December 20, 1992, pp. 59–60, *FBIS,* February 3, 1993.

No one ever expected that such a shocking event would take place at the end of the century—half of the socialist sky has collapsed. In this place, brightness turned to darkness, masters became slaves, fierce winds roared, tigers and wolves were running all over the wild fields, the capitalist bloodsucking animals came out again, and the people once again fell into the abyss of calamity.

Meanwhile the other half of the socialist sky is bathed in bright sunshine, although with some dark shadows. This is an exceedingly special situation of today. So, regarding the fate of socialism overall, what historical responsibilities should the people living under this part of the sky shoulder?

Here, I thought of the most ancient legend of our nation: The goddess restoring the crack in the sky.

According to the legend, the goddess, living somewhere around Taixing Mountain, was extraordinarily powerful. With a human head and a snake's body, she was capable of changing shape seventy times a day. It was said that it was she who created human beings. Unfortunately, the northwestern corner of the sky suddenly collapsed, and torrents of rain poured through endlessly. The sky could no longer cover the earth, and the earth was unable to prop up all things on it any longer. "The burning flames were inextinguishable, the flood water did not subside, ferocious beasts ate ordinary people, and fierce birds seized the old and the weak." It was a terrible, perilous, and astonishing scene.

However, the goddess was perfectly composed, and eventually patched up the crack in the sky with a kind of colored stone that she smelted. Afterward, she "cut the legs off a huge turtle to prop up the heavens, killed a black dragon to provide relief to the divine land, and threw reed ashes to stop the floods," so that the people were able to lead a peaceful life again. Like the stories of "Jingwei filling up the sea," "Kuafu chasing the sun," and "the foolish old man moving the mountain," the story of the "goddess restoring the crack in the sky" manifests the great spirit of the Chinese nation. When we review it today, perhaps it will give us some enlightenment!

Maybe some people will say: That is a legend, and the real sky, that half of the socialist sky, has already collapsed, and cannot be restored.

I say: No!

First, the specific road is tortuous, but the historical law of development is unchangeable. . . . Counted from the [1917] October Revolution up to the present, the socialist revolution has only been carried out for seventy-odd years. As viewed from the angle of history, the time is not very long, and the capitalist restoration that has taken place in some socialist countries is not incomprehensible, just like the restoration of the feudal classes in history. Similarly, such a restoration does not signify the ultimate victory of capitalism, still less change its inevitable decline. So far as the people in the socialist countries are concerned, this is merely a temporary setback, and it does not mean that they have finally bidden farewell to communism. In other words, this is merely the beginning of another round of struggle for the socialist revolution.

Second, we should draw lessons from the degeneration in some socialist countries, and peaceful evolution can be prevented. Now, there are three factors that have led to the degeneration in some socialist countries: 1) The strategy of peaceful evolution practiced by the imperialists in a protracted and positive way, which has influenced these countries; 2) the strong pressure exerted by the revisionist groups of some big countries on other countries that they had an influence on; and 3) the trouble stirred up by the domestic forces of bourgeois liberalization in these countries. These three factors often collaborated and coordinated with and echoed one another, and, when the opportunity arose, the political power of a socialist country was seized in one action, resulting in the fall of the country. Naturally, with regard to specific countries, there might be different centers of gravity. But we should point out that among these three factors, the most vital and decisive one was the domestic forces of bourgeois liberalization. That the evolution in some individual big countries was so vehement and rapid that they disintegrated in a very short time was mainly due to the fact that the revisionist and other anticommunist forces usurped the party and state leadership. This is the most dangerous thing of all, and is the most bitter lesson for the degeneration of the socialist countries. However, so long as the Marxist party really understands this, puts the fight against bourgeois liberalization on the high plane of strategy, and adopts a series of tough measures, peaceful evolution can be prevented.

Third, in the places where there were setbacks, the struggle will not stop, and the party and the people will be even more staunch. It goes without saying that the masses there were dragged into the deep abyss gradually by the revisionist swindlers. These political cheats used such bewitching stuff as "being open," "democratization," "multiple-party system," "new ideas," and the like to confuse people's minds so as to make them believe that if only they made one more stride, they would reach paradise. After this drastic change, their sweet dreams were shattered, and people felt painfully that they had been fooled and deceived. ... It can be stated that the people living in the drastically changed countries over the past couple of years have universally experienced the bitter results of degeneration. In these countries, society is turbulent, economies are sharply declining, inflation grows ferociously, prices are soaring sky high, and the unemployed emerge in multitudes, so that beggars appear in these countries where before there were none. We must note that those who have tasted the happy life of socialism will under no circumstances swallow this bitter fruit willingly. They will certainly rise to wage a struggle sooner or later. According to newspaper reports, wave upon wave of strikes and demonstrations have been staged unceasingly in some countries. The parties in these countries have sustained unprecedented assaults; some of them have been dissolved, others have been routed, and still others have changed their names. But the real communists will never stop fighting. They will certainly gather together and make their own ranks even more pure, firm, and combat-worthy. They will certainly sum up experiences and lessons conscientiously, rely closely on the proletariat and the masses, and seize back the state power usurped by the people who restored capitalism. We must know that these countries were, after all, socialist countries for several decades, the people's consciousness is high, the roots of communist ideology are deep, and their parties are considerably well founded. That is why we must not underestimate their potential. . . .

37
How Zhongnanhai Views Battle in Russian Capital

Lo Ping and Li Tze-ching

Source: Hong Kong, *Chengming,* #193, November 1, 1993, pp. 15–17, *FBIS,* November 12, 1993.

Jiang Zemin and Ding Guan'gen made speeches about the [October 1993] incident in the Russian capital. From their speeches and the way *Renmin ribao* reported the news, we can see that, superficially, the CCP remained "neutral" in the dispute between Yeltsin and the dissolved "parliament," but in fact, it sided with the rebellious group.

Superficially, Zhongnanhai's[1] response to the battle between those who wanted to restore the old order and those who were against the old order on October 3 in Russia was strangely calm, but the real situation was not like that.

The CCP Printed and Issued Materials on the Political Situation in Russia

On October 8, the CCP Central Committee General Office and the State Council General Office printed and issued a circular "on the recent happenings in Moscow." The content was a selection of reports by foreign media on the "large-scale conflict in Moscow," comments on Russia's situation by some Western analysts, and a forty-minute video tape about the scene in Moscow, entitled "Moscow This Week." . . . The CCP Central Committee Propaganda Department raised five topics for thought:

---

[1]The site of China's government and Communist Party leadership in Beijing.

1. The main reason for the disturbance in Russia.
2. The impact of Russia's political turmoil on the world.
3. U.S. strategy on supporting Yeltsin.
4. Why has the reform in Russia met with such big obstructions, and what is the crux of the problem?
5. The necessity to use the army for a crackdown.

Ding Guangen Analyzes the Bloodshed in Moscow

At a meeting of the party secretaries of ministries, commissions, and offices of the central authorities, convened by the CCP Central Committee Secretariat in early October, Ding Guan'gen analyzed the incident in Moscow. He said the political and military conflicts in Russia, and also the bloodshed, were in essence caused by the sudden changes in the power struggle within the leading echelon. The basic factors included the difficulties and setbacks in the political and economic reforms and the struggle between the redistribution of power and monopoly of power. The bloody military conflict, which was an outcome of the power struggle, will have a negative impact on future political stability in Russia and will cause more obstacles to the economic and political reforms. The army played a decisive role in this round of the power struggle, and, in the future, it will have a bigger role in deciding the government and the core leadership level, playing a guiding function.

Ding Guan'gen's speech mainly revealed three viewpoints:

1. The bloodshed in Moscow was a "power struggle," not a struggle between rebels and those who fought against them.
2. Yeltsin fought against the rebellion because he wanted to "monopolize power."
3. Russia's political situation in the future will be more unstable.

From this the people can see on which side the CCP stood during the battle in Moscow.

U.S. Support for Yeltsin Caused Great Resentment within the CCP

Ding Guan'gen also talked particularly about the interference by U.S.'s hegemony into Russia's situation and the consequences of such interference. He said: The United States and Western Europe openly support President Yeltsin because the development of the situation in Russia has a direct impact on U.S. global strategy. But the U.S. position toward Russia's situation contradicts the U.S. wish because it can only cause a rise of nationalism in Russia and strengthen the unity of the opposition forces—they have always opposed the involvement and interference in Russia's internal affairs by foreign forces, which do so out of their own strategic interests. In addition, Ding Guan'gen mentioned that the use of U.S. dollars to affect Russia's foreign and domestic policies is a new method of U.S. hegemony to get involved in and interfere in the internal affairs of another sovereign state under the new international condition.

U.S. support for Yeltsin caused great resentment within the CCP. The remarks by Ding Guan'gen once again revealed the CCP position toward the struggle between those who wanted to restore the old order and those who were against the old order in Russia.

Looking at such a big incident in Moscow, the general secretary of the CCP surely had something to say.

Jiang Zemin Proposes "Gun Barrel Determinism"

In early October, Jiang Zemin met the relevant personnel from the CCP Central Committee Policy Research Office and the Central Military Commission Policy Research Office. He talked about the incident in Russia and said that Russia's situation was very complicated, but the crux was the lagging Russian economy and lack of development. A power struggle at the leadership level took place, leading to an abnormal political situation in Moscow and to the military conflict and bloodshed in the city.

Precisely like Ding Guan'gen, Jiang Zemin did not point out that the bloody conflict in Moscow was caused by the leaders of the stubborn "leftist" clique who stirred up the rebellion but said it was a power struggle at the leadership level. What is noteworthy is that when the general secretary summed up Russia's experience, he proposed that it was "gun barrel determinism." . . .

The General Secretary Thinks That a Power Struggle
Will Not Take Place in China

Jiang Zemin also asked: Will a power struggle take place at the leadership level in China? I do not think it will because the leadership level within the party has fully implemented democratic centralism; every major decision or policy has to be collectively studied, discussed, and finalized by the CCP Central Committee Political Bureau, and the party's line is confirmed and adopted unanimously by the party congress.

Here, the general secretary once again resorts to "a big lie." Everyone knows that the fact that Jiang Zemin himself replaced Zhao Ziyang as the general secretary [in 1989] was an outcome of a power struggle at its peak. Indeed, China and Russia "differ in national conditions and systems" and the nature of the struggles is also different—the struggle in Russia was against a rebellion and an attempt to restore the old order, and the result of the struggle was that the diehards, who stood on the side opposite to the people, were brought under legal sanction; the struggle between the "reformists" and the conservatives in the CCP was a power struggle as well as a struggle between lines and, because the struggle itself was often a hard one, of course some leaders of the two cliques within the CCP would cease fighting from time to time and "turn their guns outside," one typical example being the [1989] June 4 Incident, but the essence of power struggle will never change.

38
Official Protest to U.S. Envoy

Source: Beijing, Xinhua, August 27, 1993, *FBIS,* August 27, 1993.

Chinese Vice-Foreign Minister Liu Huaqiu, at an urgent meeting here today with U.S. Ambassador Stapleton Roy, lodged a strong protest with the United States concerning the U.S. government's decision to impose sanctions against China on the grounds of its determination, based on its analysis of a so-called large body of evidence, that China has made M–11 missile-related transfers to Pakistan.

Liu said that the U.S. side, ignoring the repeated clarifications made by the governments of China and Pakistan and invoking domestic legislation, has willfully imposed sanctions against sovereign states. This naked hegemonic act has brutally violated the basic norms governing international relations, he noted.

The Chinese government and people express their utmost indignation at such a move on the part of the U.S. government which compromises China's sovereignty, dignity, and interests and puts Sino-U.S. relations in serious jeopardy, Liu said. "I am hereby instructed to lodge a strong protest with the U.S. government."

Liu stressed that the Chinese government has all along adopted a positive and serious approach toward preventing proliferation of weapons of mass destruction and their delivery systems.

In respect to export of conventional weapons, he said, China also strictly abides by its international commitments and its consistent principled position on transfer of such weapons. This is well-known and irreproachable, he added.

Liu pointed out that the Chinese side has told the U.S. side in explicit terms on many occasions that China has honored its commitment to acting in accordance with MTCR [Missile Technology Control Regime] guidelines and parameters and has done nothing in contradiction to that commitment.

Insisting on having its way, the U.S. side has now resumed sanctions on China, he said. This is most unreasonable and totally unacceptable to the Chinese side.

Liu pointed out emphatically that in September 1992, in blatant violation of the Sino-U.S. Joint Communique of August 17, the U.S. government decided to sell 150 F-16s to Taiwan, a move that has grossly interfered in China's internal affairs.

On the one hand, the U.S. has poured large amounts of advanced weapons into the region sensitive to China, threatening its security, and on the other hand, it has made groundless accusations and interference against China on self-invented stories. This is a show of power politics, he said.

In conclusion, Liu Huaqiu said that according to the bilateral agreement, the Chinese government's announcement that it would act in accordance with MTCR guidelines and parameters in February 1992 was predicated on U.S. removal of its sanctions imposed on China in June 1991.

Now that the U.S. side has resumed these sanctions, the Chinese government has been left with no alternatives but to reconsider its commitment to MTCR. The U.S. government shall be held fully responsible for all the consequences arising therefrom, Liu said.

39
Pakistan Admits Receiving Missiles from China

Source: Beijing, Xinhua, August 26, 1993, *FBIS,* August 27, 1993.

Pakistan Foreign Minister Abdul Sattar has regretted the U.S. decision to impose sanctions against Pakistan and China on the basis of incorrect information and groundless suspicion.

Making a statement in the Senate here [in Islamabad] today, he said Pakistan regretted the U.S. decision, especially because the sanctions affect our friend China more than Pakistan.

We deeply appreciate that China has throughout maintained a principled position in the matter, he added.

He admitted that Pakistan had acquired short-range tactical missiles from China.

He said that several years ago, when Pakistan was hit by Scud missiles, it decided to approach China for the supply of missiles to enhance the country's self-defense capability, and China kindly agreed to provide a small number of short-range tactical missiles.

When the United States raised this matter with Pakistan, we reaffirmed to Washington that the missiles Pakistan received were within the Missile Technology Control Regime (MTCR) parameters, and provided information in response to further questions, he said.

The U.S. announced economic sanctions against China and Pakistan on August 25, claiming that they dealt in sensitive missile technology in violation of international arms control. Both China and Pakistan have denied any violations.

40
UK's Cradock: PRC Prepared to "Wreck" Hong Kong Economy

Jonathan Braude

Source: Hong Kong, *South China Morning Post,* December 4, 1992, p. 1, *FBIS,* December 4, 1992.

[Excerpt] Britain's former China policy chief yesterday warned that Beijing was ready to wreck the economy of Hong Kong rather than back down in its battle to block democratic reforms.

Whoever won the battle of wills between China and Britain, Hong Kong would suffer, he said.

In a major BBC television interview, . . . Sir Percy Cradock, foreign policy adviser to two prime ministers before his retirement this year, said Sino-British tensions over Hong Kong were worse than at any time since the Cultural Revolution [1966–76].

In grim remarks that contributed to the stock market's devastating 433-point plunge, Sir Percy dismissed as an "economic fallacy" the belief that China would put prosperity above politics in its clash with Britain.

"We encountered it a lot in the main negotiations in 1983/84—the view that economic considerations come first. The Chinese made it abundantly clear then that politics comes first," he said.

"They brought Hong Kong to the edge of a serious financial crisis in September 1983 rather than accept continued British administration. The same rules apply today. This is a matter of national pride."

And in a barely disguised sideswipe at the Governor, Mr. Chris Patten, he warned that failure to cooperate with China would hurt Hong Kong, although "it might allow us to strike a heroic pose in Britain."

In blunt remarks on the BBC's influential "Newsnight," Sir Percy described the war of words between Britain and China as "the most serious crisis we've had in Hong Kong over the last ten years."

"To find anything like the same state of tension I think I'd have to go back to the Cultural Revolution in the sixties," he said. "Any situation where there is confrontation between Britain and China is bad for Hong Kong.

"It doesn't matter who wins, which of the two capitals wins or seems to be winning, Hong Kong suffers as it is suffering now."

The Chinese meant precisely what they said when they warned that they would scrap the Governor's policy innovations in 1997, he said.

"It would be a serious, indeed a fatal, misjudgment to think otherwise.

"They are very serious."

He refused to attack British policy directly or to criticize the Prime Minister, Mr. John Major, or Mr. Patten by name.

He said the Chinese might have been prepared to accept the degree of democracy already agreed to if relations had remained good. However if "those reforms" were implemented, they would be reversed.

"I'm sure they will be ready to dismantle them and impose what they think is a safer system, which, by definition, means a more repressive system," said the former Foreign Office mandarin.

41
PRC Office Reacts to Legco's Adoption of Electoral Bill

Source: Beijing, Xinhua, February 24, 1994, *FBIS,* February 24, 1994.

A spokesman for the Hong Kong and Macao Affairs Office of the State Council (HKMAOSC) of China made a statement to Xinhua here today after the Legislative Council (Legco) of Hong Kong passed this morning the partial electoral bill submitted by Chris Patten, governor of Hong Kong.

Following is the full text of the statement:

After the seventeenth round of the Sino-British talks on the arrangements for the 1994/95 election in Hong Kong was held, the British side walked away first from the negotiating table and submitted the electoral bill to the Legco despite the earlier statement made by the Chinese side, thus terminating the talks.

Even so, we made it clear repeatedly that for the Chinese side the door for negotiations was open under the prerequisite that the British side must withdraw the submitted partial bill from the Legco. However, the British side has ignored this and clung obstinately to its own course. It has not only had the partial bill passed at the Legco, but also decided unilaterally to make public the contents of the seventeen rounds of the Sino-British talks and to submit the rest of the electoral bill to the Legco,[1] thus closing completely the door for resuming the talks. Therefore, the British side should be held fully responsible for ruining the talks.

The Sino-British Joint Declaration and the Basic Law stipulate that

---

[1] The full electoral bill expanding the number of directly elected seats on the Legco was passed in 1994.

the British administration of Hong Kong will terminate on June 30, 1997 and the Chinese government will resume the exercise of sovereignty over Hong Kong as of July 1, 1997. In accordance with these provisions, the Chinese side reiterates that as component parts of the British political body administrating Hong Kong, the last British–Hong Kong district boards, the two municipal polls, and the Legislative Council will definitely be terminated together with the end of the British administration of Hong Kong. Before the Chinese and British sides reach an agreement on the arrangements for the 1994/95 elections, the three-level bodies produced on the basis of the partial electoral bill passed by the British–Hong Kong Legco or any other electoral bill possibly to be passed by the Legco cannot stand after the year of 1997. By that time, the political body of the Hong Kong Special Administrative Region will be formed according to the decisions of the Chinese National People's Congress and the relevant provisions of the Basic Law.

42
Commentary Urges End to [Taiwan's] "Three No's Policy"

Chu Ke

Source: Hong Kong, Zhongguo tongxun she, March 24, 1993, *FBIS,* March 30, 1993.

Chiu Chin-yi, secretary general of Taiwan's Straits Exchange Foundation, recently said that, at an appropriate time, Taiwan should examine its "three-no's policy" toward the mainland, because the policy "has fulfilled its duty," and that there was not much sense in upholding it.

This is a practical way of speaking, regardless of whether it is his "purely individual opinion," as he claimed it to be.

The "three no's policy" of no contact, no negotiation, and no compromise pursued by Taiwan is in fact a burden of history; it proceeds from feelings of ingratitude and resentment in history, and perpetuates long-term isolation and confrontation between the mainland and Taiwan. However, in the past two years, when real exchanges and interactions at various levels between both sides of the strait had become more frequent and when economic relations had gradually become inseparable, it actually became impossible to really implement the "three no's policy." However, the policy often still clumsily hinders the development of relations across the strait. Recently, for example, because of this outdated and impractical policy, two mainland basketball teams could enter Taiwan only after several rounds of mediation, and several eminent mainland academics almost could not enter Taiwan because they had official status.

During the "generational change," new-born politicians in Taiwan should really look calmly at the current direction in which cross-strait relations are developing, grasp the chance, cast off the old burdens of history, and take steps of a breakthrough nature. The good macroclimate for Taiwan at this time is:

First, mainland China is developing its economy "full steam ahead," and people and government officials across the whole country are responding to the call of the reform and opening up policy and are marching along the road of economic development. If various circles in Taiwan could promptly join the ranks and support it with full strength, they could get a free lift on one hand, and, on the other, enjoy "equal and preferential" policies granted to Taiwan compatriots by mainland China based on the feeling that blood is thicker than water. At present, Japanese, South Korean, and Western businessmen all envy the advantage held by Taiwan businessmen. The problem is, if the Taiwan authorities do not understand the macroclimate on the mainland and use the "three no's policy" to refuse to accept the kindness and sincerity offered by the mainland, then they may miss many good opportunities on the mainland, because the development of the mainland is very urgent, and it cannot wait for Taiwan businessmen to the extent of losing its opportunity for development; this point is very clear.

Second, at present, no matter whether in strategy or economic development, the whole world faces new integration, a so-called new world order is being deliberated, and obviously this kind of new order must "let the economy take the lead." Taiwan is small in size, lacks resources, and relies excessively on foreign-oriented economic means; whenever world markets fluctuate, Taiwan society is rocked. Recently, for example, the United States wanted to use "special article 301" [i.e., Super 301 provisions of U.S. trade law][1] to deal with Taiwan, and this greatly worried Taiwan society, which excessively depends on the U.S. market. If, through "omnipositional" exchanges, Taiwan enters the mainland market, which has 1.2 billion people, then, even if it suffers setbacks in trade with the United States, the effects would not be lethal; concerning this point, many Taiwan businessmen have profoundly realized the subtlety. To beg from other people is not as good as doing it ourselves, and while Taiwan businessmen are striving for a place in the international market, it would be unwise to ignore or deliberately avoid a readily available market that belongs to them and provides rich manpower and raw materials.

The two sides of the strait have been separated for more than forty years, and it is indeed difficult to settle quickly many political prejudices and burdens, and this is why the Taiwan authorities' mainland policy has always been dragged by the people. However, so long as those in power in Taiwan follow the development of the times, abandon their prejudices, visit the mainland more frequently, and have more contacts with mainland officials and persons in various circles, then they can surely feel the meaning of relations between the two sides of the strait.

---

[1]A provision of American trade law that allows the U.S. government to cite unilaterally another nation for trade violations.

43
Lien Chan Defends [Taiwan] Government's "Three No's Policy"

Source: Taipei, Taiwan, *Taipei China Broadcasting Corporation News Network,* November 2, 1993, *FBIS,* November 3, 1993.

While answering questions at the Legislative Yuan [Taiwan's "national" parliament], Premier Lien Chan pointed out yesterday: If it were not for the difficulties created by the Chinese communists, the Asia-Pacific Economic Cooperation forum would be a very good opportunity for contact between the two sides of the Taiwan Strait. He also pointed out: When conditions are ripe for us to join the United

Nations, it should be all right for both sides of the strait to discuss the reunification of the country in the United Nations.

However, when Legislator Cheng Chien-jen asked the government to explicitly declare the three no's policy out of date, Premier Lien Chan stated: The government of the Republic of China must be responsible to history and reality. Before the Chinese communists abandon what they call the one country, two systems and Four Cardinal Principles. . ., we should not jump to the second stage of the program for national reunification, should not hold talks with the Chinese communists, and should not compromise with them at any cost.

Legislator Cheng Chien-jen then pointed out: The three no's policy has long been impractical among nongovernmental organizations; it is no longer news that government officials have been in contact with Chinese communists. Therefore, this policy declared by [Republic of China] President Chiang Ching-kuo in 1979 has long been out of step with the times.

Legislator Cheng Chien-jen suggested that the three no's policy be replaced by a three yes' policy provided it is in the interest of the people and provided dialogue be held with the Chinese communists through a third party.

Further Readings

Black, George, and Robin Munro. *Black Hands of Beijing* (New York: John Wiley and Sons, 1993).

Dellios, Rosita. *Modern Chinese Defense Strategy: Present Developments, Future Directions* (New York: St. Martin's Press, 1990).

Dittmer, Lowell. *China under Reform* (Boulder, CO: Westview Press, 1994).

Fewsmith, Joseph. *Dilemmas of Reform in China: Political Conflict and Economic Debate* (Armonk, NY: M.E. Sharpe, 1994).

Goldman, Merle. *Sowing the Seeds of Democracy in China: Political Reform in the Deng Xiaoping Era* (Cambridge, MA: Harvard University Press, 1994).

Harding, Harry. *A Fragile Relationship: The United States and China since 1972* (Washington, DC: The Brookings Institute, 1992).

Joffe, Ellis. *The Chinese Army after Mao* (Cambridge, MA: Harvard University Press, 1987).

Joseph, William, editor. *China Briefing* (Boulder, CO: Westview Press, yearly).

Lee, Hong Yung. *From Revolutionary Cadres to Party Technocrats in Socialist China* (Berkeley: University of California Press, 1991).

Lieberthal, Kenneth, and Michel Oksenberg. *Policy Making in China: Leaders, Structures, and Processes* (Princeton: Princeton University Press, 1988).

Liu Binyan. *China's Crisis, China's Hope: Essays from an Intellectual in Exile* (Cambridge, MA: Harvard University Press, 1990).

Luk, Shiu-Hung, and Joseph Whitney, editors. *Megaproject: A Case Study of China's Three Gorges Project* (Armonk, NY: M.E. Sharpe, 1993).

Oi, Jean C. *State and Peasant in Contemporary China: The Political Economy of Village Government* (Berkeley: University of California Press, 1989).

Ruan Ming. *Deng Xiaoping: Chronicle of an Empire* (Boulder, CO: Westview Press, 1994).

Shirk, Susan L. *The Political Logic of Economic Reform in China* (Berkeley: University of California Press, 1993).

Terrill, Ross. *China in Our Time: The People of China from the Communist Victory to Tiananmen Square and Beyond* (New York: Simon and Schuster, 1992).

Unger, Jonathan, editor. *The Pro-Democracy Protests in China: Report from the Provinces* (Armonk, NY: M.E. Sharpe, 1991).

White, Gordon. *Riding the Tiger: The Politics of Economic Reform in Post-Mao China* (Stanford, CA: Stanford University Press, 1993).

Wu, Hongda Harry. *Laogai: The Chinese Gulag* (Boulder, CO: Westview Press, 1992).

Yan Jiaqi. *Toward a Democratic China* (Honolulu: University of Hawaii Press, 1992).

II

Economics

China's economic performance over the past decade of reform has been remarkable. Growth rates above 10 percent a year, a dynamic consumer market, billions in investment from abroad, burgeoning stock markets, and a rapidly growing export sector have all created an economic takeoff that has already transformed China into the world's third largest economy. Denied meaningful political participation after the 1989 Tiananmen crackdown, the Chinese people—rural and urban alike—have sought personal enrichment at a dizzying pace. The capitalist values that Mao Zedong once denounced during the Cultural Revolution (1966–76) have now become the social norm, especially in the country's vibrant coastal provinces.

Economic success did not, however, end the long-standing controversy over China's economic system. Defenders of orthodox socialism (Document 44), advocates of a mixed market/planned economy (Document 45), proponents of full marketization (Document 47), and even the nominally "retired" Deng Xiaoping (Document 46) openly debated the course of China's future economy throughout the 1989–1994 period.[1] At the same time, the growth of a modern economy forced the country to confront several crucial policy issues: What legal system should China adopt (Document 48)? What role should China's central bank play in the economy (Document 49)? How can enterprises adjust to the market (Document 50)? Should workers at inefficient state-run industries be laid off and comprehensive price reform enacted (Docu-

---

[1]For an analysis of recent debates over economic reform in China, see Lowell Dittmer, *China under Reform* (Boulder, CO: Westview Press, 1994), and Joseph Fewsmith, *Dilemmas of Reform in China: Political Conflict and Economic Debate* (Armonk, NY: M.E. Sharpe, 1994).

ment 52)? And, how should China pursue further integration into the world economy (Documents 62–65)?

The benefits of the country's economic growth for the average Chinese are many. Promises of a shorter work week (Document 53), larger per capita income, and wider availability of consumer goods have produced an unprecedented improvement in the standard of living in both the city and the countryside (Document 55). But China's new-found wealth has also created severe problems of insufficient electric power (Document 51), rapid inflation and severe disruptions in agriculture (Documents 57 and 58), a vast army of "floating laborers" (Document 59), and a growing gap between the country's richest and poorest regions (Document 61). Increased budget deficits throughout 1989–1994 have also prompted the government to reduce costly urban subsidies and propose comprehensive reform of housing (Document 60). But even as some top CCP leaders consider dismantling the entire socialist economic edifice, they have encountered stiff resistance in reforming China's industrial and agricultural economy (Documents 54 and 56).

A. The Economic Structure

44
Economic Levers Cannot Replace
Planned Economy

Wu Shiquan

Source: Beijing, *Guangming ribao,* November 11, 1989, p. 3, *FBIS,* December 5, 1989.

In the past ten years some people have proposed the establishment of a "new socialist system of commodity economy"[1] to replace mandatory plans and to fulfill state plans indirectly through economic levers. The main problem with this system is that it only stresses the law of value at the expense of the law of developing the national economy in a planned and proportionate way, thus making its function a mere formality and negating the government's functional role in directly managing the economy and the need for administrative means. As a result, it runs counter to the original idea of the "socialist planned commodity economy."

Planned economy was developed to meet the law of developing the national economy in a planned and proportionate way and belongs to the macroeconomic category; economic levers exist along with the law of value and belongs to the microeconomic category. Since their categories and characteristics are different, they cannot replace each other in terms of their mutual functions and roles. During the first twenty years of reform [1958–1978] we let the planned economy replace the readjusting market functions of economic levers. As a result, our microeconomy lost its vitality. In our reform in the past ten years, we let economic levers gradually replace the control functions of the planned

---

[1]The proposition of economic reformers that China's economy should utilize markets within a broader "socialist" economic framework.

economy, thus causing serious dislocation in the macroeconomic structure. The error of replacing one with the other violates the law of the unity of opposites. The former case pays attention to opposites instead of unity and excludes the commodity economy and the law of value outside the socialist economy. The latter case only stresses unity at the expense of opposites, and as a result, the planned economy loses its meaning. Why cannot the intermediary role of economic levers replace the role of the planned economy? This is because of the contradictions between macroeconomy and microeconomy.

First, there is a contradiction between the unified policy decision nature of macroeconomy and the scattered policy decision nature of microeconomy. The planned economy is at the policy decision level of macroeconomy, and its role is to grasp the general economic orientation and goals on a long-term basis and to implement corresponding policies and tactics. Macroeconomic policy can only be carried out through government action. Economic levers are at the policy decision level of microeconomy. Owing to the restrictions of scattered policy decisions of microeconomy, such a grand system of engineering as strategic economic development, disposition of productive forces, and readjusting the industrial structure are not only out of the question in terms of policy decision but are also unimaginable if we carry them out through "intermediaries." Over the past several years, there has been "hot" strategy but "cold" implementation. We have not been able to effectively carry out many measures precisely because we have been affected by "intermediaries." What should be pointed out is that the functions of an economic levers system and a government system are different. It is really inadvisable to impose the important task of macroeconomic management, which government departments should directly undertake, on departments in charge of economic levers because this is management that abandons the functions and roles of government.

Second, there is a contradiction between the planning of macroeconomy and the blindness of microeconomy. The goal of planned economy is to bring stability to microeconomic activities through the structural control of macroeconomy. However, economic levers are links in microeconomy that control macroeconomy. Since banks and credit loan departments have the nature of enterprises, they will of course blindly run after profits, thus running counter to macromanagement. When contradictions arise between profit-making and macroeconomic policy of banks and credit loan departments, macrocontrol will fall through if the government does not directly intervene. For instance, in the past few years, capital construction has been overextended and has cost more than our state can pay. The direct reasons are too much credit and too much money being issued. The final solution is still administrative intervention. Since "intermediaries" are unreliable, it is perfectly justified to strengthen government management over macroeconomy.

Third, there is a contradiction between the organized state of macroeconomic management and the anarchy of microeconomy. The planning and management of the national economy stress organization; otherwise it would be difficult to overcome the anarchy of microeconomy. This is especially true today when financial departments at all levels are responsible for their own budgets. When there are conflicts between local and state interests, a powerful authority is needed as a binding force. However, departments in charge of economic levers have no such authority. For example, in managing investments, the control of economic levers is often in the hands of local governments. When local interests hold sway and reach the extent of causing a shortfall in investments, the intermediary function of economic levers will become weak and ineffective. At this point, it is very necessary for the state to intervene in local affairs.

When the intermediary function of economic levers cannot replace the function of planned economy, then planning in the "new system" ceases to exist except in name. If we leave aside the question of planned economy, which serves only as a foil, what remains is a complete market economy. However, the complete market economy cannot solve the question of macroeconomy losing control.

45

Several Questions on Methods and Theory Regarding Studies in Economic Operations in China

Chen Yuan[1]

Source: Beijing, *Jingji yanjiu (Economic Research)*, #2, February 20, 1992, pp. 29–37, *FBIS,* May 27, 1992.

I. Identity of Planning and the Market

What kind of relationship is maintained between planning and the market in a socialist national economy? (Planning and the market mentioned here are in the sense of operational mechanisms.) There have been countless discussions on the question over the decades, and many views have been expressed. People generally observe the relationship as between two independent entities, believing that there is a pure planned economic model and a pure market economic model in the world, and that the task of those practicing socialism is to ingeniously put the two together. . . .

Is there any identicalness between planning and the market? I believe there is. First, planning and the market exist interdependently in a modern economy. In any society, economic planning cannot appear in a natural [i.e., underdeveloped] economy. All markets, no matter what kind, constitute a force that is divorced from a natural economy. If the market is regarded as a regulatory means for distributing social resources, it will have even less to do with a natural economy. A mature form of planning and the market can exist only in modern socialized mass production after the industrial revolution.

Second, in a modern economy, planning and the market have always accompanied each other. We have not yet seen a planned model that has no relation at all to the market. . . .

The question of a pure planning or pure market model existing in China presents even less of a problem. The founders of economic

---

[1] Chen Yuan is the influential son of China's long-time economic "czar," Chen Yun. See Glossary.

structures never proceeded from concepts. The regulation mechanism adopted by them depended on the practical conditions of the time. In most of the 1950s, market regulation accounted for a large proportion of the national economy. In the first half of the 1960s, a considerable amount of farm and sideline produce were exchanged through the market. Even during the "Cultural Revolution" [1966–76], exchanges between the state and the peasants were carried out generally according to the market. As to the unrealistic planning that appeared for a time and attempted to include everything, it was a seriously distorted, extreme practice conducted under the historical conditions at that time.

In a broader sense, planning is an arrangement made by people to attain a previously set target. The arrangement is made in advance and is active, scientific, definite, centralized, and unified. However, the market, which serves as a link among numerous economic units, makes arrangements afterward and is passive and blind. In addition, markets are independent, mutually contradictory, pluralistic, and decentralized.

To determine an economic target, we must carefully observe the activities of numerous economic units, and the market is the place for carrying out these activities. Accurate economic information basically originates from the market, and market information is quick and objective. Without a market, a planned target cannot be objective. Definite planning derives from the diversified and indefinite market environment. Conversely, a market cannot exist without centralism and planning. The market's definiteness, diversification, and plurality require a unified standard as a precondition and require a specific target as a motive power.

Judging from the global context, the precondition for a modern market's formation and existence is the arrangement of the scope and basic rules of economic links by a political authoritative power. Market activities cannot proceed without this arrangement. The formation of a capitalist unified domestic market takes the bourgeois revolution as a precondition, and the formation of a unified overseas market is an outcome of a world war. As far as various participants of market activities are concerned, external links are unplanned and indefinite. To cope with this indefiniteness, there ought to be a high degree of definiteness and planning within enterprises. The larger an enterprise is, the more it needs planning. Moreover, modern large enterprises cover a very large area of economic life. Within their scope, the allocation of resources is a nonmarket relationship. What is important is that the following situation often exists: An enterprise, a trade, or a country is not the one that brings forth new ideas for a particular kind of product, labor service, or production structure. Here there is the question of taking a shortcut, namely, studying the mature experiences of other enterprises and countries. This time, spontaneity comes in the second place, and artificial active arrangements take a leading role. Therefore, various types of strategic, economic, guidance, revitalization, and multiplication planning exist in all types of modern economies.

Planning and the market change into their opposite under given conditions. In a certain sense, planning is also a kind of market. The planned allocation of resources must still obey the law of value. In addition, if based on a poor understanding of the market and economic laws, a previously prepared, active plan will be out of touch with reality; lose its initiative; become a blind, passive, and remedial plan; and change to market characteristics in essence. Given the pattern of separation of powers, stratified plans are reflected more as pluralistic, decentralized, partial, independent, mutually conflicting, and blind in characteristics. They are also changing into the market. The definiteness of plans will also become indefinite and blind with a change in time and conditions. Conversely, a large number of random matters on the market will reflect the stability and definiteness of a long-term tendency. Under an indefinite market environment, enterprises will naturally demand that their own behavior is planned and definite, and their general demand for planning will appear particularly after a laissez-faire anarchic market eventually leads to a serious crisis.

We can see from this that planning structures the market, and the market seeks help from planning, with each existing in the other. Whenever people can make and need an artificial arrangement, the portion of planning in the economy is reinforced. Whenever there are comparatively more indefinite factors and whenever new ideas are badly needed, the portion of the market in the economy is reinforced. And indefiniteness does not remain unchanged. Once indefiniteness changes to definiteness, the object will call for planning (whatever its form), and when definiteness changes to indefiniteness, the market will become necessary again.

We can thus see that planning and the market are two poles in the modern economy. They are both methods for allocating resources in the modern economy. Here, what is of great significance to us is how China should follow its unique path of integrating planning with the market. The historical starting point of China's modernization process determines our country's Oriental nature, where, objectively speaking, the factors contributing to separation and combination are more concentrated than in the West. As a natural result, the tendency toward combination is more manifest externally in the social economy. Such a unifying factor is a precious historical legacy. To achieve modernization from a backward starting point, China must resort to the safeguard of the unifying forces and take such concentrated strength stemming from the combination as a motive power for development beyond the precapitalist stage. In the course of development, even when industrialization rises and social division of labor deepens in our country, the traits of combination will not disappear. Our country's industrialization course is bound to show features that are different from those in the West, and the development of our country's market is bound to have its unique form. These have been proven by our history. In our country's history, there has never been a stage of market development dominated by separation. Even when separatist regimes were set up in the days of political turbulence, this feature did not change. Furthermore, such a state of separation could never last long, and the inherent cohesion would lead to reunification. . . .

II. The Operation of the National Economy and Interest Entities

The question of how to study the operation of the national economy in our country as a process of socialist reproduction has not been resolved yet. Many people like to deal with the issue of economic operation simply as a technical and operational issue. They only talk about supply and demand or about production and fulfillment. They do not note the interests contradictions behind economic operations. This way of thinking may hinder the in-depth study of economic operations.

In the present economy, the movement of resources is very difficult. The entities are fixed, and the interests are rigid. Another characteristic of the present pattern of interest entities in our country is the development of decentralization, which is also a kind of pluralization trend. All institutions and entities, and even quasi-institutions and quasi-entities, are trying to turn themselves into interest entities, as long as they are performing or used to perform certain functions. These entities all take planning and market as the arena and means of contending for resources. What they are pursuing is opportunism of sorts with regard to planning and the market under the principle of furthering their interests to a maximum. A large majority of the entities coming into being in this way do not consider how to survive under the functions of the market mechanism; instead, they just try by every possible means to continue their existence by resorting to administrative force. When planning restricts their impulse to expand, they try to use "commodity" relations to break through such constraints; once they find that the market can no longer be the arena for them to scramble for resources but has become a limit to their demands, they will instinctively turn to administrative protection and intervention in an attempt to prevent themselves from being crushed by market forces. The way they come into being is not in line with the constraining terms of the market mechanism, so they instinctively fear the market. They thus stress so-called planning, which is in fact their antimarket, blind, and low-level administrative monopoly. It is precisely such planning that has seriously hindered the market's growth. The commodity relations developing under such conditions can only lead to irrepressible expansion, and are just a kind of extremely deformed and merely formalistic commodity relations. Such commodity relations cannot assume a stable state in the end and will only lead to economic disintegration and political crisis. This conclusion has been proved by history, and needs no further meaningless tests.

Since economic overheating and economic expansion are caused by the unreasonable and rigid pattern of interest entities, the restructuring of the interest pattern is the main means of overcoming the expansion. The restructuring of the interest pattern should first be aimed at breaking the illusion of equality among the various entities over the disposition of resources. It is necessary to clarify that the positions of various entities are determined by the roles and the functions they perform in the course of economic operations. Because various entities play different roles and perform different functions in economic operations, they naturally hold different positions. For example, the central government bears responsibility for directly promoting the development of basic industries, making technological progress, and guaranteeing economic and social stability, and it certainly cannot hold an equal position with enterprises and localities. The status of the local government also should not be equal to that of the enterprises with regard to public works in the locality. However, the local government should not exceed its functions and meddle in many industrial and commercial affairs, and should not use its administrative power to interfere in normal industrial and commercial activities. Enterprises should be really allowed to encounter the market, which causes the good to win and survive and the bad to be eliminated. With various entities being placed in correct positions, the root cause of economic overheating can be eradicated.

III. An Enlightenment from Western Economics: Supply-and-Demand Contradictions and Macroeconomic Regulation and Control

The economic structural changes and the intensified economic opening up since the 1980s have caused more conspicuous ups and downs in China's macroeconomy. We are thus required to carry out thoroughgoing studies as to their causes, mechanisms, and methods of regulation and control. Compared with Western countries, however, we still lag far behind in macroeconomic quantitative analysis as well as in the theory and practice of policy operation. This is precisely the reason why many scholars have turned to modern Western macroeconomic theories since the beginning of reform and opening up [in 1978], with the hope that they could either find a direct solution among those theories, or use the methods and frameworks to explain China's realities. It can be said that all these efforts have achieved some results; however, there still exist apparent defects in certain macroeconomic theoretical models that took shape in that period. Tracing their roots, these defects are attributable not only to the lack of a thoroughgoing and correct understanding of China's macroeconomy, but also to the ways in which people assimilate modern Western macroeconomic theories and methods.

In the history of economic thought, Keynes' macroeconomic analysis has undoubtedly proved to be a major breakthrough in research methodology, and his macroeconomic theory undoubtedly provided a new starting point and a new way of thinking for the development of modern macroeconomics. We can even say that the reason why the West could maintain a steady economic growth over a long period of time after World War II was that, besides such factors as scientific and technological progress, Keynes' theory did play an undeniable role in practice.

The following three major questions that China's economy is currently facing bear some resemblance to those Keynes encountered in his day: Do we dare to face squarely and admit the objective possibility and reality of an imbalance or even of China's macroeconomy being seriously out of control? What are the inherent mechanisms and deep-level structures that cause the macroeconomic imbalance and periodic fluctuations? What option should we select and what efforts should we make to ensure smooth economic operations and, in particular, to prevent vicious economic shocks, and what role should the state play in this process?

Historical experience and large quantities of proofs and studies have clearly shown that during the entire course of China's macroeconomic operation and growth, there have existed supply-and-demand contradictions, which can even become considerably intensive from time to time. That is to say, different economic systems cannot change the nature of imbalances in modern economic operations, and only the form of the imbalance is changed to a certain extent. If we say that the supply-and-demand imbalance in the Western economy mainly expresses itself in the inadequacy of effective demand, then we can also say that the aggregate imbalance in China's economy is mainly reflected in the undue expansion of total demand and the consequent inadequacy of effective supply. Such supply-and-demand contradictions existed in the past, and exist in the replacement of the old economic structure by a new one; and even for a considerable period to come, we can hardly extricate ourselves from their disturbances and influence, though the degree of imbalance may be reduced and its external form may change every now and then.

Judging from the angle of macroeconomic operations, an enlightenment we can gain from Keynes is that he dared to face the reality squarely; and what is more important, he pointed out in clear-cut terms that the function of macroeconomic quantitative regulation and control can be performed only by the government, not by market mechanisms. This reflects certain common features of modern economies. Ours is a developing country in which industrialization started rather late, and the market is still undergoing development. In China, the state also shoulders the responsibility for industrializing a backward country through catching up with and surpassing the advanced ones by "taking shortcuts," as well as the responsibility for fostering the market. It thus can be seen that in macroeconomic operation, the state is all the more an indispensable actor. The idea of excluding the state from economic operations and turning it into a passive "referee" is just a simplistic copy of the outdated Western economics prevailing several decades ago, without regard to China's national conditions. . . .

In a word, what we should assimilate from Keynes is his analysis of supply-and-demand contradictions in modern macroeconomics, as well as his exposition on bringing the state as an economic entity into the process of modern economic regulation and control; and what we should cast away is his deficit-centered financial policy.

1. Curbing inflation will be regarded as a priority goal in macroeconomic management. This implies the need to maintain a balanced budget as far as possible, and to oppose the policy of financial deficit. . . .

2. When selecting monetary policies for the purpose of preventing inflation and stabilizing economic growth, it is an enlightening point to give prominence to the role of money supply. The two major schools of Western economics, which respectively stress interest rates and money "supply," are both of considerable theoretical significance. However, judging from China's present situation, it is of greater practical significance to pay more attention to money supply in our monetary policies. In this field, many monetarist analyses merit special attention.

3. Attention should also be paid to the school advocating the theory of rational expectations and the supply-side economics school, for both of them stress the need to attach importance to studying the microeconomic elements in macroeconomics.

In contrast to the aforementioned attitude toward Keynesianism, when some people in our country show favor toward the monetarist school and the supply-side economics school, they set store by their laissez-faire economic philosophy rather than their policies for checking inflation; and the laissez-faire economic philosophy is precisely something that does not work in China. If we can put right this incorrect montage—that is, discard Keynes' expansion policy aimed at stimulating total demand, but use for reference his methodology of attaching importance to aggregate quantity and state intervention; and cast away the laissez-faire economic philosophy advocated by Milton Friedman and others, but use for reference their policies and suggestions on stabilizing currency, keeping an appropriate control over total demand, and increasing supply—we will surely discover that Western economics can be turned to serve our socialist construction.

46
Main Points of Deng Xiaoping's Talks in Wuchang, Shenzhen, Zhuhai, and Shanghai from January 18 to February 21, 1992

Source: Beijing, Xinhua, November 5, 1993, *FBIS,* November 8, 1993.

I

I visited Guangdong in 1984. At that time, rural reforms had gone on for several years, and urban reform and the establishment of special economic zones had just started. Now eight years have gone by since my last visit here. I did not realize that the developments in Shenzhen, the Zhuhai Special Zone, and other places have been this fast. After seeing these places, my confidence has increased.

Revolution can liberate productive forces; so does reform. Overthrowing the reactionary rule of imperialism, feudalism, and bourgeois capitalism to liberate Chinese people's productive forces is a revolution, and so revolution can liberate productive forces.[1] After the basic socialist system has been established, we must also fundamentally change the economic system that restricts the development of productive forces and establish a socialist economic system imbued with life and vitality so as to expedite the development of productive forces. This is reform, and so reform can also liberate productive forces. We used to stress developing productive forces under socialist conditions, and never stressed liberating productive forces through reform. This is incomplete. We should fully explain the need to liberate and develop productive forces.

The fast development that our country has achieved in just a decade or so has delighted the people and impressed the world. This is sufficient to prove the correctness of the line and the general and specific policies formulated since the [1978] Third Plenary Session, and that nobody can change them even if they want to. To put it simply, the bottom line is that there will be no change in upholding this

---

[1]The concept in Marxist theory that emphasizes the role of labor and technology in enhancing production.

line and the general and specific policies. We have drawn up many laws and regulations since the adoption of the reform and open policy, and these laws and regulations govern affairs in all areas. There are specific principles and policies governing economic, political, scientific, technological, educational, cultural, military, and diplomatic affairs, and there are even standardized expressions. The recent Eighth Plenary Session of the Thirteenth Central Committee has been successfully convened. It reaffirms that the responsibility system under which contracts are linked to rural households' outputs will remain unchanged. If this system changes, people will feel ill at ease and will say that the CCP Central Committee is going to change its policies. Shortly after reform started in the rural areas, the issue about roasted melon seeds produced by a man who called himself a "fool" occurred in Anhui Province. At that time many people felt uncomfortable, saying that this man had made a profit of one million yuan [$175,400], and they said something had to be done about him. I said nothing should be done; otherwise, the gains might not make up the loss. There are also many similar problems that, if not properly handled, will upset our policies and affect reform as a whole. The basic policies for urban and rural reform must be stabilized for a long period. Of course, following the development of our work, what ought to be improved or amended should be improved or amended accordingly, but they should basically remain unchanged. It is all right too even if you cannot come up with any new ideas. Changelessness is what is needed. We should not make people think that policies are going to be changed. If we follow this rule, China will have great hopes.

II

We should be bolder in carrying out reforms and opening up to the outside world and in making experimentations; we should not act like a woman with bound feet. For what we regard as correct, just try it and go ahead daringly. Shenzhen's experience means daring to break through. One just cannot blaze a trail, a new trail, and accomplish a new undertaking without the spirit of daring to break through, the spirit of taking a risk, and without some spirit and vigor. Who can say that everything is 100 percent sure of success with no risk at all? One should not consider oneself always in the right—there is no such thing.

I never think so myself. Leaders should sum up experiences every year. They should persist in what is right and promptly correct what is not. New problems should be immediately solved whenever they emerge. It may take thirty more years for us to institute a whole set of more mature and complete systems in various fields. Under this set of systems, our principles and policies will fall more into a pattern. Now we are better experienced with each passing day in building socialism of the Chinese type. There is a wealth of experience in this regard. Judging from newspapers published in various provinces, they each have their own distinguishing features. This is good, and creativity is just what we need.

Failing to take bigger steps and break through in carrying out reforms and opening to the outside world is essentially for fear that there may be too much capitalism or that the capitalist road is followed. The question of whether a move is socialist or capitalist is crucial. The criterion for judging this can only be whether or not a move is conducive to developing the productive forces in socialist society, increasing the comprehensive strength of the country, and improving the people's living standards. There were differing views on setting up special economic zones from the beginning, and people feared that they might involve the practice of capitalism.[2] The achievements made in the construction of Shenzhen provide clear answers to people with various misgivings. The special economic zones are socialist, not capitalist. Judging from Shenzhen's situation, public ownership is the main system of ownership, and the investment by foreign businessmen accounts for only one-fourth of the total amount of investment in the zone. As for foreign investment, we can also benefit from it through taxation and by providing labor services. There should be more three kinds of partially or wholly foreign-owned enterprises, and we do not have to be afraid of them. We do not have to be afraid so long as we keep a clear head. We have advantages, such as large and medium-sized state enterprises, and village and town enterprises. More important, the political power is in our hands. Some people hold: The more foreign investment, the more capitalism; the more three kinds of partially or wholly foreign-owned enterprises, the more capitalist things—that means

---

[2]The intense leadership struggle in China over creation of the special economic zones is analyzed in Ruan Ming, *Deng Xiaoping: Chronicle of an Empire* (Boulder, CO: Westview Press, 1994), pp. 134–141.

the development of capitalism. Those people do not even have basic common sense. In accordance with current laws, regulations, and policies, foreign businessmen running such enterprises always make some money. But the state taxes them, and they pay our workers; we can also learn from their technology and managerial expertise and get information to open up markets. So the three kinds of partially or wholly foreign-owned enterprises that are restricted by our political and economic conditions are a beneficial supplement to the socialist economy. In the final analysis, they are advantageous to socialism.

Whether the emphasis is on planning or market is not the essential distinction between socialism and capitalism. A planned economy is not socialism—there is planning under capitalism, too; and a market economy is not capitalism—there is market regulation under socialism, too. Planning and market are both economic means. The essence of socialism is to liberate and develop productive forces, to eliminate exploitation and polarization, and to finally realize common prosperity. This is the truth I want to explain to you all. Are negotiable securities and stock markets good stuff after all? Are they risky? Are they peculiar to capitalism? Can they be used in socialism? Try them out, but try them resolutely. If they prove to be correct after one or two years, let's open them up; if they prove to be wrong, let's take corrective action by closing them. Even if we want to close them, we can close them quickly or slowly; and we don't have to close them completely. There are no grounds for fear. If we persist in such an attitude, we will be all right and will not commit major blunders. In short, in order to win a relative edge of socialism over capitalism, we must boldly absorb and draw on all fruits of civilization created by the society of mankind, as well as all advanced management and operational methods and modes reflecting the law on modern socialized production in various countries of the world today, including developed capitalist countries. . . .

III

To seize the opportunity and develop ourselves, the key lies in economic development. At present, the economies in some of our neighboring countries and regions are developing faster than ours. If we do not develop our economy or if we do it too slowly, the people will complain after making comparisons. Therefore, if development is possible, we should not block the way. Localities with conditions should carry out development as quickly as they can. As long as attention is paid to economic efficiency and product quality, and as long as the economy is export-oriented, we need not be worried about anything. Low-speed development is equal to stagnation or even retrogression. We should grasp the opportunity. The present is precisely a good opportunity. I am afraid that the opportunity may be lost. If you do not grasp it, the opportunity in sight may still slip away, and we may lose time easily.

We must strive to upgrade the economy to a new level every few years. Certainly, I do not mean to advocate an unrealistically high growth rate. Rather, we should do down-to-earth work, pay attention to solid results, and carry out steady and coordinated development. Take Guangdong Province as an example. It should strive to raise itself several notches higher and catch up with the "four little dragons" [South Korea, Taiwan, Hong Kong, and Singapore] of Asia in twenty years. Take Jiangsu Province and other comparatively developed areas as another example. Their development should be quicker than the national average. It is now completely possible for Shanghai to develop more quickly. Shanghai has obvious advantages in intellectual personnel, technology, and management, and its influence is broad and wide. In retrospect, one of the great mistakes I committed was not to include Shanghai when setting up the four special economic zones. Otherwise, the present situation of reform and opening up in the Yangtze River delta area, in the entire Yangtze River valley, or in China as a whole, would have been quite different.

Judging from international experience, we can see that some countries have gone through a period of rapid development or certain stages of rapid development in the course of their development. This can be said of Japan, South Korea, and some countries and regions in Southeast Asia. Now, with the conditions existing at home, with the favorable international environment, and with the socialist system's strong point of being able to concentrate forces on handling important jobs, it is necessary for us to bring about several stages of comparatively rapid development that produce comparatively good economic results in the protracted process of modernization in the future, and we are capable of doing do. We simply must have such an ambition!

47

China Cannot Implement the Quasi-Market Economy

Xiao Liang [economist]

Source: Beijing, *Gongren ribao,* April 30, 1993, p. 3, *FBIS,* May 24, 1993.

The socialist market economy we are going to practice is a modern market economy whose main body is enterprises and individual business operators. It functions entirely in the context of the market, which is regulated and controlled by the state. It is not a completely laissez-faire economy; still less is it a quasi-market economy whose main body is the government or that is guided by the government. In view of China's actual situation, practicing a completely laissez-faire economy is almost out of the question, while the emergence of a quasi-market economy is not impossible. Therefore, we must be cool-headed and have a clear conception of what we are doing.

Of course, there must be a gradual process from the planned economy to the market economy and from a homogeneous planned economic system to the coexistence of the new and old systems and to the homogeneous market economic system. Reform is meant to complete this process. In fourteen years of reform, we have already gone through more than half of this process, and the future road will be much tougher. Because the complete negation of the planned economic system and the establishment of a new socialist market economic system involve the question of redistributing rights and interests, it is necessary to conscientiously carry out reform at a deep level and consider it a revolution.

Why is it possible for China to develop into a quasi-market economy rather than a real market economy?

First, due to the influence of several decades of the planned economic system, both the cadres and the masses are accustomed to administrative orders, which have even become a fixed norm for some people. It seems that all economic activities can only be directly commanded by the government. Now that we are practicing a market economy, enterprises and individual business operators will become the main body of interest and of the market—and they will have to make their own decisions on all activities. For some people, this is something they are not used to and is unthinkable. Why have we not been able to succeed in the separation of the functions of the government from those of the enterprise, which we have called for for many years? Why is it that, when we are experimenting with the joint stock system, many places still use the same management method for joint stock companies as for enterprises owned by the people [i.e. state-owned firms], whereby their chairmen, directors, and general managers are appointed by the personnel department, but shareholders are deprived of their rights? Why is it that, up to the present time, leaders of the collective enterprise are still appointed and dismissed by its supervisory department rather than being elected and discharged by the enterprise's staff and workers? Why do so many comrades think it inconceivable that an enterprise could be an independent commodity producer and operator and should not have a supervisory department over it—that it should become an entity without a supervisory department in the future?

We clearly recall that, for some time after the CCP approved the "Decision Regarding Economic Restructuring" in 1984 to confirm that the socialist market was a planned commodity economy, it seemed that no one was outwardly opposed to the commodity economy any longer, but they had very different ideas and understanding of it. Comrades favoring the commodity economy from the start maintained that the planned commodity economy should be based on the commodity economy, while those who were originally opposed to it held that the planned commodity economy should be based on planning. After [June 4] 1989, some people even said that the socialist economy was in effect the planned economy with a commodity nature. Some published articles to criticize viewpoints that put a high value on the commodity economy, saying that the extinction of the commodity economy, as Karl Marx had predicted, was becoming a reality.

Now that the [October 1992] Fourteenth CCP National Congress confirmed that China will practice the market economy, people will—of course—no longer publicly oppose this type of economy. But it is very normal and not strange at all that people have different ideas and understanding of it.

We will give two examples here.

First, in recent months, some people have suddenly and fully affirmed the pattern under which "the state regulates the market and the market guides the enterprises." They argue that the market economy should use this mode of operation. I hold a different view on this issue. I think that, when the Thirteenth CCP National Congress proposed this pattern five years ago, it represented great progress at that time, because it gave prominence to the role of the market. Since the Fourteenth CCP National Congress, however, this pattern no longer works, because, under the pattern of "the state regulating the market and the market guiding the enterprises," the state is still the initiator, organizer, and decision maker for economic operations and is the main body, while enterprises can only be passive executors and regulated entities and are not the main body of the market. Moreover, under this pattern, there is only one-way state regulation of the market and enterprises rather than two-way regulation of the state by the market and enterprises. Under a true market economy, state regulation must be built on the foundation of the market economy, and state regulation should be adaptive regulation.

Second, to some people's surprise, some comrades who were originally opposed to the market economy now feel interested in the relationship between planning and the market and are beginning to advocate that the market be integrated with planning. They originally stressed that the planned economy should be the primary element and eloquently argued that planning and the market could not be on the same footing. What does this mean? I guess they still want to retain some room for the planned economy. I think that discussion on the relationship between planning and the market should have been settled with the Fourteenth CCP National Congress, which confirmed that we will practice the socialist market economy. As a system, the socialist market economy is a total negation of the previous planned economy. The two are no longer integrated; one has replaced the other. Although the future socialist market economy does not rule out state regulation and government management, we are not saying that we need no planning, but rather that it can only be based on the market economy.

Third, some comrades are still maintaining that China's market economy should be guided by the government. I think this question can be discussed. A government-guided market economy will probably retain some practices of the previous planned economy, mainly the method of using administrative orders to allocate resources, affecting the role of the market and restricting the formation of the main body of the market.

I think that, if this question does not draw attention, according to the understandings and views of some comrades mentioned above, it will be very possible for China to develop a quasi-market economy, rather than a true market economy.

A true market economy differs from a quasi-market economy primarily in the following three points:

First, in a true market economy, the operation of the entire social economy is based on the market and takes it as the foundation. State regulation proceeds on the basis of market economic operations. To separate the functions of the government from those of an enterprise, the object to be regulated and controlled by the state is a matter of macroeconomic economic relationships, not direct administrative interference in activities. Whereas, in the quasi-market economy, although the scope of market regulation is already very large and enterprises are to a very large extent geared to the needs of the market, the state often interferes with enterprises' activities, external environments, and internal mechanisms, making it impossible for them to completely gear themselves to the needs of the market.

Second, in a true market economy, enterprises and individual business runners are the main body of the market. They have complete operating rights and can start competition on an equal footing, whereas the government is only the monitor, manager, and servant, rather than a commander and initiator. In the quasi-market economy, enterprises and individual business operators already have considerable self-operating rights and launch competition within a certain scope, but the government is still the initiator, organizer, decision maker, and commander of the entire social economy and is the leading force of social economy.

Third, a true market economy totally negates the previous planned economy, while the quasi-market economy primarily uses state regulation and control and retains a considerable proportion of the planned economic system.

Proceeding from improving efficiency, rationally allocating resources, and invigorating the entire social economy, I think that China can only take the path of the true market economy and must guard against becoming a quasi-market economy.

B. Economic Policy Issues

48
Qiao Shi on Legal System for a Market Economy

Source: Beijing, Xinhua, January 13, 1994, *FBIS,* January 21, 1994.

Qiao Shi, Standing Committee member of the Political Bureau of the CCP Central Committee and chairman of the National People's Congress Standing Committee, said recently: The establishment of a socialist economic structure is a great pioneering undertaking, and the establishment and development of a socialist market economic structure requires standardization and perfect legal guarantees. . . .

Qiao Shi said: There is no precedent in the world for a smooth transition from a planned to a market economy, no ready formula for establishing the legal system of a socialist market economy. . . . The [recent] enactment and enforcement of laws have guided, standardized, guaranteed, and regulated the creation of a socialist market economic structure. However, because the legislation for the socialist market economy covers extensive areas, there are numerous laws that need to be enacted. We must pay close attention to planning in our legislation. Judging from the present situation, the NPC and its Standing Committee must act promptly to formulate laws designed to standardize norms for the market, keep the market orderly, perfect macroeconomic control and regulation, and improve social security. The enactment of laws in these areas is essential to the establishment and perfection of a socialist market economy, which requires standardization and perfect legal guarantees. We should accelerate the pace of economic legislation and update the backward legal system in the spirit of reform so that people can be aware of legal and illegal behavior under the conditions of a market economy, and can use laws to guide, promote, and guarantee the smooth progress of reform and to provide a legal basis for the growth of the market economy. Meanwhile, we should revise or abolish in time laws and regulations that are incompatible with the establishment of the socialist market economic structure so as to ensure the consistency and coordination of the legal system of the market economy. . . .

Qiao Shi pointed out: Drawing up laws concerning the socialist market economy is something new for us. While we must consider China's actual situation when we draw up laws and regulations, we must also broadly study and borrow other countries' legislative experiences and learn about those that are useful to China. All the laws must be conducive to developing the economy and safeguarding China's stability and unity. While we must consider China's actual situation when we make a law, this does not mean that we can ignore foreign experiences. We must dare to assimilate that in foreign laws which is good and useful to us. We should also learn from their mistakes. We may directly transplant those articles that we can use, and then reinforce and improve them during their application. Because the market economy is an open, worldwide economy, our laws relevant to the market economy must be compatible with certain foreign laws. This compatibility not only can speed up our process of creating market economic laws but can also link our economy with the world economy and enable us to compete in the world.

49
Properly Serve as Banks' Bank—Thoughts on Monetary Problems

Shi Mingshen

Source: Beijing, *Renmin ribao,* November 3, 1993, *FBIS,* November 30, 1993.

Since the reform and opening up, a notable change in China's financial structure has been the change from a unified banking structure, which is suited to the product [i.e., backward] economy, and the establishment of a central bank system. The People's Bank has become the banks' bank and that of the government. It has exercised the special functions of a central bank.

In recent years, the People's Bank has boosted economic growth by approving, in a planned way, the establishment of various new monetary establishments; nurturing securities, capital, and foreign exchange swap markets; and expanding monetary opening to the outside world. In terms of macroeconomic regulation and control, it has also started paying attention to the use of interest rates, reserves, and other economic means to regulate financial activities. However, as China is in the midst of making the transition from a planned economic to a market economic structure, it lacks experience, and there is also the influence of the old planned economic structure. As a result, the various relationships between the central bank on the one hand and the governments, treasuries, and specialized banks at all levels on the other have not been fully straightened out, and mandatory credit quotas are principally used to exercise financial regulation and control. These are no longer suited to the development of a market economy. With the growth of a socialist market economy, an urgent subject of the financial reform is to perfect the central bank structure and improve the means of financial macro-regulation and control.

Bank credits are generally divided into two categories. The first are credits that must be guaranteed, such as those for grain and cotton purchases and reserves and for key state construction projects; the second are those independently issued by the banks according to their capabilities. To ensure guaranteed credits, to prevent credits from surpassing deposits, and to avoid excessive currency issuance, the central bank has exercised "dual controls" over specialized banks; that is, they should have both scope and funds. Just as people in the past had to take along grain coupons and money to buy grain in a grain shop, specialized banks at present must have both the scope and funds when issuing credits. Some bank presidents cannot grant more credits even if they have ample funds, and so they are worried because they have to pay interest for nothing. Despite their large scope, some other banks cannot support economic growth because they cannot raise the funds. Overall, this state of affairs boosts the expansion of credit. As a result, the state credit plan worked out at the beginning of the year is often outstripped during the year and has to be readjusted at the end of the year.[1]

On the other hand, for a long time in the past, as the central bank's principal targets of regulation and control, specialized banks did not have a clear status. They were both institutions and enterprises and were both policy and business-related banks. In most cases, specialized banks passively issued credits according to administrative organs' requests rather than to the efficiency, liquidity, and security of the credits. On the surface, it was a very "smooth" situation. In effect, however, not only has it resulted in banks being less concerned about the safety and efficiency of their credits, but it also has made it more difficult for the central bank to exercise macroeconomic regulation and control. When their economic interests came into conflict with their policy-related business, some specialized banks put their money in more profitable areas and projects. When there was a shortfall in policy-related funds, they would ask the central bank for money.

According to a rough estimate, the People's Bank spends about 70–80 billion yuan [$12–14 billion] per annum making up funding shortfalls for the purchase of agricultural and sideline products and for the export trade, key construction projects, and key enterprises. Moreover, for a long time in the past, state-owned enterprises have relied on specialized banks for funds. This has also increased the dependence of the specialized banks on the central bank for funds. Over the years, with all quarters asking for money, the central bank has been reduced to stricter circumstances.

The hardest thing for the central bank to handle is that it has to assume the function of paying financial expenses. When there is a deficit, the state treasury either creates an overdraft or obtains credits from the bank without giving a mortgage or a guarantee or specifying a repayment time. Since financial expenditures are always greater than receipts, debts are naturally not repaid.[2] The consequence of linking the bank with the state treasury is obvious: Issuance of cur-

---

[1] In fall 1993, the central bank created $17 billion (97 billion yuan) in credits to meet the cash shortfall of China's 11,000 state-owned firms, two-thirds of which lose money. Total employment at these firms is 109 million workers and 20 million pensioners. See *New York Times*, May 5, 1994.

[2] The cycle of debt between banks, factories, and their suppliers in China is now so large that a major portion of the banking system would have to declare itself bankrupt if the losses were recognized.

rency in excess of economic growth makes it impossible for the central bank to control the supply of money and credit.

Due to the lack of coordination in external reforms, the central bank does not have enough powers of macroeconomic regulation and control. Furthermore, it should also improve its own work. Since taking up the special function of a central bank in 1984, the People's Bank has not genuinely detached itself from the past. Not only has it set up economic entities, it has also handled some direct investments. Naturally, its ability to stabilize the currency's value and develop the economy has been affected.

An important task for the financial structural reform is to change the functions of the People's Bank. It should shift the focus of its work from determining the scope and distribution of funds to working out and implementing money and credit policy and stepping up the supervision and management of monetary institutions. It should attach importance to the use of economic, legal, and the necessary administrative means to regulate and control financial activities, and it should serve well as the bank of the banks and the government and as an issuing bank.

Practice at home and abroad and historical experience shows that it is impossible for a central bank to effectively exercise indirect macroeconomic regulation and control without a relatively independent status. For this reason, some relevant economists call for the speedy formulation of a "Central Bank Law" to define the functions and status of the central bank in a legal form. In particular, it should be made clear that financial deficits should be made up in full by issuing government bonds to society rather than by continuously creating overdrafts or by borrowing from the central bank. By plugging this hole, pressure on the bank to issue currency in excess of economic growth will drop substantially. A senior leader recently suggested the establishment of a regulation and control system for the central bank that is directly led by the State Council and carries out monetary policy independently. Taking advantage of the opportunity to rectify the monetary order and supported by the coordinated reforms of the financial, planning, investment, and foreign exchange structures, the People's Bank should replace current planning, which is based on credit ceilings and administrative and management means, with such economic and legal means as reserve deposits, discount bills, open market business, interest rates, exchange rates, and legislation, and should gradually change from direct to indirect regulation and control.

50
On Bringing Enterprises into Direct Contact with Market

Source: Beijing, Interview with Dong Fureng, *Jingji cankao bao (Economic Reference News),* March 15, 1992, p. 4, *FBIS,* April 2, 1992.

Dong Fureng, renowned economist and vice chairman of the Financial and Economic Committee of the National People's Congress, was interviewed . . . the other day. He offered his opinion on what kind of enterprises should be brought into direct contact with the market and how this can be done.

Dong Fureng said: I look at the state-owned enterprises in two broad categories. One of them covers competitive enterprises that aim at profit making and operate according to market conditions. The other category covers noncompetitive enterprises, which can be further classified into two subcategories. In one subcategory, there are enterprises that enjoy natural monopolies over railways, electric power, urban natural gas, and so on. Their operation cannot be totally or almost totally regulated by the market like that of competitive enterprises. In the other subcategory, there are enterprises that take care of public welfare, such as bus companies. Often, enterprises in this subcategory do not make high profits, or cannot make profits at all, and may even suffer losses that entail government subsidies. The state-owned enterprises in these two subcategories cannot be subjected to market regulation. Only the competitive state enterprises should be brought into the market.

To bring the competitive state enterprises into the market, the first problem to solve is the excessive number of goals the enterprises are required to fulfill. For example, an enterprise may be required to make higher profits; guarantee the fulfillment of the prescribed contributions to state revenue; ensure employment; guarantee certain benefits for its workers, such as housing, medical care, and care of the elderly; undertake the task of urban construction; maintain social stability; and safeguard the stability of the market. The many goals set for enterprises are weighing them down to an unbearable extent. In solving the problem of excessive tasks for enterprises, the most important measure that can be carried out now is to reform the housing, medical insurance, and old-age pension systems, and to establish a social security system and labor transfer system. In this way, these social tasks on the backs of enterprises can be detached from their own goals. Some of them can be taken up by the government, some by individual workers, and some by the enterprises, individual workers, and the government together.

In my opinion, at present, when the new and old systems coexist, the enterprises can be divided into two categories: The tasks assigned by the state under its mandatory plans can be put together and given to some enterprises, and the rest of the enterprises can set their sights on profit making and come into direct contact with the market as competitive enterprises.

At the moment, it is necessary to give full decision-making power to the competitive enterprises in direct contact with the market. In the meantime, we must also resolve the issue regarding the enterprises' sole responsibility for their profits and losses. Without enterprises that operate independently, make their own decisions, and take sole responsibility for their profits and losses, where would be the market to speak of? Naturally, however, without a developed competition-oriented market, it would also be difficult for enterprises to act as the main body of the market. Enterprises and the market are like the two sides of a shield and cannot be separated. In my opinion, bringing enterprises into the market requires some vigorous efforts to improve the market in the following respects:

First, it is imperative to make it possible for production essentials to circulate freely in the market;

Second, enterprises should be able to sell their products freely through the market;

Third, prices should be determined by the conditions of market supply and demand;

Fourth, it is imperative to have well-developed market regulations and market organization.

51
Electric Power: Another "Bottleneck" in China's Economy

Jiang Shijie

Source: Beijing, *Renmin ribao,* October 11, 1993, pp. 1, 2, *FBIS,* October 27, 1993.

In the first half of this year, we devoted much space to coverage of China's railway transportation dilemma, which causes grave concern among our readers and the relevant authorities. Beginning today, we bring you a series of reports on the problem of electric power supply, starting with "Electric Power—Another 'Bottleneck' in China's Economy." . . . In order for the national economy to maintain a sustained, speedy, and healthy development, it is imperative to adjust the industrial structure in real earnest and make substantial efforts to solve the restrictive factor of "bottlenecks." This is an important issue of immediate significance affecting the whole situation. Authorities at all levels and in all departments should pay attention to it. The discussion, concern, and support from various quarters may contribute to a better and more unified understanding so as to pool the wisdom of the masses and find more and better approaches and methods for solving these problems. . . . At the moment, if one says that railways are a "bottleneck" that throttles the national economy, everybody would nod their heads in agreement.

However, if one says that electric power is another "bottleneck" that restricts the development of China's economy, it may not be an accepted truth for everybody. Many comrades would be taken aback and question: Is it?

Is it not true that China's electric power production and installed capacity leaped to fourth place in the world in 1987 and has stayed in this position?

Is it not true that since 1988, the total installed capacity has been increased by 60 million kW, which is equivalent to the total capacity installed in the thirty years before reform and opening up [1948–78]?

Is it not true that today, the average amount of energy generated in two days is equivalent to that of the whole country in the whole of 1949?

It must be affirmed that the grounds of the above questions are all factual. However, this is not the whole picture of China's power supply today. The following are some other facts that are also very important:

The Power Shortage Is Like a Specter That Has Been Pacing Up and Down and Loitering on the Land of China for over Two Decades. Frequent Power Cuts to Enforce Power Rationing Indicate That This "Vanguard" Is "Debt-Ridden" and Limping Along

The shortage of China's power supply began as early as 1970, when the situation of "little food and many mouths to feed" appeared. Because the production, supply, and marketing in relation to the operation of electric equipment must be kept in balance at all times, the main expedient to fill the gaps in power supply was cutting power to enforce power rationing. Thereupon, the offices for planning utilization of electric power, which in time became known as the "three electricity offices" after the regulatory functions for efficient utilization of electric power and safe utilization of electric power were added to them later, emerged in all parts of the country as a product of that age. Under the meticulous arrangements of the "three electricity offices," factories, mines, government organs, and urban and rural residents began to experience suspension of power supply, once a week or several times a week.

In order to change this unbearable situation, for more than two decades the party and the government have adopted a series of measures that truly brought much progress to the power industry, alongside a fair rate of economic growth each year. Therefore, the debate over whether the development of the power industry was lagging behind became intermittent, off and on.

The comrades in the State Electric Power Distribution Communication Center told this reporter:

- At present, the per-capita electric power production in China is only 644 kWh [kilowatt-hours], representing 40 percent of the world average and ranking eightieth in the world.
- Among all the thirty administrative regions at the provincial level on the Chinese mainland, except for Ningxia Hui Autonomous Region, where power supply has a small surplus, all other provinces,

autonomous regions, and municipalities are currently experiencing various degrees of "deficit" of power supply.

- In Guangdong Province, the foreground of China's reform and opening up, the power shortage is as "outstanding" as its economic growth. For over a decade, the gap of power supply in this province has been around 30 percent. Buying electricity from Hong Kong, a practice that started in 1979, will continue in future, and the amount of buying has increased more than tenfold.
- The northeast supply network, which did not have a shortage two years ago, will have a gap of 900 million kWh this year, and it seems that consumers who used to suffer from frequent power cuts will have to "go through the misery all over again."

A host of facts that have emerged or are emerging indicate that as far as the ever-growing demand for electric power by enterprises and residents is concerned, our power industry is indeed too much "in debt." . . .

The Power "Famine" Not Only Hampers Sustained, Steady, and Healthy Development of the National Economy, but Also Brings Much Inconvenience to the Public and Creates Many "Roots of Trouble" in the Power Industry That Are Hard to Cure

Electric power is sometimes compared to the "blood" of the national economy. A power shortage means a blood shortage. Obviously, it is absolutely impossible for an "anemic" patient to be rated as healthy and fit.

The development of the national economy is a systems engineering project. The "bottleneck" of power supply very often forestalls such development. For example, the number of railways in China is small, their technical standard is low, and their carrying capacity is small. There is an urgent need to build new electric lines and electrify the existing lines. However, in areas where this is necessary, no electricity can be spared for this purpose. Therefore, electrification of the railway system has no basis. Who can tell how many projects there have been that could not be carried out in time or at all because of this reason in the past two decades or so when China was suffering from power shortages?

In addition, the negative effect of electric "bottlenecks" is in most cases visible and tangible.

First of all, power cuts cause enormous damage to the total industrial output value. It is common sense that without electric power, almost none of the modern production equipment can work. Major industrial consumers bear the brunt of the power cuts arranged by the "three electricity offices" around the country. In Guangdong Province, factories often "stop for three days and run for four days" or even "stop for four days and run for three days" per week because of power shortages. At least 30 percent or more of their production capacity lies idle. It is estimated that idle production capacity nationwide as a result of power shortages nationwide is no less than one-third. According to a comrade in the Ministry of Electric Power Industry, power shortages in our country each year are about 15 to 20 percent. In 1992, for example, the gap was 111.7 billion to 148.9 billion kWh for the whole year. Given that each kilowatt-hour generates 4.9 yuan in industrial output value, last year's industrial output value was reduced by 547.33 billion [$96 billion] to 729.61 billion yuan [$128 billion]. What an astronomical economic loss!

Three Feet of Ice Is Not Formed Overnight; Insufficient Investment in Electric Power Industry and Inadequate Scope of Capital Construction Are the Real Cause of Power Shortages; "Supernormal, Accelerated Development" Is a Way to Break the "Bottleneck" of the Power Industry

In late autumn 1991, Huang Yicheng, minister of energy resources, went to Hunan and Hubei provinces to inspect the construction of the power industry. Wherever he went, provincial governors and city mayors asked him for electricity. Even the folks from his home town, Zaoyang, who specially visited him also asked him for electricity point-blank. As the person in charge of China's energy industry at that time, Huang Yicheng was very aware of the fundamental reason for the power shortage in central China. He said: "Power shortages in central China are by no means a fortuitous phenomenon. It is all because the scope of capital construction for the power industry here is too small." . . .

In fact, this pertinent conclusion applies to all other areas in the country with power shortages and to the whole of China as well.

"Increased oil output primarily depends on drilling more wells; increased electric power primarily depends on expanding installed capacity." This unsophisticated remark made by veteran workers in the power industry deserves to be called an indisputable truth.

There is an international gauge for measuring the development of the power industry, called the "power elasticity coefficient," which is the ratio of the annual growth of the power supply to the growth rate of the gross output value of industry and agriculture. When this coefficient is 1, it means that the growth of the power supply is basically synchronous with economic development. When it is bigger than 1, it means that the power industry is genuinely "taking the lead," but when this coefficient is smaller than 1, it will be a cause for concern, and frequent arranged power cuts will be certainly inevitable. Since the 1970s, the power elasticity coefficient in China has never reached 1. Most of the time, it has been fluctuating between 0.7 and 0.75. Even in the period 1986–92, when installed capacity and electricity output both grew relatively fast, plus the three years of improvement and rectification, the average power elasticity coefficient in these seven years was under 0.9. The coefficient for Guangdong during the periods of the Sixth and Seventh Five-Year Plans was 0.56 and 0.76, respectively. With such low power elasticity coefficients, it would have been a miracle if there had been no power shortages!

Perhaps someone would chant this line: "So vast is the scenery that one should take a broader view." There were power shortages in the past, there are power shortages today, and will there be power shortages by the year 2000 when the Eighth and Ninth Five-Year Plans have been completed?

An authority in the power industry replied: According to the revised development plan of the national economy, it is estimated that the total demand on power nationwide will be 920 billion kwh in 1995 and 1.34 trillion to 1.47 trillion kWh in 2000. If in the Eighth Five-Year Plan period [1991–95] additional large and medium-sized generating units with a total capacity of 68 million kW are installed, plus the power output of some medium-sized and small units, the target of 920 billion kWh for 1995 can be achieved. If in the Ninth Five-Year Plan period [1995–99] large and medium-sized generating units with a total capacity of 20 million kW are installed each year on average, the total installed capacity of the country will reach 307 million kW and power output of 1,400 billion kWh by the year 2000. To reach this target, great difficulties in fund raising, equipment supply, progress in the initial period, and the balance of various external conditions required is foreseeable. Moreover, even if the above target is fulfilled, it is hard to say that it will thoroughly relieve the power shortage for the whole country, because by that time, given that the population will be 1.25 billion,[1] the per capita installed capacity will be only 0.24 kW and per capita power output 1,096 kW. These figures are not only way below the corresponding figures of Norway and Canada, namely, 26,000 and 18,000 kWh per capita, respectively, but also quite far behind the per capita generated energy of 2,000–6,000 kWh in East European countries at present.

---

[1]See Document #80 on the population problem in China.

52
Coal Sector Shedding 140,000 Workers in 1993

Chang Weimin

Source: Beijing, *China Daily,* August 16, 1993, p. 2, *FBIS,* August 16, 1993.

At least 100,000 coal workers have been laid off this year and 40,000 more will leave the coal industry before the end of 1993, Coal Industry Minister Wang Senhao says.

The layoffs are an effort to streamline the coal-mining industry, Wang said at a coal-industry reform conference early this month.

The industry, which employs seven million employees to produce 1.1 billion tons of coal a year, plans to cut its workforce by 400,000 workers during the Eighth Five-Year Plan (1991–95).

Coal mines have been encouraged to open service businesses to employ those workers who lose their jobs. Workers have been told that they should try to go into business.

The reduction in force is expected to reverse the industry's decades of losses within three years, Wang said.

The latest statistics show that the country's largest state coal mines suffered losses totaling some 2.4 billion yuan ($421 million) in the first six months of this year.

The losses for the same period in 1992 were 920 million yuan ($161 million).

Decades of rigid central planning weakened the coal mines' ability to upgrade technology and equipment and to improve their employees' standard of living.

In 1992, 100,000 workers were moved out of coal mining and into the service sector.

The central government has promised to provide preferential loans to help laid-off workers get jobs in other industries.

Another measure that has helped the industry cut its losses is coal-price reform.

The central government allowed the price of 20 percent of the coal to be regulated by the market in 1992.

That percentage was supposed to increase to 37 this year, but a ministry official said that quicker reform will allow the market to determine the price of an even greater percentage of the coal.

It's possible, the official said, that coal prices will be set entirely by the market this year.

Coal prices, under government control for decades, used to be too low to meet production costs.[1] At the same time, the cost of materials used in mining, such as steel and wood, have risen several times.

Wang said that reforms will move faster, so that in three years, the coal industry will stop bleeding and start profiting.

Wang said the coal industry will be in a difficult position in the second half of 1993 in the wake of railway freight fee increases and higher prices for electricity and work materials.

Wang urged coal-mine officials to make additional reforms to meet requirements of the market economy.

Wang promised that the ministry will delegate more decision-making power to help state-owned enterprises' administration become more autonomous.

Stifled by central planning for decades, enterprises in China, particularly state-owned ones, could not make their own business decisions. They were required to meet government production quotas, regardless of profits or losses.

---

[1]In Beijing in the 1980s, a truckload of sand cost more than a comparable truckload of coal.

53
China May Adopt New Five-Day Work Week

Source: Beijing, *China Daily,* January 7, 1992, p. 3, *FBIS,* January 17, 1992.

Enterprises and institutions in China are likely to adopt a new work timetable very soon, which will shorten the current six-day working week to five and a half days, a Labor Ministry official disclosed to *China Daily.* . . . Developed countries such as the United States, Japan, and France and some developing countries have long made a five-day, forty-hour week their normal legal working maximum.

A feasibility investigation group coorganized by the Labor Ministry and the Personnel Ministry has recently completed a trip throughout China and submitted a report in favor of a five-and-a-half-day working week to the central government for approval, the official said.

However, he didn't say when the scheme would be implemented.

Government specialists have long advocated a shorter working week, citing that a forty-hour week, replacing the present forty-eight-hour week, would be in the interests of improving productivity and efficiency, reducing material and power cost, propelling service industries, and developing the characters of workers by giving them more leisure time.

China has tried out various methods to cut work hours. Statistics show that about 1.9 million workers in large and medium-sized firms across the country are now working fewer than forty-eight hours a week.

Workers in textile mills and metallurgical plants have two days off after working eight consecutive days; and some chemical factories and oil fields allow their workers to work only six hours a day.

Five-day working week experiments have demonstrated a large increase in output value and profits and an improvement in efficiency and product quality despite the cut in working time.

54
Industry Should Learn from Capital Iron and Steel, Rural Areas Should Learn from Huaxi

Source: Beijing, *Jingji guanli (Economic Management)*, #9, September 5, 1993, p. 7, *FBIS,* October 15, 1993.

In Issue No. 81 of *Internal Reference Materials on Industrial Economics,* published by the Industrial Economics Association of China, it was reported that not long ago, Comrade Wu Dazhen of the Metallurgical Economic Development Research Center under the Ministry of Metallurgical Industry had proposed that the central authorities put forward the call: "In industry, learn from Capital Iron and Steel Corporation; in agriculture, learn from Huaxi." He said: In the sixties, Chairman Mao put forward the call that industry should learn from Daqing and agriculture should learn from Dazhai.[1] At that time, this was completely correct. At present, we should, as before, advocate the spirit of arduous efforts like that seen at Daqing and Dazhai.

At present, the situation is far more prosperous, diverse, and complex than it was at that time. However, with respect to an orientation and a road, I believe that our party can still put forward a similar call, a call for industry to learn from Capital Iron and Steel Corporation and for rural areas to learn from Huaxi.

First, let us talk about the Capital Iron and Steel Corporation's road. After Comrade Deng Xiaoping inspected Capital Iron and Steel Corporation and affirmed that the Capital Iron and Steel Corporation's road was correct and good, there seem to have been no dissenting opinions on this point. However, it is possible that people do not have a common understanding as to what the Capital Iron and Steel Corporation's road actually is. My own understanding is as follows: Capital Iron and Steel Corporation has, through the two "bases" ("contracts as a base and the people as a base"), at the same time as swiftly developing

---

[1]Daqing and Dazhai were a model oilfield and agricultural brigade, respectively, that during the Maoist years stressed moral and political incentives rather than material interests to increase production. After Mao's death in 1976 it was revealed that both Daqing and Dazhai had, in fact, received heavy state subsidies.

production and continually improving economic results, prominently manifested the following two characteristics:

First, it has greatly strengthened the economic power of the whole-people ownership system, powerfully consolidated and strengthened the economic basis of socialism, and fully brought into play and effectively demonstrated the superiority of the socialist public ownership system.

Second, it has given prominence to the position of the working class as masters and strengthened the consciousness of the masses of staff and workers as masters of their own affairs.

The first characteristic is necessary so that, in a situation where diverse economic components coexist and the proportion of the nonpublic ownership components is swiftly increasing, we can maintain the prime position of the public ownership system. The second characteristic is necessary so that in a situation where there have appeared quite a number of millionaires and even those who have hundreds of millions of yuan, we can maintain the leading position of the working class and maintain the essential nature of our country. It is based on this understanding that we believe that the road that Capital Iron and Steel Corporation follows is the true road of socialism with Chinese characteristics. The model provided by Capital Iron and Steel Corporation is a model that implements the basic line of the party in an overall way.

Now, let us look at Huaxi Village. Comrade Li Peng wrote an inscription for the village: "Where the hopes of China's rural areas lie." I believe that this statement is both proper and accurate. My understanding is as follows: These words by Comrade Li Peng indicate that the model constituted by Huaxi Village provides the development orientation for China's rural areas. Everyone knows that Huaxi Village was one of the first villages in the country to become a "100-million-yuan [$17 million] village." We need say nothing here about the speed of its economic development. Huaxi Village was originally named the Huaxi Production Brigade. Back in the seventies, *Renmin ribao* systematically introduced it as one of the brigades with the highest production in Southern Jiangsu. . . . During the process by which Huaxi Brigade changed from being a poor brigade to being a rich brigade, I visited it on numerous occasions. I believe that in the process by which it has seen speedy economic development, Huaxi has also displayed two major characteristics:

First, common prosperity. On the several occasions I visited Huaxi, Wu Renbao, the party branch secretary of the village, and the deputy secretary Mao Meiyi stressed: "We are all well-off households here, and there is only a difference in the degree of wealth. There are no households in economic difficulty, and no households that have become suddenly and exceedingly wealthy." All members of the village draw wages, regardless of whether they work in agriculture, industry, commerce, or other spheres. Under the precondition of the tasks of the work posts being completed, the greatest proportional differential between the highest and lowest wage is 3:1. The bonus awards are about one-half the wage amounts, and the differential between bonuses is a little smaller than that between wages. Thus, in the 1987 distribution, the lowest average incomes of households were not less than 1,000 yuan [$175], while the average incomes of the highest-earning households were no higher than 10,000 yuan [$1,754].

The second characteristic is that they have greatly raised the socialist consciousness of the peasants and strengthened their concept of the collective. I visited dozens of families, and all of them lived in houses in the village built jointly by the villagers and then sold to the respective village families. The size of house varies in accordance with the number of household members. The smallest house has three rooms downstairs and another three upstairs, while the largest has five or six rooms upstairs and another five or six downstairs. Every family has a telephone and a hotel-type bathroom with hot water. None of the members of the village has built their own house, and none has engaged in individual operations. It is not that they are not allowed to. Rather, they choose not to, preferring to put all their efforts into collective undertakings. Their slogans are: Love the party, love the country, love Huaxi, love one's family, love one's neighbors, love oneself. They ingeniously blend love for the country, love for the collective, and love for the people of the village with a self-respect involving self-strengthening and self-love. In Huaxi Village, no one has exceeded the family planning standards [i.e., one child per family], there is no feudal superstition or gambling, and everywhere there is a new atmosphere of a socialist new village. In brief, the continuous strengthening of the collective economy and the continued deepening of socialist education promote each other and permeate each other. In this way, Huaxi Village has traveled a long way along the road of gradually eliminating the differential between industry and agriculture and the differential between urban and rural areas, and of ensuring that the ideology of the masses gradually advances to the level of the working class. Chairman Mao long ago pointed out: "A serious problem lies in educating the peasants." The most important contribution of the Huaxi Village party branch lies in having done this.

55
Development in Two Tianjin Villages Viewed: Xiaojinzhuang and Daqiuzhuang

Shi Conglin

Source: Beijing, *Jingji ribao (Economic Daily),* August 28, 1992, p. 2, *FBIS,* September 16, 1992.

Tianjin has two villages that are well known in the whole country. One is called Xiaojinzhuang, the other, Daqiuzhuang. Xiaojin- zhuang had an extremely high reputation in the Cultural Revolution period [1966–76] because its people sang songs, which made their village very famous north and south of the Yangtze River. It is now a poor village. Daqiuzhuang was also a poor village with people "drinking bitter water and eating vegetables"; however, it has devel- oped its economy since reform and opening up, using good manage- ment methods to improve itself. The village's industrial and agricultural output value in 1991 was 1.8 billion yuan [approxi- mately $316 million], making it the first village in China to become rich (see *Jingji ribao,* July 24).

Xiaojinzhuang and Daqiuzhuang are the outcome of history. One was a pet in the time of ultraleftism [i.e., during the Cultural Revolu- tion]; the other is a favored son in the period of reform. We should treat them with a "normal attitude," but the things happening between these two villages create a desire within me to write about my feelings. Wang Zuoshan, the village head of the miserable Xiaojinzhuang, sought help from Daqiuzhuang. Daqiuzhuang responded enthusiastically and tried to meet his urgent needs; it immediately promised to let Xiaojinzhuang do some processing jobs, to send some technicians to give guidance, and to give 60,000 yuan [$10,524] to Xiaojinzhuang so as to let it pay the outstanding wages to workers. Apart from helping it to solve urgent problems, it also promised to help Xiaojinzhuang to develop enterprises. According to normal reasoning, this is something that is too good to be true. However, when Wang Zuoshan excitedly reported the situation to the upper level, he suffered a staggering blow. The superior said: "Stop saying it. It is all about the 60,000 yuan! I'll give you 600,000 yuan" [$105,240]. Thereafter, three opinions came from the upper level, one of which said: The [Leftist] Gang of Four[1] had not made Xiaojinzhuang stink, but Daqiuzhuang made it do so.

The things that happened between these two villages have nothing to do with gratitude or resentment involving "the treating of kindness as a donkey's lung [something worthless]," but profoundly illustrate that today, as we are carrying out reform and opening up, some people are still stubbornly embracing the old face of "leftism," and getting enmeshed in a web of their own spinning.

A tree is known by its bark, and a person by his face; the demand for face is not a bad thing, and in particular, we, the Chinese, attach great importance to face, but the demand for face must be judged by how it is done. People compare their methods in work, and try to show off a bit; some tell some lies but are discovered by others, so their faces turn red—all these are a result of man's desire to show off and of their conscience, and this is a good thing. However, asking for face at the expense of deliberate backwardness and stubbornly refusing to learn from the advanced and refusing help from other people is "dying for face and living for sorrow."

It is naturally very important to unbind our hands and feet in order to build the economy and to untie the rope around our bodies, but it is similarly important to give up face and abandon the psychological burden left behind by history. Wang Zuoshan, who gave up the "face" of Xiaojinzhuang and humbly sought assistance from Daqiuzhuang,

---

[1]The radical faction during the Cultural Revolution led by Jiang Qing, the wife of CCP Chairman Mao Zedong.

can learn the good things from Daqiuzhuang; the leader of Xiaojin-zhuang, who stubbornly embraces his old face, which is not so grace-ful, can only look at the increasingly bustling activities in Daqiuzhuang.[2]

---

[2]The glamour surrounding Daqiuzhuang was marred in early 1993 when, fol-lowing the murder of an itinerant worker at one of the village's busiest enterprises, residents conspired to prevent Tianjin police from investigating the case. The leader of this "model" village was sentenced to twenty years in prison for corrup-tion. *New York Times,* March 30, 1993.

56
Liaoning Province Orders Halt to Tearing Up Contracts

Source: Beijing, Xinhua, May 14, 1992, *FBIS,* May 14, 1992.

Northeast China's Liaoning Province has ordered a halt to the practice by local authorities of taking back contracted farmland from farmers.

Today's *Renmin ribao* reported that a dictate came recently in the form of a notice that accused some village authorities in the province of terminating land contracts and taking back contracted farmland in violation of government rural policies and local legislation.

In the late 1970s, China began to allow farmers to grow whatever they like on contracted land after fulfilling the government mandatory purchasing plan. The major change in rural economic policy improved the country's agricultural performance.

In September 1990, Liaoning Province promulgated a set of rules regulating contracts in the rural collective economy in an effort to stabilize and improve the system.

However, some local authorities have recently torn up agreements with farmers under the pretext of "strengthening the collective economy."

57

Farmers Holding IOUs, While Pesticide Prices Stay on Rise

Wu Yunhe

Source: Beijing, *China Daily (Business Weekly)* April 4, 1993, p. 8, *FBIS,* April 5, 1993.

Farmers need to spend money on chemicals that ensure their crops are not damaged by weeds, pests, and plant diseases.

But the increased use of chemicals is creating a vicious circle for farmers who are faced by spiraling prices for both foreign and domestic pesticides.

Farmers, many holding government IOUs instead of cash, suffer from a shortage of funds.

The problem could bring about an undesirable situation in agricultural production this year, some officials have warned.

Pests wrecking crops may force farmers to raise their chemical consumption this year, the Ministry of Agriculture predicts.

Chinese agricultural officials say farmers may this year use more than 190,000 tons of various pesticides, germicides, and herbicides to prevent their crops from being damaged by plant diseases and pests such as moths and locusts.

As the spring arrives, plant diseases and pests tend to become a greater problem. . . . The country's more than 17.3 million hectares of farmland are being overgrown with various weeds, which are checking the growth of agricultural crops.

The situation will add to the difficulties for farmers to sustain a steady agricultural production, not to mention the spiraling prices of farm chemicals this year.

This year, the Ministry of Chemical Industry has decided to call off its subsidies for imported farm chemicals in order to lighten the financial burden on the State.

It also plans to introduce a market mechanism for setting prices for domestic agricultural chemicals, which have, for years, been under the control of a state monopoly system.

58
A Weak Foundation Should Not Be Overlooked

Source: Beijing, *Liaowang (Outlook Weekly),* #44, November 1, 1993, *FBIS,* November 22, 1993.

"The question of rapid industrial growth, agricultural stagflation, and the unbalanced development of industry and agriculture has become prominent." This is the conclusion drawn by many economists and rural experts after conducting thorough investigations and studies. It shows that the weak foundation in China's national economy is a very important question. It has been manifested prominently once again in the course of socialist market economic development. Unless effective measures are adopted to resolve the problem, it will affect agricultural development and the normal operation of the national economy as a whole.

What is more serious is that the question has not drawn due attention from some departments and localities. Some people still have a muddled understanding of the current status quo in agriculture and misunderstand the situation. Some of them believe that the problem of China's agriculture has been resolved as the rural areas took the lead in reform following the [1978] Third Plenary Session, rapidly boosted production, and turned out a large amount of surplus grain, which exceeded demand. Others say that problems in agriculture in the past were immediately reflected in the market: Grain prices would rise at county fairs and there would be short supplies of meat, eggs, and milk, which are exchanged for grain. However, grain prices are stable in the market at present and there is an ample supply of meat, eggs, and milk, so there is no problem at all.

The supply of farm produce in the market is indeed a barometer of agricultural production. The current market status quo is the achievement of a decade of rural reform, with which urban people are satisfied. However, agricultural production requires a long production cycle and produces results very slowly. The market today reflects only the production situation of yesterday or the day before. Our forecast of agricultural prospects cannot merely be based on current market supply. Instead, we should draw conclusions after a thorough observation of agricultural production and the rural economy as a whole. A large number of problems in the rural economy are prominently exposed, and some latent problems are expanding further. We can say that a signal of a crisis has appeared. The alarms sounding in the fields merit our attention. It will be too late if we wait for the problems to appear in market supply. . . .

China has a large population with limited arable land, and its per capita grain output is lower than the world's average.[1] If such a state of affairs is allowed to develop unchecked and if there are problems in grain, this will be desperately serious. China has a large population with limited arable land, which is one of its unique characteristics. This is the reality we must face. There is no country in the world that does not attach importance to agriculture. To give more attention than any other country to agriculture and grain production, we should protect and make use of every inch of land. Zones that have been blindly developed in recent years have occupied a large amount of fertile farmland. We should not let this farmland lie idle and grass grow there. Naturally, we should protect the enthusiasm of the peasants for farming. This is an outstanding problem demanding a prompt solution in current rural work and rural economic development.

It is also noteworthy that growth in peasants' incomes has slowed down in recent years. The gap between peasants' average net income and the incomes of urban inhabitants for living expenses is widening and has basically returned to the same level as before the rural reform. No wonder peasants say that the benefits brought by rural reform over the past decade or so have all been taken away by certain departments, units, or trades.

The drop in peasants' incomes also reflects the low efficiency of agricultural production, the widening price scissors of industrial and farm produce, and excessive burdens. But the most important thing is the limited prospects and lack of depth of agricultural development. This is the picture in the rural areas of a number of localities. Apart from a few *mu* [0.0667 hectares] of land, there are no other resources for farming. How then can peasants become prosperous? Compared with the period before reform, peasants' living standards have improved remarkably and the number of peasants living below the poverty line has decreased. However, we should also be aware

---

[1] Only 13 percent of China's total land area is arable.

that apart from a small number of regions, peasants in most regions have no access to prosperity after getting enough to eat and wear. If we cannot put an end to such a state of affairs, how can we attain China's target of a comparatively well-off level and the modernization program?[2]

---

[2]In June 1994, the Chinese government increased prices paid to farmers for basic grains by 40 percent to stem the decline in overall grain production.

59
Labor Tide Calls for Great Efforts to Develop Rural Employment Channel

Source: Beijing, *Liaowang,* #8, February 22, 1993, p. 3, *FBIS,* March 16, 1993.

This issue of *Liaowang* gives prominent coverage to reports on the recent labor tide.

At the heels of Spring Festival [Chinese New Year] of the Year of the Rooster, millions of peasants again packed their luggage and left their home towns for coastal open areas and a number of large and medium-sized cities to look for jobs. Thus, communications lines, including train stations and piers, again came under the pressure of another big tide of floating laborers.

Reflecting a new situation wherein China's surplus laborers are badly in need of employment opportunities, this labor tide of a considerable size is making this appeal: Vigorously developing rural employment channels is necessary for deepening rural reform and further promoting agricultural production; it is also a major event in the course of the socialist modernization drive.

Ever since the beginning of reform and opening up, especially with the continued deepening of rural economic restructuring, China's rural areas have seen the rise of a trend in which large numbers of rural laboring forces, who were just liberated from the old operational system of production, are rapidly moving toward coastal open areas and a number of large and medium-sized cities. This trend is attributable to many factors, among which one major factor is that China's farmland is overloaded and there are large numbers of surplus laborers in rural areas.

During the period from 1949 to 1991, China's total acreage under cultivation was reduced from 1.468 billion *mu* [241 million acres] to 1.435 billion *mu* [236 million acres], while the total number of rural laborers during the same period increased from 173 million to 428 million. Putting other issues aside, calculated at the agricultural productive level of 1949, the total number of existing surplus laborers has reached 260 million in China's rural areas. Township and town enterprises, which were first set up in the 1980s, have recruited nearly 100 million rural laborers. However, there are still over 150 million surplus laborers remaining in China's rural area, with an increase of over 6 million each year. Peasants need to find jobs. However, when they cannot find opportunities in their local areas, it is natural for them to look for jobs in other parts of the country. On the other hand, coastal open areas, economically advanced regions, and a number of large and medium-sized cities stand in need of laborers at the same time. When there is both demand and supply, a channel linking up the two is floating laborers. Therefore, such a situation has given rise to the trend of a large number of surplus rural laborers flowing from inland and mountainous areas to coastal open areas, and from less advanced areas to fairly advanced areas. . . .

By working and doing business in other parts of the country or engaging themselves in the tertiary industries in urban areas, the vast numbers of the surplus rural laborers have not only helped, with their cheap labor services, accelerate the economic development of the regions and cities into which they have flowed; but also have earned money for themselves, learned new knowledge and techniques, changed their old concepts, and enhanced their awareness of the commodity economy. Consider the case of Henan Province. The province has 3 million peasants working in other parts of the country. In 1992, these peasants sent or brought home about 2 billion yuan worth of belongings. Such support is very helpful to rural areas in their efforts to change their backward outlook. In some localities, peasants who have returned after working in other places for several years are setting up factories or shops in their home towns. By so doing, they have actually played the role of spreading information, technologies, and new concepts; promoting the commodity economic development of their localities; and rejuvenating the economy of their own home towns. . . .

The practice by which peasants work and do business in other parts of the country has its inevitability and positive significance. However, we should also notice at the same time that it is impossible to provide employment to China's 100 to 200 million surplus rural laborers through the method of "laborer flows" alone. According to an estimate made by relevant departments, the over 10 million rural laborers working in all parts of the country has made up only about 10 percent of the country's total surplus rural laborers.[1] Even at such a scale, the country's existing communications and transportation capacities have found the load unbearable. In addition, because working posts are limited in regions into which laborers flow, many peasants who come from afar are unable to find any jobs, yet they have spent much money on their fruitless trips. What is more, such a situation is harmful to the traffic control and public security of these regions. Therefore, it has become extraordinarily important to strengthen the organization of and guidance to the flow of rural laborers. . . .

To solve the problem of China's large number of surplus rural laborers, the only way out is to closely integrate the method of settling problems in local areas with the social and economic development of rural areas, and place our focus on creating more jobs through accelerating rural economic development. This is a method that can reach the root of the problem. To achieve this goal, a great deal of work needs to be done. At present a considerable number of peasants fail to show high enthusiasm for growing grain; some are no longer willing to undertake farming under contracts; while others have abandoned their farmland. A major cause for such a situation is that the economic returns of farming are very low, while burdens borne by peasants are heavy. To put an end to such a situation, we need to carry out comprehensively the policies and measures made by the party Central Committee and the State Council on lightening the burdens of peasants, and help solve a number of problems currently plaguing peasants, such as "difficulties in buying and selling" and "IOUs"; and to work out poli-

---

[1]Other estimates of China's total migrant population run as high as 50 million people. *New York Times,* June 29, 1994.

cies that tally with local conditions and are beneficial to the cultivation of the market, and that guide peasants to gear themselves to the market needs. . . .

60
Several Key Issues Involving Housing Reform

Source: Beijing, *Gongren ribao,* May 3, 1991, p. 3, *FBIS,* May 28, 1991.

Housing reform in China's urban areas has lasted for a decade or so. During this period, we experienced high tides as well as some setbacks. Although the public has reached some common understanding of the necessity for housing reform and its basic policies and targets, and also summed up and explored effective housing reform methods in practice, on the whole, the pace of housing reform is still slow nationwide, which is far from our anticipated target. Leading comrades of the central authorities recently stressed on many occasions the necessity of attaching more importance to reform. To attach more importance to reform, I think we should step up efforts to resolve the following key issues:

First, leading cadres at all levels and principal provincial and city leaders should pay great attention to housing reform. As the old housing system has lasted forty years, the problems piled up are deep-rooted. Because housing reform involves the vital interests of all workers, the structure of interests to be readjusted is rather complicated. Hence, it will be impossible to carry out work in this respect without due attention of leaders from the top levels. As a matter of fact, in places where housing reform has developed rapidly in recent years and which have achieved marked results, the leaders have paid great attention to and personally taken a hand in the work. Similarly, people have witnessed in the course of housing reform that obstruction comes from vested interests, that is, the families with large living areas. Who has vested interests in the current housing system? Who occupies a housing area larger than others? They are mainly the cadres at all levels, particularly leading cadres. They live in larger houses, and the quality of the houses is also better than others. It should be noted that the party's cadres at all levels, leading cadres in particular, have high party spirit. Once they have understood the purpose and significance of housing reform, they will take practical action to promote housing reform. However, we also cannot deny the fact that in actual life, there are a handful of leading cadres who lack self-consciousness. They always obstruct or drag down the progress of housing reform under one excuse or another. Moreover, some leading comrades are not yet determined for fear that housing reform would affect social stability. Unless we put an end to this state of affairs, it will be impossible to push forward housing reform.

To attach great importance to the work, first, leading cadres should be determined and bold in making policy decisions for housing reform. With a clear target, they should unswervingly continue the work through to the end. In light of the spirit of the speeches made by central leading comrades, policy decisions can be made and experiments can be conducted so long as the housing reform schemes conform to the basic spirit of the State Council's stipulations. If the experiments conducted prove that housing reform can be accepted by the workers and masses, can be undertaken by enterprises, can ease the financial burden, and can speed up the settlement of housing problems, it should be vigorously spread. It is also necessary to urge cities, counties, enterprises, and institutions under one's jurisdiction to step up housing reform work. And, finally, we must establish and perfect forceful housing reform organs at all levels as quickly as possible. . . .

Second, accurately select the breach. The essence of housing reform is to increase responsibility of individual workers in settling the housing problem and increase their expenses in housing. There are three ways of reform: First, sell houses; second, raise rent; and third, organize workers to build their own houses. Viewed from the practice of housing reform at the previous stage, housing reform involves many problems and the vital interests of almost all the workers and inhabitants in cities and towns. Hence, it is a systematic social policy construction project. Where to start with the reform will be very important for the smooth progress of reform. It is also related to the success or failure of reform. In my opinion, housing reform should adopt the strategy of overall design, development from easy to difficult, progress in stages, and gradual completion.

Under the guidance of such strategic thinking and in connection with housing reform practice over the years, I think "new houses" should be the breach of the current housing reform. First, it is necessary to plug the holes of the old system and never let the newly built houses to follow the track of the old system, or sell the houses at preferential prices, or impose high rent for new houses so that the houses newly built every year will first be put on the track of housing commercialization. Through accumulation for some years, a new housing system will gradually take shape. Then it will be far easier to effect a change in the old houses. The advantage of this tactic is that the reform involves a limited field and obstruction is limited. The principle of voluntary purchase can easily be accepted by the workers and masses, and be well received by those who have housing difficulties and are willing to buy houses. Hence, the reform can be easily implemented, cause limited shock at the beginning, and produce practical effect, speeding up the pace of resolving housing difficulties. Conversely, if the method of increasing rent in a comprehensive way is adopted, it will create difficulties. Increasing rent in a comprehensive way seems fair, but it cannot turn out practical effects. First, it is unlikely that the current housing rent will be raised to a new level and will reach the level of rent cost.[1] Second, subsidies will have to be granted to raise rent, which will be difficult for the state and enterprises to bear. Third, funds collected from the increased rent are not enough to expand housing reproduction. Fourth, "high rent" has a mandatory nature that is psychologically not accepted by the workers and masses. While choosing the method of selling houses first, we should also consider the problem of duly raising the rent. Moreover, the workers and masses should be vigorously organized to muster funds for housing or to build houses in cooperation.

Third, take the bearing capacity of the workers and masses fully into account. Since reform and opening up over the past decade or so, the capacity of enterprises and workers has continued to increase on the whole. However, such capacity is uneven in different regions and trades and among workers at different posts. The capacity of workers of the enterprises that are operating at half capacity or that have

---

[1]Rents in urban China have been very low since 1949, generally less than 10 percent of average household incomes.

suspended production, those with low incomes, and those in strained circumstances is particularly limited. Therefore, the raising of rent or selling of houses should not exceed such bearing capacity. Taking the bearing capacity of enterprises and workers fully into account refers to raising rent and selling houses at appropriate prices. It is also necessary to formulate preferential policies for houses built by workers with pooled funds or in cooperation. When necessary, workers should be given some financial and material support. In some places, the market price of housing has reached over 3,000 yuan [$526] per square meter, which is far beyond the capacity of salaried workers. The price of houses should be reduced, and buffer measures should be adopted.

61
Gap between Eastern, Other Regions "Widening"

Source: Hong Kong, Zhongguo tongxun she, April 1, 1993, *FBIS,* April 5, 1993.

The gap in economic development between China's eastern region and the central and western regions, whose area comprises 88.6 percent of the country's total and whose population accounts for 63.1 percent of the country's total, is visibly widening with every passing year. An Agriculture Ministry official has pointed out that if this state of affairs is allowed to continue, it will be disadvantageous to China's economic development and political stability.

According to a division by the relevant mainland departments, the eastern region includes [nine] provinces and municipalities: Beijing, Tianjin, Liaoning, Shandong, Hebei, Jiangsu, Zhejiang, Fujian, and Guangdong. The central region includes ten provinces: Heilongjiang, Jilin, Shanxi, Shaanxi, Sichuan, Henan, Hubei, Hunan, Jiangxi, and Anhui. The western region includes ten provinces and autonomous regions: Inner Mongolia, Ningxia, Gansu, Qinghai, Xinjiang, Yunnan, Guizhou, Tibet, Guangxi, and Hainan.

A quantitative analysis shows that the gap between the eastern region and the central and western regions can be seen through the rural population's per capita agricultural product, the output value of township enterprises, the per capita income of the rural population, and the per capita income of the peasants from township enterprises.

According to information provided by the Agriculture Ministry, the per capita agricultural product of the rural population in 1985 was 1,450 yuan [$254] in the eastern region and 716 and 630 yuan respectively [$125, $110] in the central and western regions. In 1990, the figure rose to 2,929 yuan, 1,382 yuan, and 976 yuan, respectively [$513, $242, and $171]. In other words, the gap between the eastern region and the central and western regions grew wider by 110 and 150 percent.

Of the total output value of township enterprises in 1991, the eastern region accounted for 65 percent; the central, 30 percent; and the west, only 4.2 percent. Moreover, while the three eastern region provinces of Jiangsu, Zhejiang, and Shandong had a total output value of over 100 billion yuan [$18 billion], nine provinces and autonomous regions in the western region produced a total output value of less than 10 billion yuan [$1.8 billion].

In 1985, per capita income of the rural population was 497 yuan [$87] in the eastern region and 343 and 355 yuan, respectively [$60, $62] in the central and western regions. In 1990, the figure rose to 812, 538, and 497 yuan [$142, $94, $87]. In other words, the gap between the eastern region and the central and western regions grew wider by 80 and 120 percent.

The statistics also indicated that the wider gap between the eastern region and the central and western regions was primarily due to the uneven development of township enterprises. In 1990, the rural population's per capita income from township enterprises in the eastern, central, and western regions accounted for 25, 18, and 11 percent, respectively.

To reduce the negative effects, the Agriculture Ministry official pointed out that, while continuously maintaining growth in the eastern region, it is necessary to accelerate the development of township enterprises in the central and western regions. Otherwise, "it will be disadvantageous to the economic growth of the central and western regions and will also affect the economic development and political stability of the country as a whole."

C. China and the World Economy

62
Thoughts on Measures for Rejoining GATT

Wang Haiyan

Source: Beijing, *Guoji shangbao (International Commerce),* February 20, 1993, p. 3, *FBIS,* March 8, 1993.

I. Macroscopic Measures

1. Accelerate reform to enable China's economic operational pattern to converge with international practices as quickly as possible. The basic provisions of the General Agreement on Tariffs and Trade [GATT] are based on the establishment of a market economy; and the restoration of China's status as a signatory to GATT is, in essence, a return to the operational orbit of the international market economy.[1] By setting forth the establishment of a socialist market economy in China, the Fourteenth Party Congress [October 1992] has provided the most fundamental precondition for China's entry into the operational orbit of the international market economy. To achieve the development objective of the socialist market economy, we must increase the intensity of reform. Therefore, it can be that GATT has given us the greatest challenge; that is, we must quicken the pace of economic restructuring.

In developing a socialist market economy, aside from changing enterprises' operational mechanisms and establishing and improving the market, we also should quickly establish a macroeconomic regulation and control system with indirect regulation and control as the main content. By indirect macroeconomic regulation and control we mean that the government chiefly will rely on economic means to regulate

---

[1]China under Nationalist (Kuomintang) rule was a founding member of GATT after World War II, but withdrew in 1950.

economic life. It should be particularly pointed out that we should gradually abolish the practice of conducting different reforms in different localities and enterprises, increase the transparency of policy,[2] and shift the emphasis from short-term policies to statutes and standardized long-term policies so that our statutes and standardized policies can converge with international practices.

2. Concentrate on making a major breakthrough by selecting and quickly developing some trades and forming our export industries. In selecting the export industries, we should keep abreast of changes in the consumption demand pattern and production structure of the developed countries and, at the same time, vigorously bring along the optimization of China's industrial structure. In these trades, we should selectively import advanced foreign technology and production and processing equipment, should implement a special preferential policy for attracting foreign capital and introducing technology, should expand the import and export ability of enterprises in these trades, and should provide export credits and other financial support. Unlike the policy of import substitution, the main purpose of importing equipment and turning out products is to serve export needs and thus reach a positive import and export situation.

3. Develop export-oriented enterprise groups. GATT's challenge to our enterprises has two aspects: First, enterprises should be export-oriented; second, enterprises should attain economies of scale. For this reason, we should vigorously develop export-oriented enterprise groups, such as foreign trade enterprise groups, industry and trade enterprise groups, technology and trade enterprise groups, and export-oriented township and town enterprise groups.

---

[2]"Transparency" *(toumingdu)* is a code word for allowing greater press freedom in China.

63
Coastal Areas Close Several Development Zones

Source: Beijing, Xinhua, August 11, 1993, *FBIS,* August 12, 1993.

The coastal areas of China have closed down three-fourths of their economic development zones, in the wake of a State Council decision.

According to a report from the State Council's Special Economic Zone Office, seven provinces and one autonomous region along the coast of China have reexamined all development zones set up by local authorities. At the behest of the State Council, they have reduced the number of such development zones from 1,200 to 200. . . . The reexamination work is still under way.

The objective is to stop land that has little prospect of development in the near future being cordoned off, when it could be used for crop growing.

There has been a rush to set up economic development zones all over the country, especially in the coastal areas, in recent years.

According to Hu Ping, director of the Special Economic Zone Office, only one-tenth of the local economic development zones have turned out beneficial for the local economy. About one-fifth of the development zones are still waiting for funds to start planned projects.

The State Council has approved only 30 economic and technological development zones in the country's coastal areas.

It is also prohibited for localities to adopt investment incentives and tax exemptions beyond their authority.

64
Currency System Adjustments
Need to Be Accelerated

Source: Beijing, *China Daily,* November 13, 1993, p. 4, *FBIS,* November 19, 1993.

Since the overseas market of *renminbi* (RMB) yuan [China's currency] has already taken shape, it is necessary to guide it in a direction that is good for China's expanding trade with other countries.

This was the conclusion of Jiao Jinpu, an official with the People's Bank of China, in the monthly magazine *Finance Research*.

Adapting to the situation that RMB is already circulating outside China, the State Council issued a regulation on the management of taking RMB into or out of the country on March 1.

For the first time, people officially crossing the border can take with them a maximum of 6,000 yuan ($1,035).

The implementation of the regulation ended China's previous ban on bringing RMB out of the country.

The existing rules stipulate that a certain amount of foreign exchange has to be converted to RMB at the official exchange rate to be brought into China, and vice versa for renminbi going abroad.

But foreigners dislike the exchange procedure since the official price of RMB overstated its value on the market, Jiao said.

The rapid increases in capital construction, burgeoning domestic consumption, and expected inflation have also contributed to the actual devaluation of the RMB, placing foreign businesspeople at an unfavorable position in exchanges.

After China's opening, foreign-funded enterprises have expanded rapidly in number on the mainland, reaching a total of 84,000 by the end of 1992. Foreign investment equivalent to about $100 billion has been introduced into China.

To skirt round the official exchange rate, many foreign investors wanted to convert their currencies into RMB before they invested them in China, causing great demand for RMB outside the Chinese mainland.

Meanwhile, as the inflation rate in China has risen with the rapid growth in recent years, many Chinese residents have preferred to hold some foreign currencies for fear of the devaluation of their cash assets.

The black market, in which both the overseas demand for RMB and domestic demand for foreign exchange can be met, has increased circulation of RMB outside the Chinese mainland.

In some countries and regions, such as Russia, East Europe, and Southeast Asia and Hong Kong, the RMB has already been accepted by the residents in circulation.

Meanwhile, some foreign exchange, such as Hong Kong and U.S. dollars, has also been circulating in China, especially in some coastal areas, which, under the existing foreign exchange control system, is forbidden.

The rapid expansion of the overseas market of RMB indicates that the value of RMB has been recognized in the international market. This has been brought about to a large extent by the steady economic growth of China.

With RMB's circulation in the world market, part of the domestic purchasing power can be transferred outside the country. Thus the problem of excess demand over supply of many commodities on the domestic market can be eased and the double-digit inflation can be cooled down.

As the RMB has become a freer currency in the overseas market, its market exchange rate can be used as reference by the State's financial organization in deciding the official exchange rate. This will help the government adopt measures to change the RMB into a convertible currency.

To make the RMB more widely accepted in the world market, its value must be kept stable through the implementation of macro financial policy.

65
One Should Not Be Optimistic about the Prospects of China's Labor Export

Source: Beijing, *Jingji cankao (Economic Reference),* August 6, 1990, p. 4, *FBIS,* September 10, 1990.

At present, surplus labor tends to be increasing daily around the world, and its growth rate has exceeded its demand. On the international labor market, supply, on the whole, is larger than demand, and this situation will continue and gradually become obvious. More and more surplus labor from developing countries will enter the international market, and therefore acute competition will be unavoidable. As far as labor-exporting countries are concerned, they will meet many more challenges than opportunities.

As for the actual national conditions of our country, our labor does not have more advantages on the international labor market.

By advantages we do not only mean the advantage of cost. In fact, in recent years, the cost of primary labor on the international market has been decreasing, while ours has been increasing. In comparison with other labor-exporting countries such as India, Pakistan, and the Philippines, our country has lost the advantage of low cost. The overall quality of our country's surplus labor is comparatively low, and most of it is low-level primary labor. Large-scale export of primary labor is impossible once the advantage of cost is lost. However, one should see that the cost of our relatively high-level technical labor is more competitive compared to that of developed countries. On the international market, the demand for technical and management personnel possessing medium and high technical and expertise levels is increasing. However, one should also see that the absolute amount of our technical personnel is not excessive; in fact, we have very few. Moreover, most of the technical personnel are the backbone on all fronts of economic development and production at home. What we should now do is to vigorously train comparatively high-level and high-level personnel on the one hand, and make rational allocation and use of technical personnel on the other hand, so that they can be fully and effectively utilized. If we jump to the conclusion that we have excessive technical personnel and begin exporting them in large numbers, we will obviously not only incur losses but also inevitably affect our own long-term development.

Therefore, one should be objective in estimating the export of our surplus labor.

Further Readings

Byrd, William. *China's Financial System: The Changing Role of Banks* (Boulder, CO: Westview Press, 1983).

Kao, Michael Ying-Mao, and Susan H. Marsh. *China in the Era of Deng Xiaoping: A Decade of Reform* (Armonk, NY: M.E. Sharpe, 1993).

Lardy, Nicholas R. *China's Entry into the World Economy: Implications for Northeast Asia and the United States* (New York: The Asia Society, 1988).

Nee, Victor, and David Stark, editors. *Remaking the Economic Institutions of Socialism: China and Eastern Europe* (Stanford, CA: Stanford University Press, 1989).

Nolan, Peter. *The Political Economy of Collective Farms: An Analysis of China's Post-Mao Rural Reforms* (Boulder, CO: Westview Press, 1988).

Parish, William L., editor. *Chinese Rural Development: The Great Transformation* (Armonk, NY: M.E. Sharpe, 1985).

Perkins, Dwight. *China: Asia's Next Economic Giant?* (Seattle: University of Washington Press, 1986).

Riskin, Carl. *China's Political Economy: The Quest for Development since 1949* (New York: Oxford University Press, 1987).

World Bank. *China: Long-Term Development Issues and Options* (Baltimore: Johns Hopkins University Press, 1985).

Yeung, Yue-man, and Xuwei Hu, editors. *China's Coastal Cities* (Honolulu: University of Hawaii Press, 1992).

III

Society and Culture

Crime, drugs, guns, sex, violence, and AIDS. Since 1989, these have become the stuff of news in China as the puritanical, closed society of Mao Zedong has given way to the traumas of modern life. In a Hunan Province town, armed miners attack government offices (Document 69); in northern China, an irate peasant detonates a bomb to protest excessive taxation (Document 72); and in China's western provinces, non-Han minorities resort to terrorism in their struggle for greater independence from Beijing (Document 95). The economic progress documented in the previous section has given rise to a level of social disorder that has unsettled the population and provoked political attacks on the entire reform process (Document 76). The level of crime, drug use, and other social ills in contemporary China is still low by the standards of most industrialized nations. But in a country that since 1949 was generally free of such maladies and/or generally ignored them, the shock of the new has led many Chinese to believe that their society is spinning out of control.

Social dislocation in China has also spawned a crisis of belief. As Mao Zedong's vision of an ideologically pure society has faded, Chinese have turned to religion (Document 66) and old customs (Document 75) that now threaten traditional Communist hegemony over thought (Document 67). On the one hand, government propaganda has sought to fill the spiritual void (Document 73) by publicizing official role models (Document 74) and promoting art forms (Document 100) reminiscent of the Maoist era. On the other, Chinese listeners to state-run radio can tune into sex talk shows (Document 90) and read in the Party-controlled press about train robberies, gun proliferation, and the sale of women (Documents 70, 71, and 78). Taboo topics have also recently surfaced, such as homosexuality (Document 91) and the threat—real and imagined—of AIDS (Documents 87, 88, and 89). By democratic standards, China's state-controlled media, and intellectual and artistic circles, are still subject to stifling political censorship (Documents 97, 98, 99, 101, 103, and 105). Yet some subtle openings have occurred as Chinese government officials hold news conferences (Document 93) and appear on local TV and radio call-in shows (Document 104).

The documents in this section also address China's perennial problems of population control, pollution, and minorities. Chinese policy on coercive abortions, forced sterilizations, and "eugenics" (Documents 81, 82, 84, and 85) have been severely criticized abroad. But the Chinese government can still take pride in its comprehensive population control program (Documents 80 and 83) and its education of women (Document 79). Whether China has seriously confronted its growing environmental problems (Documents 92 and 93) and addressed the tense relations between Han and non-Han peoples (Documents 94, 95, and 96), however, are still open questions.

A. Social Changes

66
Peasants' Daily (Nongmin ribao) Article Attacks Religion

Source: Hong Kong, AFP, October 18, 1989, *FBIS,* October 18, 1989.

In a strong attack on religion, a Chinese newspaper Wednesday urged farmers to stop worshipping Buddha and "seriously study" the words of Communist Party chief Jiang Zemin instead.

In a front-page article, the *Peasants' Daily* said that a revival of traditional forms of worship in the countryside was a symptom of lax ideological education in rural areas, where four out of every five Chinese live.

"We cannot underestimate such bad influences," the newspaper said.

"All these feudal and superstitious activities have poisoned the masses, affected young people, polluted social morals, and upset the building of socialist spiritual civilization in the countryside,"[1] it said.

The "most urgent" task, it said, was for rural dwellers to "seriously study" a September 29 speech by General Secretary Jiang that spells out the new hard-line policies of the Chinese leadership [see Document #5, Section I].

Farmers were the first to prosper from senior leader Deng Xiaoping's economic reforms, launched a decade ago, which enabled them to sell surplus produce on the free market for profit.

At the same time, a relaxed state policy toward religion led many farmers to revive centuries-old forms of worship that were abandoned during the Cultural Revolution (1966–76).

The attack in the *Peasants' Daily* began with a detailed account of

---

[1] See Document #73 for a description of "socialist spiritual civilization."

farmers who have flocked to Hengshan Mountain, in Mao Zedong's southern home province of Hunan, to worship at Buddhist temples there. . . . It cited as "rare cases" a former farmer turned construction squad leader who bowed three times before a Buddha, lit "lucky" incense sticks, and burned forty 10-yuan ($2.70) banknotes as an offering.

Li Xiangshen was quoted as saying that after four years of poverty, he wanted to give thanks to Buddha for good fortune.

The newspaper also described a vice-mayor of a Hunan village who led a group of 200 local people to Hengshan to give thanks to Buddha for an exceptionally good harvest.

"Everyone says that (farmers are rich) thanks to the good policies of the Communist Party, but we cannot forget the Buddhas who protect us," Li Xiangsheng, vice-mayor of Loudi Village, was quoted as saying.

67
Wang Zhen Decries Loss of Party Influence

Willy Wo-lap Lam

Source: Hong Kong, *South China Morning Post,* March 12, 1991, *FBIS,* March 12, 1991.

A senior Chinese leader has warned that the nation's villages are being overrun by the forces of Western religion, capitalism, and the clans.

In an internal speech, the vice-president, Mr. Wang Zhen,[1] also said that the prestige and vitality of the Chinese Communist Party had fallen to a record low, with practically no desire among young rural folk to become party members.

In the speech, entitled "The Challenge of Feudalistic Forces in Villages," which is being sent to senior officials nationwide, Mr. Wang said that in rural areas, where more than 75 percent of the population lives, party organizations and activities were being disrupted and broken up by the influence of religion, the developing capitalistic class, and clans.

---

[1] Wang Zhen died in March 1993.

"Fewer and fewer people want to be enrolled in the party or the Communist Youth League, yet more and more people want to join religious groups.

"Many people in the villages, particularly young people, have absolutely no desire to join the party or the [communist youth] league," Mr. Wang said.

In Handan County, Hebei Province, last year, 813 people had become Catholics while only 270 people had joined the party, he said.

And from 1982 to 1990, the number of Christians in central Henan Province swelled from 400,000 to more than one million.

Many of these new converts had made the previously unheard-of decision to voluntarily withdraw from the party. Sixteen did so in the Langfang district in Hebei last year.

The vice-president, known as one of the "eight major elders" of the party, particularly deplored the fact that "while political activities are cold-shouldered, religious ones are drawing large crowds."

He said that the eight places of worship in a village in Chengan County in Hebei were bustling with life during the twice-daily Bible classes, and weekly masses, as well as at major festivals such as Easter and Christmas.[2]

"We take part in church activities of our own free will. Nobody needs to notify us, and we want no recompense," he reported one convert as saying.

In comparison, attendance at meetings organized by party cells was unsatisfactory, despite the fact that proceedings were relayed by broadcast system and each attendee was paid one yuan [$0.18].

Mr. Wang said he was equally disturbed by the fact that "while the words of CCP cadres in the villages have little appeal, the response to religious figures is overwhelming."

Recently in Chengan, 500 people had given money and 600 had donated their labor toward the building of a 4,000-square-meter church, which was finished in one month. However, response to appeals for public duty by party units was tepid.

Last summer, party authorities in Ningjin County in Hebei had resorted to asking a Catholic priest to persuade farmers to sell their grain to the government.

---

[2]This process was accelerated by the proliferation of Christian "house churches" in China, now banned by the CCP.

In many counties in remote Qinghai Province, party organizers practically depend on church networks to promote party activities.

"The approval of church leaders is required before (party-related) mass meetings can be called," he said.

Some party officials even had to make use of the opportunity of a church gathering to talk to their people.

Mr. Wang admitted that some people had joined the "religious army" to "absolve themselves of the pains of reality."

"To consolidate their economic positions and to make further advances, they (the capitalists) have an increasing motive in seeking political status," Mr. Wang said.

For example, the so-called 10,000-yuan or 100,000-yuan house-holders [$1,754, $17,545] engaged party cadres as consultants to their businesses. They gave generously to charities and built up their "masses network" by dispensing loans and creating jobs.

Quite a few had become deputies to the People's Congress, and the political consultative conferences, and some had even become village administrators.

To supplement their meager incomes, many cadres had teamed up with the capitalists or otherwise offered them illegal protection and "conveniences."

Mr. Wang disclosed that one-third of the 611 party cadres in seven villages in Linxiang County, Hunan Province, had become partners or consultants to private entrepreneurs and had all but abandoned their party-related work.

The rising clout of the "converts to Adam Smith" has further undermined the prestige of the party.

"Some peasants openly say, 'We would rather follow the money-splashing rich households than offer our allegiance to the poor government,'" Mr. Wang said.

The third evil he turned on was the revival of the influence of clans, which were supposed to have been wiped out by the revolution.

He cited the popular adage, "We would rather depend on the clans than on village governments. We would rather salute the chief clansman than the village chief."

One-third of the villages in the outskirts of Yueyang City in Hunan had resuscitated clan organizations, he said.

Partly as a result of the warnings sounded by Mr. Wang, the party's

Organization Department has listed as its top priority for 1991 the building and strengthening of party cells in rural areas.

In a recent speech, the new party secretary of Guangdong Province, Mr. Xie Fei, said the construction of grass-roots party units was the basic objective of agrarian work in his province.

Governor Mr. Ye Xuanping added last week that ideological indoctrination should be beefed up in rural areas.

"Development in villages should not be solely money-oriented," he said.

68
Analysis of "Abrupt Incidents" in Rural Areas

Liu Hexin [County Party Secretary in Shanxi Province]

Source: Beijing, *Renmin ribao,* April 28, 1992, *FBIS,* May 15, 1992.

In recent years, abrupt incidents like group appeals and group fights with weapons have occurred from time to time. According to our country's statistics, from 1990 to October 1991, a total of eight fairly big abrupt incidents involving 3,000 people took place. Thanks to the high degree of attention paid by the county party committee and county government and to forceful measures adopted, the aforementioned incidents were dealt with promptly and appropriately.

Generally speaking, the abrupt incidents in the rural areas may be classified into the following categories based on their natures:

Clash-of-interest type. People in the countryside often have disputes over issues that involve their self-interests, such as land ownership and contracting of orchards. However, they do not resolve the problem by going through the normal channel and legal process. Instead, the conflicts are intensified through man-made reasons, turning normal disputes into vicious incidents.

Cadre-people-conflict type. In recent years, a few incidents where peasants burned down the houses of village cadres, poisoned their livestock, and destroyed their young crops have occurred in our county. On the other hand, a handful of village cadres have also abused their powers by illegally detaining and beating people, thus leading to the escalation of conflicts between cadres and the people.

Clan-disputes type. Because of the influence of the traditional clan concept, some disputes over otherwise minor and trivial matters often develop into fights between clans. Even in disputes involving clans of the same family name, factions often form along the lines of proximity or distance in blood relations and would be engaged in acts of revenge.

The reasons for disputes and abrupt incidents in the rural areas are multifaceted:

1. Dishonesty and poor quality on the part of some grass-roots cadres is an important factor causing disputes and abrupt incidents in rural areas. Some cadres greedily take over collective properties, abuse power, and bully others by acting illegally on matters of popular concern—such as family planning, examination and approval of residential sites, distribution of materials, and assignment of contracts— creating resentment among the people.

2. There is a failure to do solid work and strengthen work styles. On the one hand, some judicial departments show tendencies of "stressing criminal cases and making light of civil cases" in the process of law enforcement. They do not act promptly on civilian disputes and on civil cases, and even shift responsibility to others. Meanwhile, some peasants lack confidence in seeking legal protection and resort to making trouble and to willful acts when disputes arise. On the other hand, some of our party and state leading cadres do not pay enough attention to letters and appeals by rural folks, considering them to be trivial matters and refusing to conduct intensive investigations and understandings, much less meticulous ideological education work.

3. A lack of sound organization and forceful measures exists. A considerable number of the people's self-rule organizations, such as rural security and popular mediation organizations, are in a state of paralysis and semiparalysis because of unsound structures and an imperfect system. No one is in charge in the village, and the peasants have nowhere to air their complaints. Hence, some people mistakenly think that the solution to problems lies in fists and sticks.

In general, every big dispute and every abrupt incident that arises in the rural areas has the participation, either overtly or covertly, of cadres who are party members, with some even playing a pivotal role. In resolving disputes in the rural areas, cadres who are party members should be the focus and efforts should be made to step up realistically their education on party regulations, party discipline, policies, and the law so they can be taught to take the lead in observing the law and in upholding the political situation of stability and unity. . . .

69
Hunan Province Mining Towns' "Bloody Clash" Investigated

Source: Hong Kong, AFP, November 7, 1992, *FBIS,* November 9, 1992.

The central government was investigating a bloody clash between two rival mining towns in central China that left scores injured and ended with one mine being blown up, a newspaper reported.

The dispute in Hunan Province culminated on June 23, when more than 100 miners from the Yaogangxian Tungsten Mine, wearing helmets and armed with iron rods, attacked the government compound of rival Chukou town. The miners surrounded the compound and then went on a rampage of violence that lasted forty minutes, the official *Tianjin Evening News* said. "They hit everyone they saw, robbed every house they passed, and smashed every object they came across," it said.

Government officials were brutally hit, and one was even pushed from the third floor of a building. The elderly and children were forced to kneel facing a wall and were threatened with death if they moved. Vehicles and offices were badly damaged before the attackers then went to Chukou's mine, blew it up with explosives and then set it on fire. When the rampage was over, twenty-three officials were injured, seven of them seriously, while damages totalled 500,000 yuan [$87,700].

The dispute dated to 1985, when 7,000 Chukou farmers were forced to move off their land to make way for a national-scale hydropower station.[1] Yaogangxian agreed to allow the farmers to take over one of its smaller mines, but when it later reneged on the deal, the Chukou authorities refused to hand back the mine. Two days before the attack, the two towns also had an all-out clash at a swimming hole, with local police and militia joining the fracas. Several people were injured.

A Chinese Communist Party commission led by Qiao Shi, who is in charge of internal security, finally intervened and together with the Hunan authorities opened a major investigation into the incident. Investigations were still going on, the report said.

---

[1]Violent outbreaks by rural and urban residents slated for resettlement to make way for massive hydropower projects, such as the 1.3 million people to be relocated out of the Three Gorges Dam area in south-central China, has led the Chinese government to strengthen police and paramilitary control of affected areas.

70
CCP Secretariat Member Comments on Train, Highway Robbery

Source: Beijing, Xinhua, March 12, 1993, *FBIS,* March 17, 1993.

In a telephone conference held today, the Central Committee for Comprehensive Control of Public Offenses exhorted people nationwide to round up and annihilate train and highway robbers. Ren Jianxin, member of the CCP Central Committee Secretariat,[1] spoke at the conference. Ren Jianxin said: In recent years, under the guidance of party committees and governments at all levels, public security, railway, and communications departments have achieved noticeable success in their sustained efforts to crack down on robberies committed on trains and

---

[1]The administrative organ of the CCP.

highways. While order along parts of most railways and highways is satisfactory, robberies are still rampant on certain railway and highway sections. These crimes have seriously endangered people's lives and property as well as the nation's reform, opening up, and modernization endeavors. The Central Committee for Comprehensive Control of Public Offenses maintains that train and highway robberies constitute an outstanding public offense; and it is imperative to launch a special, nationwide struggle to round up and annihilate train and highway robbers over a period of one year, starting now, so as to deal crushing blows to train and highway robbers.

71
Journal Analyzes Causes of "Gun Proliferation"

Duo Duo

Source: Beijing, Zhongguo xinwen she, June 11, 1993, *FBIS,* July 7, 1993.

The June issue of *Zhonghua wenzhai [Chinese Digest]* published here carries an article entitled "Perspectives of Gun Control on the Chinese Mainland" revealing the negative effects of gun proliferation on society, while analyzing the causes of gun proliferation.

The article states that there are four causes of serious gun proliferation:

1. In recent years, there has been a rise in the incidence of people outside the border, such as from Hong Kong and Macao, purchasing guns in the hinterland, and some lawbreakers have specialized in trading and trafficking guns across borders to reap staggering profits.

2. In the wake of opening up the border, people living along some borders have traded daily necessities with Chinese residents along the border of Guangxi and Yunnan Provinces. Some lawbreakers saw huge potential profits and started to recklessly engage in transporting goods for sale and speculation.

3. Affected by armed robbery in foreign society, some thugs inside the borders have also followed suit, thus greatly increasing the demand for guns and munitions.

4. Some units or individuals possessing guns, especially in some border areas, are not good at keeping their guns under control; consequently, some of their guns have been stolen or lost.

The article states that carelessness in control over guns has already resulted in negative effects on social order on the Chinese mainland, which should rouse the attention of related departments.[1]

---

[1]The shooting deaths of fourteen people in Beijing by a lone gunman in September 1994 verified this threat.

72
Peasant Blows Himself Up to Protest Tax Burden

Xiu Kang

Source: Beijing, *Beijing qingnian bao (Beijing Youth News),* January 19, 1994, *FBIS,* January 31, 1994.

Liu Shu, a peasant from Yantai's Jianggezhuang Town, refused to pay tax every year since 1980; by 1992, the amount of tax in arrears had accumulated to 470 yuan [$82].

Shortly after tax-collecting work began in 1993, Liu Shu publicly announced that he would refuse to pay, while instigating other villagers to do the same, thus directly affecting the unfolding of tax collection in the village. To ensure the smooth operation of tax-collecting work, town Vice Governor Zhang Xiao came to the Guanghe Village's village committee office, accompanied by comrades from the county public security bureau and town police substation. Then they sent for Liu Shu. Together with the village committee director Xu Shiyou, they did ideological work face to face with Liu Shu, hoping that he would promptly pay the arrears. Liu Shu rejected the criticism, while growing very angry; he flung abuse at the town vice governor as well as the cadres and policemen from the public security bureau and police substation. Quickly, Zhang Xiao and the public security bureau cadres and policemen made a decision: Liu Shu must immediately go home to get the money to pay the tax; otherwise, he would be solemnly dealt with according to the relevant law. The ferocious Liu Shu became mad and pretended that he would go home and fetch the money. When he arrived home, he got some explosives (7 kg), which he had concealed in his house, wrapped them around his body with a fuse, and covered them with his overcoat. At around 10:20 P.M., Liu Shu returned to the village office, and suddenly sprang at the town Vice Governor Zhang Xiao, holding him tight, then he pulled the fuse. . . .

The explosives erupted, and Liu Shu had his body blown to pieces, with his crime and hatred for the times, and Vice Governor Zhang Xiao unfortunately died at his post. In addition, three other public security cadres and policemen along with a villager were badly wounded. . . .

73
On Building Spiritual Civilization

Source: Nanjing [Jiangsu Province], *Jiangsu Provincial Radio Service,* December 11, 1990, *FBIS,* December 14, 1990.

A four-day meeting on building spiritual civilization and antipornography work[1] in the province ended in Nanjing on the afternoon of December 10. Shen Daren, secretary of the provincial CCP committee, delivered an important speech at the meeting.

He pointed out: The key to furthering the building of spiritual civilization and antipornography work in the province lies in the full implementation of relevant policies. Shen Daren said: It is our unswerving principle to pay equal attention to persisting in building both socialist material and spiritual civilizations. When pursuing our socialist modernization drive, we must persist in making the economic construction our central task and strive to develop social productive forces. Making economic construction our central task, however, does not mean we can be lax about building spiritual civilization. The build-

---

[1] A reference to the recent spread of pornography in China, one of the "six vices."

ing of spiritual civilization will guarantee that we take the correct direction in building material civilization. The development of material civilization requires spiritual and intellectual support from spiritual civilization. Generally speaking, our province has achieved notable results in building spiritual civilization in the last several years. We should note, however, the inconsistencies inherent in sometimes taking a decisive approach and sometimes taking a half-hearted approach when building spiritual civilization. We should fundamentally reverse those inconsistencies. There remains a great deal of work to be done. To solve this problem, it is necessary to heighten our awareness of the strategic position of spiritual civilization building, implement well the policy of paying equal attention to building the two civilizations, and do a still better job of building the two civilizations.

Shen Daren also stated: Party committees and governments at all levels should launch the activities of building spiritual civilization and carry out antipornography work on a regular basis and implement relevant policies well. First, we must formulate a good plan for building spiritual civilization and include it in the overall scheme of the Eighth Five-Year Plan [1991–1995] and the ten-year strategy for economic and social development. Second, we must pay particular attention to doing well in ideological and moral education. Third, we should organize well the activities for launching the building of spiritual civilization among the masses, continue proven methods for activities, constantly enlarge the scope of activities, and improve the forms of activities. Fourth, we must continuously do a good job in antipornography work. Great efforts should be made to effect a thriving socialist culture.

74
Cleanse Our Minor Surroundings—Learning from Comrade Zhang Zixiang, Living Lei Feng in the New Era

Source: Beijing, Commentator, *Jiefangjun bao,* March 2, 1990, *FBIS,* March 20, 1990.

Since February 19, this newspaper has been giving continuous coverage to the deeds of Comrade Zhang Zixiang. At a February 24 briefing on the National Auditing Work Conference, Premier Li Peng called upon the people to learn from this "living Lei Feng[1] in the new era" and to develop their spirit of selfless dedication. Premier Li said that the press and broadcast coverage in the last few days of Comrade Zhang Zixiang's deeds was very touching, and that the most touching aspect was that at a time when a negative social mood prevailed, Comrade Zhang strove to cleanse his immediate minor surroundings and proceeded to influence a group, a company, and even a larger group of people. That is a development of the spirit of Lei Feng. Apart from recognizing Zhang Zixiang as a model of learning from Lei Feng and extolling the former's virtues, Premier Li Peng also pointed out in his call and speech the direction in which we are to strive to launch our "learn from Lei Feng" activities.

The extensive reinforcement of socialist spiritual civilization construction is the party Central Committee's unswerving guiding principle, and the cleansing of our surroundings is the common hope of the whole party, the whole military, and the entire population of the country. How do we go about implementing this guiding principle and realizing this hope? One feasible and effective way is to learn from Lei Feng as Zhang Zixiang has and to strive to cleanse our immediate surroundings. Major and minor surroundings influence each other and are closely related. They form a dialectical unity. The objective of cleansing minor surroundings is to gradually realize the cleansing of major surroundings, and the cleansing of major surroundings is carried out by the earnest cleansing of minor surroundings. Without cleansing our immediate minor surroundings, it would be impossible for us to cleanse our major social surroundings. Taking the issue from the people's field of vision in observing their surroundings, minor surroundings are a "window" looking out toward major surroundings. If the minor surroundings have spotless windows and shining furniture, not only do the people inside feel happy, they are also able to get a clearer and wider view of the world outside the window. If this "window" is caked with dirt, it narrows the people's field of vision in observing their major surroundings, and, more importantly, sunlight is not able to pass through the window. Taking

---

[1]Lei Feng was a peasant soldier during the Maoist era who after his death became the Chinese Communist model of a socialist man and a paragon of such values as courage, selflessness, and, above all, absolute loyalty to the CCP.

the issue from the effects of changing our surroundings and the bearing of such a measure on the people, the cleansing of minor surroundings is something tangible and actual. The people's perception of such a measure is direct, it leaves a deep impression in the people's mind, and it is often very effective in strengthening the people's confidence in cleansing major surroundings. Zhang Zixiang's perseverance in learning from Lei Feng and doing good deeds is most touching. The fact that he has influenced and motivated people in his immediate surroundings and even people on a larger scale is sufficient indication of the impact of the cleansing of minor surroundings.

On a more realistic and practical plane, it is difficult to rely on one or two persons to cleanse major social surroundings, but cleansing one's immediate minor surroundings is physically feasible and possible to achieve. A group, a family, or even a unit or society is formed by people, and people are always needed in the cleansing of surroundings. When we learn from Comrade Zhang, we should also start with our immediate surroundings and cleanse the ground under our feet. "A nine-tier platform is built from accumulated soil; a thousand-mile journey starts under one's feet." We should commence our cleansing work in our immediate surroundings. We should devote ourselves entirely to helping our comrades-in-arms, loving the people, upholding righteousness, fighting evil, and we should do so with perseverance and determination. When we cleanse the ground under our feet, we are actually practicing and developing the spirit of Lei Feng, and we are contributing to the cleansing of the major surroundings. If each and every one of our millions of soldiers learns from Lei Feng in doing good deeds as Zhang Zixiang has, then the military would take on an entirely new look and the general social mood would be improved. Our party has a membership of more than 40 million persons. If each and every one of our party members, like Lei Feng, put the interests of others before his own and devoted himself selflessly to other people, then there would be basic changes in the general mood of our party, and the party would effectively initiate changes in the general social mood of the population. The cleansing of our surroundings is not merely carried out through good intentions; there have to be strong public opinion and concrete measures. Such a cleansing cannot be achieved by one or two acts; it is achieved, as in Zhang Zixiang's case, by faith and long-term perseverance. As Premier Li Peng said in a State Council executive meeting, as long as we share Comrade Zhang Zixiang's spirit and as long as we behave like him, we can surely reverse the undesirable social trends that have materialized in recent years. . . .

75

The Chinese Authorities Take Action to Purge the "Qigong Party"

Chi Ta

Source: Hong Kong, *Tang tai,* #39, August 25, 1990, pp. 14–15 *FBIS,* September 13, 1990.

In China, the number of people practicing Qigong [a health regimen involving breathing exercises and meditation] and believing in Qigong exceeds 200 million, and various types of "Qigong institutes" have over 50 million members throughout the country. Ordinary Chinese people have already replaced communism with Qigong in their minds, and the political old men in Beijing also depend on Qigong to sustain their lives. Recently, however, the CCP has become aware of the threat posed by the Qigong party, and is purging the Qigong circles.

Qigong has an enormous power and market in today's mainland China. According to official CCP bulletins, 50 million people around the country practice Qigong exercises. However, this is only a conservative figure. In China, the number of people directly practicing Qigong exercises and believing in Qigong exceeds 200 million, and they are called the "Qigong party." Recently, the CCP has begun to purify the Qigong party and arrested some "Qigong masters" who are celebrated across the country. Numerous people are also involved. In these circumstances, "Qigong" has become an incomparably hot topic and has drawn people's particular attention.

Many Leaders Also Believe in Qigong

Besides the CCP, the only legitimate association that has spread most successfully throughout the country is the "Qigong Association." It is a nongovernmental organization. Among the believers in the country are supreme leaders like Deng Xiaoping, Yang Shangkun, Wang Renzhong, Public Security Minister Wang Fang, and Political Bureau member Hu Qili ... medium-level leaders such as ministers at all levels, provincial leading cadres, intellectuals, grass-roots leaders; and ... workers and peasants.

The reason "Qigong masters" are celebrated is that in the first place they pay medical attention to senior CCP leaders. Celebrated Qigong masters Yan Xin, Zhang Xiangyu, Zhu Heting, and others won their fame across the country after curing senior leaders in Beijing by using their Qi [power of breath]. Some famous Qigong personalities said: Each of the eight "old ones" (Deng Xiaoping, Chen Yun, Yang Shangkun, Deng Yingchao, Li Xiannian, and others) has by their side four to five Qigong experts allocated by the state. They use Qi on them, cure them, and predict the future for them. Moreover, since Qigong masters practice divination according to the *I-Ching [Book of Changes]*, they can carry on political struggles with their opponents. Some politicians in [the central leadership compound at] Zhongnanhai always take counsel with their Qigong masters in "making a move," "changing it," and "running to the defensive." Now in Zhongnanhai over 200 Qigong masters, or "body-protecting doctors" and "advanced brain trusters," are employed. They go with their leaders on their trips and visits, and live with them. . . .

Since 1985, Qigong has become popular in China, and "Qigong teachers" have become special personalities. Any celebrated Qigong performer definitely comes from a certain important figure. They are well informed, live an easy life, and are invited here and there by officials at all levels. Whenever a big event occurs or a very sensitive problem crops up in the mainland's political circle, relevant people frequently ask the help of Qigong masters. In fact, it is rare for medium-level and senior officials in China to have no Qigong masters by their side or no friends in the Qigong circle. In China, Qigong has become a kind of politics. Those who know nothing about China's Qigong and the *I-Ching* have much difficulty becoming senior officials or making a fortune. A senior official of the State Commission for Restructuring the Economic System said: "There is endless wonder in it. If you are conversant with Qigong and the rules of change, you will be as good in China as a fish swimming in the water, controlling things as you please."

Members of Qigong Bodies throughout the Country Total More than 20 Million

The common people think that since "public officials" set store by Qigong, it must be "genuine." Moreover, since old times people have had the tradition and custom of using *wushu* [martial arts] and Qigong for healing purposes, and ordinary Chinese people have esteemed it and ardently loved it. In every province and city, special nongovernmental "Qigong bodies" have been set up. Now there are over thirty bodies, similar in nature to the "Qigong Association," across the country, having over 20 million members. In Beijing and Shanghai, they have several hundred members each. The *Qigong yu kexue [Qigong and Science]* monthly magazine published in Guangzhou (Canton) sells nearly one million copies per issue.

Qigong in some places of China is not only limited to hard exercises such as cutting gold and cracking jade, grappling with and overpowering others, leaping onto roofs and vaulting over walls, or even to the soft exercises such as healing and keeping people fit and healthy. It also includes the mainland's numerous mystical knowledge and arts such as *I-Ching* studies, fortune-telling, divination, special human functions, as well as witchcraft, psychic arts, and *fengshui* [Chinese geomancy]. They all consciously or unconsciously fall into the boundary of Qigong functions.

The CCP No Longer Publicly Promotes Qigong

As a matter of fact, at the back of Qigong functions lies a whole set of cultures totally different from communism. Those practicing Qigong believe that there are gods and spirits in the heavens, and that all people have souls. They also believe that the world is neither physical nor conceptual, but is the indescribable "word" *[dao]* and elements, or the "elementary breath." To the modern man, they are "nonexistent," while on a certain level of Qigong they really exist. On this level, people can directly perceive the world and simply and accurately master it. Human birth, age, illness, and death and the world's meeting and separation all have become simple and understandable. All are inevitable and fatalistic, and void and empty. The Chinese people have lost confidence in the CCP's promises, and so they use Qigong or similar beliefs to fill the vacuum in their souls. This is, indeed, a great satire on the fundamental tenets of Marxism.

The CCP takes a very utilitarian and practical attitude toward Qigong. Within the six months beginning from the time before "June 4" [1989] to the time after it, the CCP encouraged and supported people to practice Qigong. Newspapers and magazines frequently promoted and introduced Qigong knowledge, and the government also held symposiums on Qigong frequently. At that time Qigong was not involved in politics. It neither attempted to overthrow the CCP nor demanded that it speed up reform in any form. In these circumstances, the Qigong craze spread as never before. Since "June 4," the Qigong party has become more widespread, and people generally believe that the lives of the several old men in power are sustained by Qigong masters. Some inner information spread that they knew beforehand that within a certain time the CCP would definitely lose more of the people's support, and that "June 4" would be "redressed." It also disclosed the life spans of the political old men of the CCP. In October 1989, a number of national celebrated Qigong masters announced that they would return to the hills and continue to live the hermit's life. They estimated that they would leave the hills again after "June 4" has been redressed. These kinds of mysteries have caused more people to join the Qigong party. Moreover, since "June 4," industrial production has slowed down and intellectuals have become silent. Therefore people have more spare time for concentrating on Qigong exercises.

In recent months, however, the CCP top hierarchy has come to know that this Qigong party, which appears not to interfere with politics, embraces large numbers of people as its basis on the one hand, and is actually playing a role of causing people to wait negatively and not to cooperate with the CCP by peaceful means on the other. Now the people have lost the morale and enthusiasm to respond to the CCP's appeals, causing difficulties for the national economy. Moreover, politically speaking, in the eyes of the CCP, once these kinds of bodies, which are not politically oriented and have nearly 200 million members, become an independent organizational system, their very existence poses a threat. They are afraid that these national celebrated Qigong masters will play a part in waking the people up.

The "Natural Center Association" Disbanded

The CCP is beginning to purge some Qigong bodies, and the most far-reaching case was the arrest of "Qigong master" Zhang Xiangyu in in Beijing. The CCP has stipulated that no interprovincial and inter-city Qigong associations be allowed to be established, that no Qigong professionals be allowed to start up businesses without med-ical diplomas awarded by the state, and that large public Qigong lectures no longer be allowed. The governments of all provinces and cities have taken emergency measures by promulgating the "Tempo-rary Suspension Management Regulations for Qigong Physical Training." . . .

Ordinary Chinese people hold the government's action in con-tempt, generally believing that the government "only allows itself to do a lot of unreasonable things but does not allow the people to do a single reasonable thing." The CCP top hierarchy still worships Qigong and is vigorously looking for gifted Qigong people. It is said that Zhang Xiangyu got into trouble after sneering at Yang Shangkun for ordering soldiers to fire at students and warned him that he would end up bad, at a medical consultation after "June 4." Since too many people believe in Qigong, the government was more careful in making this move and dared not be reckless this time. . . .

76
Sociologists Say Market Economy Not Linked to Crime

Source: Beijing, Zhongguo xinwen she, July 6, 1993, *FBIS,* July 22, 1993.

A number of sociologists attending a forum on juvenile delinquency today said that the market economy does not necessarily bring about crime.

"The Juvenile Delinquency and Moral Building Academic Forum" sponsored by the China Contemporary Society Research Center, among other organizations, was held today. Specialists attending the forum maintained that the establishment of the market economic struc-ture is conducive to promoting the exchange of equal values, fair com-petition, equality, and mutual assistance, and is not necessarily the root cause of crime. On the contrary, it can enhance the establishment and development of new ethics in society.

At the same time, however, the sociologists were full of worry because statistics have shown that the rate of juvenile delinquency in the 1990s has increased 1.26 times since the beginning of the 1980s.

Professor Tian Sen, president of the China Contemporary Society Research Center, delivered his keynote speech at the forum and said that the new characteristics of juvenile delinquency are as follows: Offenders are younger in age, the percentage of female offenders is increasing, the number of mobile offenders is increasing, crimes involving gangsters are increasing, the degree of desperation is higher, the percentage of crimes committed in urban areas is rising, and the number of crimes committed by underground societies and transnational gangs is increasing.

Analyzing the causes of juvenile delinquency, Professor Tian said: First of all, Chinese society is experiencing a deepening of reform. The old social norms have been weakened, but the new ones have yet to be consolidated. Great changes have taken place in the concept of value. Money and commodity worship has corroded people's minds and has affected people's behaviors. Moreover, backwardness in education has given rise to approximately 300 million illiterate or semiliterate people, and illiteracy has been linked with ignorance of the law.

77
Household Registers to Be Retained Indefinitely

Source: Beijing, Zhongguo xinwen she, June 17, 1993, *FBIS,* June 18, 1993.

China will not do away with household registers[1] in the foreseeable future, according to an official from the Ministry of Public Security.

---

[1]The *hukou* system of household registration in China divides the population into two basic categories: urban and rural. People with rural registration are effectively blocked from moving permanently into cities, and urban residents are prevented from moving from one city to another without a formal change in urban registry from, for example, Shanghai to Beijing. The *hukou* determines an individual's access to food rations and housing, though the growth of free commodity markets has weakened this enforcement mechanism. Urban residents who engage in dissident political activity often are punished by having their household registration transferred to the countryside.

Speaking in an interview with this agency, the official said that the registration of households and of the total population is an important part of the administration's work. China, he said, could not do away with this practice at this time. Instead, it should further perfect the registration of the population so as to guarantee further reform and opening and to safeguard the public's legitimate rights and interests.

China introduced identity cards in 1984, and this has been seen as a major reform of the administration of the household register system; such cards and household registers run in parallel, enabling the department concerned to keep up to date on population trends.

With the ongoing economic development, a massive flow of surplus workers coming from the rural to the urban areas, and the establishment of a socialist market economy system, the administration of a population register has to deal with many new problems, and a restructuring of the existing administration is necessary. . . .

China is now using modern methods to administer household registers with the introduction of computers in many provinces and cities.

B. Women and Population Policy

78
Li Tieying Speaks at Meeting on Sale of Women

Feng Yuan and Sun Yong

Source: Beijing, Xinhua, December 20, 1990, *FBIS,* December 21, 1990.

Today, at the national work meeting on striking at crimes of kidnapping and selling women and children, and checking and clamping down on prostitution and visiting whores, Li Tieying, member of the CCP Political Bureau, said: During this winter and next spring, we must concentrate our efforts on launching a specific campaign to crack down on criminal activities involving the kidnapping and selling of women and children, and on checking and banning prostitution and visiting whores in key districts in conjunction with wiping out pornography and the six vices. We must forcefully and effectively do this.

Li Tieying said: In recent years, various localities have done a lot of work in cracking down on activities such as abducting and selling people as well as prostitution and visiting whores, and have achieved remarkable results. However, at the same time, we must be aware that illegal activities, such as kidnapping and selling women and children as well as prostitution and visiting whores, presently are still very rampant. Therefore, we must take firm, resolute, practical, and effective measures against them.

Li Tieying pointed out: At present, party committees and governments at all levels must first of all be fully aware of the importance of cracking down on the criminal activities of kidnapping and selling of women and children as well as of prostitution and visiting whores. They must also be soberly aware that clamping down on the rampancy of kidnapping and selling of women and children as well as prostitution and visiting whores, and the eradication of these vile social phenomena, is a significant struggle in protecting the personal interest of the masses, in maintaining social stability, and in straightening up current social practices. We must adopt a serious attitude and be responsible to the party, state, people, nationality, and history in this respect. We must carry out this task with a strong sense of responsibility and urgency.

79
Education Promotion Planned for Women

Wang Rong

Source: Beijing, *China Daily,* August 24, 1991, *FBIS,* August 28, 1991.

The All-China Women's Federation (ACWF), which represents the country's 400 million women, will focus its efforts on raising women's education levels and living standards in the coming five years to further promote their social status.

ACWF plans to have 3 million illiterate women educated every year in the five-year period, and to make more efforts to get as many girls of school age as possible to receive school education in order to prevent new illiteracy.

These, as discussed at the two-day meeting of the federation's standing committee that started yesterday in Beijing, are the priorities of the five-year plan.

Chinese women, in many cases independent and growing more important in social life, still do not enjoy true equality with men, especially when it comes to opportunities for promotion, education, and employment. Women make up 70 percent of the country's 220 million illiterates. These are mostly from the countryside, where illiteracy develops from economic dependence on husbands or parents.

The ten-point plan covers all aspects of women's development and sets goals on women's participation in State affairs, the protection of women and children's legal rights and interests, broadening of exchanges with overseas women, and the development of women's studies.

The plan also proposes that at least 60 million rural women should be given farming technological training by 1995 and grasp at least one advanced technique of farming or handicraft. Some 240,000 rural women have already received and were found to have benefited from such training.

As part of a new drive to help improve women cadres' art of leadership, the present school for women cadres in Beijing will be expanded to a university, with a 1,000-student capacity. Teaching staff and basic construction will be finished by 1995. The university students will be women administrative officials ranking above county magistrate level.

As to women participating in policy making, the plan says the ACWF will strive for more seats in policy-making groups for a louder voice from women.

The ACWF's plan proposes that in the 1993 election of the National People's Congress, women delegates should not account for less than 25 percent.[1]

---

[1]Presently, approximately 12 percent of the NPC Standing Committee members are women.

80
Make the Greatest Determination to Control Population Growth

Source: Beijing, Xinhua, April 28, 1991, *FBIS,* April 29, 1991.

The "Outline for the Ten-Year Program and Eighth Five-Year Plan for National Economic and Social Development," adopted by the Fourth Session of the Seventh National People's Congress, noted the need to unswervingly implement the basic state policy on family planning, and to bring the average annual natural population growth rate to within 1.25 percent in the next ten years.[1] To achieve this goal, the party

---

[1]In 1993 China's population growth rate was approximately 1.1 percent. This figure is, however, expected to rise in the next few years.

Central Committee and the State Council recently held a discussion meeting on family planning, which stressed that the whole party should take actions, the whole people should be mobilized, and top party and government leaders at all levels should take personal interest in the work, and that the greatest determination should be made to bring China's population growth under control.

A huge population and its rapid growth have always been a heavy burden restricting China's economic and social development. Now, the population on mainland China exceeds 1.14 billion. Even if we closely attend to our work according to the requirements of the Ten-Year Program and the Eighth Five-Year Plan, the total population on main-land China will exceed 1.2 billion by 1995, and will near 1.3 billion by the end of the century. A slight relaxation in our efforts may cause it to break the 1.3 billion mark. If we let the population grow without effec-tively controlling it, the realization of the second-step strategic goal for China's modernization drive will be directly affected, and the efforts to further improve the people's living standards will be thwarted. This will create heavier pressure on economic and social development in the next century, further reduce China's per capita resources, worsen its environment, and bring endless misery to our posterity. Therefore, it is an important thing indeed to practice family planning and control pop-ulation growth. The whole party and the people of all nationalities throughout the country should immediately take action and strive to strictly control China's population growth, improve the quality of the population, and fulfill the population plans for the next five and ten years, respectively.

The key to success in family planning lies in the leadership. Party committees and governments at all levels should realize the strategic significance of controlling population growth, fully understand its tre-mendous importance and urgency in China's economic and social de-velopment as a whole, and further enhance their population awareness, the per capita concept, and the sense of responsibility toward popula-tion control. They should stop the one-sided view and shortsighted behavior of some comrades, who concentrate on the economy to the neglect of population control, and overcome the laxity and fear of difficulties in family planning. . . .

We should persistently stabilize and strictly implement the current family planning policy and manage the work of family planning ac-cording to law. At present, the key to strict control over population growth is to seriously . . . make every effort to ensure that the current family planning policy is truly put into practice at the grass-roots level. It is necessary to resolve to form a family planning work team at the grass-roots level characterized by a good state of mind and a correct work style and with professional knowledge and management ability; to speed up the establishment of family planning networks covering counties, townships, and villages; and to strengthen the family planning personnel of various villages and work groups so that there are always some people at the grass-roots level in charge of the various tasks related to family planning. In addition, we should ensure that necessary funds are put into this work. . . .

To make a success of the family planning work, we must adhere to the mass line, fully trust the masses, and rely on them. Because our country is still rather backward economically and culturally and is still subject to the influence of the traditional concept to a relatively great extent, and because an integrated social insurance system has not been established in our rural areas, it is understandable that some people among the masses may not be able to comprehend the need for family planning for the time being because practical difficulties and problems still exist in their production work and life. It is precisely because of this reason that we should make unremitting efforts to do successful propaganda and education work.

81
Man Executed for
Family Planning–Related Murder

Source: Urumqi, *Xinjiang Province Television Network,* April 25, 1991, *FBIS,* April 30, 1991.

The Changji Hui Autonomous Prefectural Intermediate People's Court held a sentencing meeting in Manas on April 23, at which Li Xinming was sentenced to death, executed immediately after sentencing, and deprived of political rights for life in accordance with the law for violating family planning policy and committing murder. (Video opens with long shots of the open-air meeting site, cutting to show a banner reading: Long Live Proletarian Dictatorship!)

Murder convict Li Xinming's wife delivered a third baby intentionally, and the (Lanzhouwan) Township Government in Manas County subsequently made a decision on dealing with the latter. (Ma Fengxian), chief of (Jiahezi) Village, forwarded the township government's decision to Li Xinming on February 27. Hatred began to well up in Li Xinming, who thought that the village chief was attempting to harm him. On the afternoon of the same day, he used a kitchen knife to slash to death (Ma Fengxian's) two sons, who were over ten years old, and seriously wounded the village chief's wife. (Video shows Li, flanked by two police officers, standing with his head bowed and a placard hanging around his neck identifying him as murder convict Li Xinming. Shots of a uniformed officer announcing the verdict and spectators are also shown.)

Family planning is our country's basic national policy. Li Xinming received due legal punishment for having violated family planning policy and having committed murder in disregard of national laws.

82
Population Minister Defends Abortion Policy

Bruce Shu

Source: Hong Kong, AFP, June 9, 1991, *FBIS,* June 13, 1991.

China's population minister defends the use of social and psychological pressure to persuade women to have abortions and advocates sterilization of the mentally handicapped.

She hopes her Western critics will come to understand China's perspective on human rights, which demands individual sacrifice for what the communist authorities deem the greater good.

In an interview with Agence France-Presse, Peng Peiyun, minister of the State Family Planning Commission, said contraception was a constitutional duty in China.

"People have rights, the right to reproduction, but they are constrained by law," she said. "Couples all have a duty to practice family planning. This is stipulated in our constitution."

That duty includes obeying the state on when to have children and how many to bear—one per family in the cities and up to two in the countryside—and voluntarily aborting babies conceived outside the quota system.

It is a system whose critics, notably the U.S. anti-abortion lobby, say has produced documented cases of forced abortions into the ninth month of pregnancy, infanticide, and economic coercion.

For the minister, there is no alternative for a country feeding 21 percent of the world's population with 7 percent of its arable land and overexploited water, forest, and mineral resources.

"If you have too many children, they won't have enough to eat, they won't have a good education," she said. "If a person doesn't have the most basic right, the right to life, how can you talk about human rights then?"

Mrs. Peng, a jovial, bespectacled sixty-two-year-old, oversees the sex lives of a fifth of humanity and calls on people to marry late and have "fewer but better babies."

China's official population was 1.14 billion at the end of last year. The government hopes to keep it below 1.3 billion in the year 2000.

The number of children the average Chinese woman bears fell in the last decade to 2.3 from more than five, and Mrs. Peng said the next target of 1.62 could be reached just by carrying out current policies to the letter.

China enforces its well-known one-child policy in the cities, but in the countryside, home to four out of five Chinese, peasants are allowed a second child if the first is a girl, and the rules are even looser in minority areas.

"We couldn't make the policy any more strict. It is a question of implementing it," Mrs. Peng said. "Currently, we are not really implementing it with success."

The minister reacts with emotion to those who accuse China of forcing people to practice family planning: "They do not understand. How could we possibly have carried out family planning only by coercion and commandism?"

But when asked to specify how much force a family planning official may use to convince a woman to abort, Mrs. Peng said it was "very hard to draw the boundary line."

"Simply said, you can't tie her up and make her do it," she said, but officials should create a "general mood" favoring abortion in their communities and bring pressure to bear to "mobilize" the woman.

"If it doesn't work the first time, the woman must be mobilized a few more times. It may take dozens of tries at persuasion for some," the minister said.

"I talk reason with you. I clearly reason with you. If you aren't convinced, then we'll have a few more ideological work sessions."

"If she was not willing to do it originally, she will do it in the end after giving it some thought. This is all right, and it is no good to insist on calling this coercion or commandism," Mrs. Peng said.

Western diplomats describe China's stated national population policy—which is voluntary and stresses education—as "progressive and enlightened."

But they warn that local enforcement may be overly zealous, with local-level family planning workers pressed to meet quotas.

The population control hierarchy matches China's political structure, with central planners issuing birth quotas to each province, provinces issuing quotas to counties, and down the line to individual work units.

Western reports regularly quote Chinese medical workers saying they are forced to perform abortions against women's will and to kill unwanted newborns by suffocation or injection.

Although the extent of the practices is difficult to gauge, discipline of couples who violate the population policy include financially debilitating fines, the withholding of social services, demotion, and other punishment.

When asked if the government ensured the civil rights of clients by penalizing family planning workers who went beyond the stated national policy, Mrs. Peng said only that the law was applied in cases in which it was violated.

"If the family planning worker does not violate the law," she said, "if she uses measures that are too simple—taking too harsh an attitude, scolding—if she has a rigid work method or style, then we try to educate her."[1]

---

[1]For a recent analysis of Draconian family practices in China, see Steven Mosher, *A Mother's Ordeal* (New York: Harcourt Brace, 1993).

During the interview, Mrs. Peng denied that China's "eugenics" program was a human genetics plan, but she defended laws in at least five localities requiring sterilization of mentally handicapped people.

While acknowledging that a mental handicap was not necessarily hereditary, the minister said China approached the problem from a "social viewpoint."

"The mentally retarded really place a heavy burden on their family and society. They can only eat, but cannot work, and they can bear children," she said.

"Some retarded women are taken advantage of and have children. They cannot keep themselves alive, let alone care for children," Mrs. Peng said. "We think one cannot call this (their sterilization) a violation of human rights."

The minister said she did not expect to convince everyone.

"A small number of people in the U.S. Congress don't understand the situation and constantly attack us," she said. "There is a type of person who attacks us with ulterior motives, and it will do no good to explain things."

"But most people just don't understand the situation," she added. . . .

83
Birth Control Card for Roving Workers

Zhu Baoxia

Source: Beijing, *China Daily,* December 27, 1991, p. 1, *FBIS,* January 3, 1992.

Members of the transient population in China are now required to produce "family planning cards" when they apply for residence permits or business licenses or seek jobs, according to new rules made public yesterday.

The rules governing family planning among the transient population—the first to be enforced in this country—are aimed at controlling rampant childbirth among the millions of itinerant Chinese tradesmen or workers who are constantly on the move away from their home counties.

The card is supposed to carry detailed information on the holder's marriage and childbirth status, and those for married couples will also indicate the measures they are taking for birth control.

Peng Peiyun, minister of the State Family Planning Commission, told a press conference yesterday in Beijing that family planning among the transient population remained a "hard nut to crack" and one of the key tasks faced by China's family planning workers.

Data shows that the country's transient population numbers some 70 million, one-fourth of whom are women of child-bearing age, between fifteen and forty-nine.

She said that though only some of the transient people have had multiple births and married below the age of twenty, it affects the implementation of the country's family planning policy.

84

Some 6,000 Child-Bearing Retarded Adults Undergo Sterilization Operation in Gansu Province

Chiang Fu-mei

Source: Hong Kong, *Ming Pao,* January 31, 1992, p. 9, *FBIS,* February 12, 1992.

According to statistics of Gansu Province's related departments, the province made 6,271 child-bearing retarded adults undergo a sterilization operation between January 1989 and June 1991.

As relevant data disclosed, Gansu had a population of 23 million, but with a populace of 260,000 retarded people. Furthermore, an additional 2,000 retarded babies were born each year, whereas the relief grain for populace in this category involved some 40 million kg, accompanied by some 14 million yuan [$2.5] of relief funds.

The retarded are intellectually disabled, but many of them are normal in their sexual development and reproductivity. When they bear children, they do not take care of the babies, and naturally become a burden to their families.

A survey showed that most children of the retarded are likewise retarded. Even when some children of the retarded are normal intelligence-wise, they usually have a low IQ simply because of failure in their parents' care and enlightenment.

At the first session of the Seventh Gansu Provincial People's Congress, the Pinglian [County] delegation submitted a bill for the first time on banning the retarded from bearing children. In April of the same year, Gansu People's Government officially submitted the provisional regulations on banning the retarded from bearing children to the provincial People's Congress, while suggesting that the Gansu Provincial People's Congress formulate local decrees on this issue.

According to the "Regulations of Gansu People's Congress Standing Committee on Banning the Retarded from Bearing Children," the retarded are allowed to get married on condition that a sterilization operation is performed on them. Should both partners in a marriage be retarded, sterilization can be confined to the female party; should only one of the couple be retarded, sterilization will be performed on the retarded person only.

The decree only bans the retarded from bearing children, but not from marriage. And measures of planned parenthood are implemented among the retarded between the ages of fifteen and forty-nine who have child-bearing capability, but not among the entire retarded populace.

85
Government Revising Draft Eugenics Law

Geoffrey Crothall

Source: Hong Kong, *South China Morning Post,* February 2, 1994, p. 11, *FBIS,* February 3, 1994.

Stunned by Western criticism of its proposed law on eugenics, the Chinese government is revising the draft legislation in an attempt to make it less contentious, according to Beijing sources. The original draft submitted to the National People's Congress Standing Committee for deliberation last December appeared to advocate the forced sterilization of mentally and physically disabled people and led to an outcry of protest from many Western countries.

The criticism came as something of a surprise to the Ministry of Public Health, which drafted the legislation, since China had practiced eugenics for the past five years and the new law was designed simply to codify existing practices. However, the State Family Planning Commission, which had borne mainly American criticism of China's one-child policy and was more aware of how the legislation would be received abroad, quickly voiced its concern over the proposed law, particularly its use of language such as "inferior births."

A source at the commission said the draft law was seen by many within the government as "very contentious" and possibly damaging to China's international reputation. There was also concern that it would place additional burdens on the work of the commission without providing any extra resources, the source said. All government agencies concerned with the proposed law are now refusing to discuss the legislation publicly for fear of creating more controversy, but it is understood that the draft is being reworked into a less contentious form.

Sources said that while the basic aim of the law, to slow the rapid increase in the number of children born with disabilities, remained the same, the language used would be altered and the proposed regulations watered down so as to appear less Draconian. The word "eugenics" would not appear anywhere in the new draft, a source said.

The new draft would make it clear that no one would be forced to have an abortion or be sterilized and that the emphasis would be placed on improving medical and social welfare care. "The new draft will focus on the positive aspects of the program rather than those negative, prohibitive aspects," the source added.

The law is now unlikely to go before the full session of the NPC, which meets in Beijing on March 10. The legislation is still considered too controversial to be discussed at the NPC, which attracts national and international media attention. He pointed out that the last time a controversial law was discussed at the NPC—namely the Three Gorges Dam project [see Documents #34 and #35]—the voting session ended in chaos, with a deputy from Taiwan storming out. It was more likely that the government would wait for a smaller standing committee meeting of the NPC before putting the legislation to the vote, he said.

C. Public Health and Environment

86
He Zhiqiang Addresses Rally to Combat Drugs

Source: Kunming, *Kunming Yunnan People's Radio Network,* October 26, 1991, *FBIS,* November 5, 1991.

The Yunnan provincial authorities and the Kunming city authorities jointly held a public sentence pronouncement rally in Kunming's Dongfeng Stadium this morning.

The rally, which was attended by over 40,000 people of all nationalities, passed sentences on and punished criminals involved in drug-related crimes in accordance with the law and burned confiscated drugs in the presence of all.

Today, three eye-catching, huge slogans were hoisted inside Dongfeng Stadium which read: Fight Drug Abuse and Punish Drug Trafficking, Drug Addiction, and Drug Plantation; The People of the Province Take Immediate Action to Resolutely Fight Against Drug-Related Crimes; Wage a Struggle Against Drugs to Ensure Smooth Progress in Reform, Opening Up, and Four Modernization Building.

After Kunming Mayor Wang Tingchen declared the rally open, Governor He Zhiqiang delivered a speech in which he said: Today, the Yunnan Provincial Higher People's Court is holding a public sentence pronouncement rally here to punish criminals involved in drug-related crimes in accordance with the law and publicly burn a batch of confiscated drugs. This is another major move aimed at severely cracking down on drug-related criminal activities, serves as a powerful deterrent to criminals at home and abroad, fully embodies a common aspiration of the people of all nationalities, and demonstrates the solemn and just stand of our party and government.[1]

---

[1]China's concern for drug addiction reflects the country's experience in the late nineteenth century when approximately 10 percent of the entire population was addicted to opium that was imported largely from abroad after the mid-century opium wars.

He Zhiqiang noted: In order to thoroughly wipe out the existing drug scourge, party committees and governments at all levels must earnestly strengthen organization and leadership and continually adhere to the principle of simultaneously eradicating drug trafficking, cultivation, and abuse; blocking drug sources; checking drug proliferation; strictly enforcing laws; and eliminating both root causes and symptoms. . . .

87
China Strengthens Prevention and Control of AIDS

Wang Nan and Li Wei

Source: Hong Kong, Xinhua, November 8, 1990, *FBIS,* November 16, 1990.

Since China discovered its first AIDS patient in 1985, the government has strengthened the comprehensive prevention of AIDS primarily by controlling its sexual transmission. They have firmly banned prostitution and whoring, and have achieved initial success in the monitoring of and scientific research into AIDS.

He Jiesheng, vice minister of public health and chairwoman of the China AIDS Prevention and Control Committee, said at the Chinese-American Symposium on Countermeasures against AIDS, which opened today, that the chief measures China has adopted to prevent and control AIDS are: strengthening examination and monitoring of AIDS, enhancing the general public's awareness of their own health protection, strengthening legal building so as to eradicate the root of AIDS and other venereal diseases, strengthening drug fighting and detoxification so as to stop the spread of AIDS through intravenous drug injection, and controlling other venereal diseases so as to prevent the spread of AIDS by sexual transmission.

He Jiesheng said: Since 1985, AIDS has been rated by the state as one of the infectious diseases that is given top priority in prevention and treatment. Up till now, almost all provinces, autonomous regions, and municipalities directly under the central government have carried out check-ups and monitoring of AIDS. The Ministry of Public Health has set up three laboratories for confirming positive results in testing for the AIDS virus antibody. A monitoring network has taken shape.

By the end of September of this year, 446 AIDS virus carriers had been found, of whom 68 were from abroad, and five were diagnosed as AIDS patients.

Said He Jiesheng: Under the present circumstances whereby effective medicine and preventive measures for treating AIDS are absent, propaganda and education on AIDS figure largely in the effort to prevent and control it. While stepping up comprehensive improvement in the social environment, China is also striving to implement, in a substantial way, effective measures to prevent and control AIDS and other venereal diseases.

She said: Apart from promulgating a series of laws and regulations for firmly cracking down on prostitution and whoring, and strengthening public order, the state has also promulgated "A Number of Regulations Regarding the Examination and Monitoring of AIDS" and the "Law of the People's Republic of China Governing the Prevention and Treatment of Infectious Diseases." They provide a legal guarantee for the successful prevention and treatment of AIDS.

He Jiesheng also said: In recent years, there has been a rapid increase in the number of drug addicts in some regions of China, especially in the southwestern frontier areas.[1] This has become a focus of attention of the Chinese government. Public security and customs departments have strengthened drug fighting in the frontier areas, and public health departments have established three kick-it centers to provide treatment for drug addicts.

He Jiesheng emphatically said: Venereal diseases are a premonitory sign of the spread of the AIDS virus. In recent years, venereal diseases have been spreading in a geometric progression in some regions, especially in some cities that are open to the outside world, and have gradually extended to towns and townships. In 1986, the Ministry of Public Health started to restore the system for preventing and treating

---

[1]The 1994 AIDS International Conference held in Yokohama, Japan, identified Asia as the region most likely to experience the fastest growth in AIDS cases in the near future.

venereal diseases and to integrate the prevention of sexual transmission of AIDS with the control of venereal diseases.

He Jiesheng said: China has scored great achievements in controlling infectious diseases. She expressed her conviction that China is bound to achieve more in preventing and controlling AIDS.

88
Officials Warned on AIDS, Threat to Reform

Source: Hong Kong, AFP, February 8, 1993, *FBIS,* February 9, 1993.

The Chinese cabinet met recently to discuss a growing AIDS threat after a report warned that the killer disease threatened to disrupt the country's economic reforms, a newspaper said Monday.

"AIDS is the big enemy of opening and reform (and) we cannot tolerate AIDS obstructing opening and reform," prominent Chinese economist Ma Bin wrote, in a report to the central authorities, the official *Health News* said.

Opening and reform must continue, Ma added, but not if the price to pay was an explosion of Acquired Immune Deficiency Syndrome.

Ma, an adviser to the cabinet's Development Research Center, suggested implementing a systematic program to fight against AIDS, including stepping up measures against drug abuse, prostitution and pornography.

Premier Li Peng paid great attention to Ma's report, and the cabinet met recently to specifically discuss ways to combat AIDS, the newspaper said. . . .[1]

---

[1]The absence of a nationwide system of checking blood donors and the unavailability of disposable syringes in rural and even some urban hospitals heightens the risk of contracting the HIV virus in China.

89
State to Build First AIDS Hospital in Yunnan Province

Chen Wei-chiang

Source: Hong Kong, *Ming Pao,* September 23, 1993, *FBIS,* October 8, 1993.

China's first AIDS hospital will have been built in Ruili city of Yunnan province by the end of the year. The hospital will provide a total of fifty beds. However, Zhao Shangde, member of the China AIDS Experts Commission, worried that lack of medical personnel will undercut the hospital's normal operation.

When interviewed by reporters, Zhao Shangde said that as mainland medical personnel are generally afraid of AIDS, the hospital will probably find it difficult to find sufficient medical personnel at the outset. Zhao noted that although the hospital will probably find it less difficult to find doctors, the majority of the mainland nurses are thought to be afraid or unwilling to have any contact with AIDS patients.[1]

Zhao Shangde added that the Chinese government has decided to build the AIDS hospital in Yunnan because Yunnan has the largest number of people infected with the AIDS virus in the entire country. The number of HIV carriers in Yunnan accounts for 75 percent of China's total. . . .

Zhao Shangde explained: Since it borders on Burma, Thailand, and Laos, which are known as the "Golden Triangle," Yunnan Province has been suffering from a very serious drug problem. The majority of the HIV carriers, 80 percent of whom are peasants, have become infected with HIV by sharing syringes. Some HIV carriers are women who had been lured by drug syndicates into prostitution into Thailand.

Zhao Shangde said that in the face of this serious problem, Yunnan Province has set up a transdepartmental working group composed of a

---

[1]This fear of even casual contact with HIV-infected people is a common problem throughout Asia, where general knowledge of how the virus is transmitted is very poor and often surrounded by myths. In Japan, for instance, bellboys and hotel staff have refused to carry the luggage of known HIV-infected guests out of misplaced fear of being infected. Similarly, before visiting the West, Chinese have been instructed to avoid contracting the virus by wearing rubber gloves when touching doorknobs!

vice governor, the provincial public security department director, and a representative from the provincial public health department. The working group will discuss and map out measures for resolving the AIDS problem. In order to combat narcotics, apart from conducting education and propaganda to urge people not to take drugs, as well as launching large-scale antinarcotics mopping-up operations in the border areas, the Yunnan provincial government has also set up some drug addict rehabilitation centers in which drug addicts can find ways to quit drugs.[2]

In order to check the spread of AIDS, apart from carrying out propaganda and education among the masses, the Yunnan provincial government has also started conducting research work with a view to verifying symptoms of AIDS, the period between HIV-related infection and sickness, and reaction of AIDS patients to medicines. Zhao Shangde stated: Although the majority of HIV carriers in China have become infected with HIV by sharing syringes, the number of HIV carriers who have become infected with HIV through human contact is steadily increasing. This group of people is becoming the principal source of AIDS in China.

---

[2]Breaking drug addiction, often through highly coercive means, was one of the most notable accomplishments of the Chinese Communist government following its takeover in 1949.

90
Radio Sex Education Programs Popular

Li Jianchang

Source: Beijing, Xinhua, May 9, 1993, *FBIS,* May 12, 1993.

Chinese people, whose countenance changes when they talk about "sex," can today listen to special radio programs about sex, family, marriage, and other topics.

A program called "Pillow Talk" is carried by radio stations in the three municipalities of Tianjin, Beijing, and Shanghai as well as Hangzhou [Zhejiang Province] and a number of cities.

The Tianjin People's Broadcasting Station took a great risk four years ago when it began to discuss "sex" on radio for the first time.

At first, the program, which lasted only ten minutes, was aired late at night at 11:00 PM. As the announcer said at the start: The children are enjoying sweet dreams, and now their parents have a chance for some pillow talk.

Recalling the situation at that time, editor Wang Guizhi said: Although the program is designed for "night talk," they still had some misgivings. The program will be suspended immediately if it encounters censure.

As expected, some people accused the "Pillow Talk" sex education program of being pornographic.

Nevertheless, letters from listeners poured in, expressing their support for and trust in the program.

A twenty-two-year-old young man revealed a history of masturbation over the past decade. He was worried about his thin figure, yellow hair, and failing sight.[1] He dared not tell his parents or go to a hospital. But he told the radio station the truth.

A construction worker from Canton felt wronged and hid in Shandong when his wife blamed him for their disharmonious sex life. When he came across the "Pillow Talk" program by chance, he poured out his grievances to the radio station and asked for advice. . . .

Noted sex expert Wu Jieping vouched for the station's programming and praised it for "resolving difficult problems and transforming social traditions."

Professor Chen Zhongshun, a noted psychologist from Tianjin, said that many Chinese people, including intellectuals who have completed higher education, are ignorant about sex because they feel it is shameful to talk about it. The psychological problems arising from this belief account for half of all mental diseases. Radio is an appropriate means for carrying out education in this regard.

Tianjin radio's "Pillow Talk" program has already covered more than eighty special topics, such as "the criteria for sexual problems and sexual harmony," "the necessity of sex education viewed from the

---

[1]Sexual activity, including masturbation, is believed in China to cause a loss of the body's vital force of *qi,* which leads to physical deterioration.

perspective of the divorce rate," "sexual taboos," "the harm of one-minute lovemaking," "women's sexual problems," "what should be done if children happen to find their parents having sex," and "what a husband should do if his wife has a hypoplastic vagina." These programs have been repeated three times, and the books that have been compiled in light of these programs are selling well.

Today, "Pillow Talk" is not limited merely to sex. All localities have included issues relating to the family, marriage, love affairs, and sex after marriage. Tianjin radio also offers live programs, inviting scholars and experts to talk to listeners directly on the air.

In any case, the appearance of sex and related topics on mainland radio stations—from taking the risk to start the program to its popularity—shows that the mainland's opening up is continuously expanding to all fields.

91
Beijing's First Homosexual Salon Has Been Banned for Disseminating Wrong Ideas

Ching Chi

Source: Hong Kong, *Ming Pao,* May 19, 1993, *FBIS,* May 28, 1993.

An informed source disclosed that the first homosexual salon in mainland China, which emerged in Beijing late last year, was banned by the Ministry of Public Health last week. An official of the ministry said that this club, sponsored by the China Health Education Research Institute, must cease operation.

This salon, named "Men's World," officially came into being on November 22 last year. The person in charge of the salon is a young research fellow of the China Health Education Research Institute.

According to a physician who wants to remain anonymous, a high-ranking official complained: "That salon has been disseminating wrong messages; it is not opposed to, but is encouraging homosexuality, which is contradictory to China's aim and purpose in health education."[1]

The informed source said: The purpose of the salon at the outset was the prevention and control of AIDS in mainland China. Clinical records provided by hospitals show that more than 30 percent of the patients infected by the AIDS virus who have been discovered on the Chinese mainland are homosexuals. Of the ten cases of AIDS virus infection and AIDS patients discovered in Beijing Municipality in recent years, four have been verified to be related to homosexuality.

In order to prevent and curb the AIDS virus from spreading in mainland China, preventive medicine experts proposed to launch a health education drive on the prevention of AIDS among homosexuals as a special population group. It is just because of the existence of this special population group vulnerable to AIDS infection that the China Health Education Research Institute decided to set up the homosexual salon called "Men's World" to promote health education related to prevention of AIDS among these people.

It is reported that the first function of the homosexual salon was held on November 22 last year, sponsored by the China Health Education Research Institute; thirty-five male homosexuals attended the function; specialists on the topic voiced their opinions on homosexuality from the medical and social behavioral points of view, and the homosexuals present at the function also talked about their views and frustrated feelings. The atmosphere was harmonious and good during the three-hour meeting.

On Valentine's Day this year, "Men's World" held another function for homosexuals at the Sea Horse Ballroom in Beijing, the first homosexual gathering ever held in a public place.

During a symposium on the spread and prevention of venereal diseases, held in Beijing's Liangma Hotel from March 15 to 18 of this year, Chen Bingzhong, director of the China Health Education Research Institute, and Wan Yanhai, a research fellow of the institute, jointly presented a thesis entitled "Let Us Sow Seeds on Fertile Land—Homosexual Culture and AIDS Education." They suggested a view "to treat the phenomenon of homosexuality with the sense of ordinary people

---

[1]Homosexuality has generally been taboo in puritanical socialist China, although it was the topic of Chen Kaige's recent film, *Farewell My Concubine,* which the CCP subsequently banned.

and homosexuals and the homosexual culture with a sense of equality."
They held that homosexuality, as a natural form of human sex, has
drawn increasing concern and gained tolerance in the Chinese community; there is no ground for regarding homosexuality as a morbid psychology, crime, or immorality; and it is necessary to recognize the value
of homosexuality and the need for developing a homosexual culture.
They also called for a more tolerant attitude toward and more assistance
to those who are in a morally and legally unfavorable position.

This homosexual salon held another function in early April. But this
time the gathering was spoiled by disputes and clashes among homosexuals and unpleasant incidents between reporters and homosexuals
present on the occasion, because of poor organization of the function.

92
Environment Considered "Secondary" to Development

Stanley Leung

Source: Hong Kong, *Hong Kong Standard,* June 12, 1992, *FBIS,* June 12, 1992.

China apparently regards environmental protection as a "luxury" that
should not threaten the basic survival of the nation.

The attitude of China toward environmental issues is quite different
from that of Western and developed countries that are enjoying a high
degree of industrialization and high income per capita.

China, which has emerged as the leader of the developing countries,
takes a cautious view on the question of environment.

Apparently China attaches more importance to economic and industrial development. Environmental problems caused by economic and
social development appear to be secondary.

To some extent, China's attitude toward the environment is similar
to the case of human rights protection. Without "survival," China finds
it difficult to give full consideration to human rights.

China maintains that environmental issues can hardly be separated
from principles governing world politics such as national sovereignty

and territorial integrity, mutual nonaggression, and noninterference in each other's internal affairs.

China's stance on the relationship between "development and environment" was explained by Mr. Song Jian, head of the Chinese delegation, who delivered a speech earlier this week at the current plenary meeting of the United Nations Conference on Environment and Development (UNCED) in Rio de Janeiro.

To achieve its purpose, the preparatory committee for the conference has called for the establishment of a "new global partnership" and has written it into the draft "Rio Declaration on Environment and Development."

Among other things, Mr. Song said that countries have the right to exploit their own natural resources according to their own needs, without causing damage to other nations.

"Any attempt to impose certain political and economic models on other countries or to attach unreasonable conditions to cooperation will undermine the basis of this partnership," he said.

Mr. Song, State Councillor and Minister in charge of the State Science and Technology Commission, said China holds that a "new global partnership" should be established on a firm and solid basis fully reflecting the common understanding of the international community on environment and sustainable development.

He said the new partnership should be aimed at enhanced international cooperation in the preservation, protection, and restoration of the global ecosystem as well as in economic development.

"Without steady economic development, it is impossible to meet the people's basic needs in life, let alone protect the ecosystem and environment." He said the new partnership must cover both the environment and development and be designed to properly handle, in particular, problems relating to trade, debts and funds and to improve the international economic environment.

Mr. Song said that as countries are in different stages of economic and social development, they are entitled to choose their own ways of economic development and environmental protection that best suit their own national conditions.

He said the new partnership must also be fair and just and should be able to handle properly problems of funds and technology transfer.

Without a guarantee of funds and technology transfer, international cooperation could only be a mirage.

Without the effective participation of developing countries, establishment of such a "new global partnership" is impossible, Mr. Song said.

He said the development modality, in particular the production and consumption pattern that has prevailed since the Industrial Revolution, cannot continue.

93
National People's Congress News Conference on Environment

Source: Beijing, *Beijing Central Television Program,* March 15, 1994, *FBIS,* March 16, 1994.

[Qu Geping, chairman of the National People's Congress Environmental Protection Committee (EPC)]: Today, we are very glad to have this opportunity to meet you and exchange views with you on China's environmental protection. I have already given you my written statement. Now my two colleagues and I are ready to answer your questions.

[Dong Zhixiang:] I am a *Keji ribao [Science and Technology Daily]* reporter. What plans does the EPC have for China's future environmental protection? What will China's environment be like in the future? Thank you.

[Qu:] China faces many environmental issues today, and the situation is quite severe.[1] So we must take a series of effective measures to deal with problems in this area or it is unlikely that China will continue to have sustained, rapid, and healthy economic growth in the future, especially in the next century. To protect the environment, we must take measures in several major respects. First of all, the NPC must intensify legislation and come up with the laws that are urgently needed today. During our present term of office, the NPC will revise or draw up fourteen

---

[1]For an analysis of China's growing environmental problems, see Vaclav Smil, *China's Environmental Crisis: An Inquiry into the Limits of National Development* (Armonk, NY: M.E. Sharpe, 1993).

laws for control of environmental pollution and protecting natural resources. But it is important that these laws are enforced after they have been enacted. We have to urge the government to come up with effective measures for carrying out strict supervision of the environment according to law. Second, as far as protecting the environment and natural resources is concerned, the state must appropriately increase spending. Generally, China's environmental condition is severe. But we hope that, after taking necessary measures, we will have an environment favorable for our natural resources as well as for sustained economic development.

[Unidentified correspondent:] I am from Associated Press. Local Chinese governments at various levels have now given greater priority to economic development than to environmental protection. How serious is the problem? Moreover, the fines imposed on the polluters are quite low. What measures do you have planned to correct the situation?

[Qu:] We have conducted many years of investigation and study on the economic losses that environmental pollution has caused in China. The approximate annual economic losses caused by pollution amount to 100 billion yuan [$18 billion]. As far as your second question is concerned, the fees levied for pollution discharge are indeed too low. Some enterprises would rather pay the fees than take measures to control pollution. We have taken note of this problem. We are ready to raise the rates to force these enterprises to take remedial measures.

[Unidentified correspondent:] I am a reporter with the Hong Kong *Sing Pao Daily News.* I have something to ask related to a question from the AP correspondent. You said you plan to raise pollution discharge fees. Can you tell us something about the collection of the fee? How big will the increase be? . . .

[Qu:] The total figure of pollution discharge fees we collect each year is less than 3 billion yuan [$52 million], or a little bit more than 0.1 percent of our gross industrial output. This is a very small figure. Therefore, the State Environmental Protection Bureau raised the rates by one-third last year. But it seems the new rates, which are being implemented, are still too low. So they will be raised further. Another measure adopted last year was the establishment of higher standards, by nearly 50 percent, for pollution discharge by all newly built factories. So the standards for pollution discharge are much higher now.

[Unidentified correspondent:] I am a China Central Television reporter, and I have a question for EPC Vice Chairman Yang Jike. You have been engaged in making economic laws for many years. The way certain impoverished areas have chosen to develop their economies has had a big impact on the ecology. Can you tell us whether legislation can be passed to control these areas? Do you have such a plan? Thank you.

[Yang:] The NPC plans to establish a legislative system compatible with (?sustainable) development by the end of this century, or a little later. This means that (?sustainable) development should be incorporated with our legislative system. Our work will include improving the Environmental Protection and Resources Protection Laws; speeding up economic legislation; and applying the (?sustainable) development principles to legislative affairs concerning development, population, production, and social security. China is a sprawling country. Different regions have different characteristics. And so local authorities should also have their own laws about the environment. So we hope that, around 2000, local authorities will have improved their legislative affairs relevant to (?sustainable) development. We hope our laws can converge with similar international laws. We will also adopt as many legal provisions that have proven to be effective in other countries as possible. Of course, China has its own specific situation. Since China has a large population, our population-related legislation may be different from that of developed countries. Except for this, we will do as much as we can to adopt the good experiences of countries in the West and learn from them. Finally, we will also propagate the ideas and information of (?sustainable) development, and train the personnel we need to make laws in this area.

. . . I am a Hong Kong Wireless Television reporter. You mentioned that China has sustained economic losses amounting to 100 billion yuan annually [from environmental pollution]. How did you come up with this figure? My second question is: In recent years, the Chinese government has planned to develop its nuclear power industry and has built some nuclear power stations, especially in southern Chinese provinces, such as Guangdong. These nuclear power stations are potentially dangerous with respect to their nuclear materials and wastes, which have to be properly treated, and accidents that might occur. Is there a contradiction between environmental protection and the development of nuclear power? As a state organ in charge of environmental protection, what is your comment on the policy of developing nuclear power?

[Qu:] Your first question is about how the pollution-caused losses are calculated. It is a figure that experts have come up with through extensive investigation and study. The losses include those of material resources and the damage caused to the ecology, as well as the calculable harmful effects on physical health. This is a very complex issue. I can only give you a general picture. As for your second question about nuclear power development, it should be answered by [EPC Vice Chairman] Lin Zongtang, as he is an expert in this area, but he asked me to comment on it briefly. China has only two nuclear power stations—the Dayawan and Qinshan Nuclear Power Stations. We also plan to build more nuclear power stations in Guangdong and energy-deficient areas along the coast. Compared with traditional power plants that generate electricity by burning coal or oil, nuclear power stations should be considered a source of clean energy. The key requirement is that these stations must have safety measures. So when the nuclear power stations were built, China attached top priority to their quality and safety. The two nuclear power stations are very safe. They have the highest safety coefficient in the world. As long as we strengthen management, nuclear power stations will not endanger the environment. The two nuclear power stations are now operating very well. As for the problem of treating nuclear wastes, this is a global problem. But this is not a big problem for China. Why? We have only two nuclear power stations. In addition, China has very large, very efficient, and very safe vaults for the storage of nuclear wastes. So the treatment of nuclear wastes is not a problem as far as China is concerned.

[Lin Zongtang:] We have very good storage facilities in the Gobi Desert [laughing heartily].

[Qu:] So, countrymen in Hong Kong do not have to worry about this problem at all.

[Yang Jike:] Just recently I invited six professors—prestigious experts in the fields of energy and environment—from Sweden, the United States, Britain, Italy, and Canada to inspect the Dayawan Nuclear Power Station. We found that this station has the world's best system for ensuring security. This system can continuously monitor the way nuclear wastes are treated and how the hardware installed in the station can cope with nuclear accidents. Moreover, all the personnel in the station must receive rotational training every year to make sure they can deal with any accident. So we were very impressed. All the professors were very satisfied. So countrymen in Hong Kong can feel at ease.

[Unidentified correspondent:] I am a *Fangzhi ribao [Textile Daily]* reporter. I want to ask Vice Chairman Lin Zongtang this question. During last year's (?campaign) for enforcing the law for environmental protection, some rhinoceros' horns and bears' gallbladders were found. How were these findings handled? What is the result of the handling?

[Lin:] China attaches very great importance to protecting wildlife and enforcing the Wildlife Protection Law. Last year, China joined the Convention for Protecting Endangered Wildlife and Plant Species. We are earnestly implementing this convention, which we joined in 1980 [as heard]. Last year, the State Council formally issued a circular to strictly ban the illegal hunting and trading of tigers, rhinoceros, and other wildlife. For those rhinoceros horns already imported through normal channels, they are all sealed up and properly kept, pending handling. As for bears' bile, it is a very important ingredient in Chinese medicine, and it plays a significant role in ensuring people's health. In the past, a bear had to be killed for its bile, which would later be processed into medicine. Now we keep the bear alive and draw the bile from the bear. So there is no need to kill the bear when obtaining its bile for medicinal purposes in such a manner is available. By raising one bear, we can prevent the slaughtering of 220 bears. However, we are still studying whether or not we can use another substance to replace bears' gallbladders.

[Qu:] China has large numbers of bears. When the number of bears becomes too high, they have to be (?thinned). I think this is a principle commonly followed by the International Fund for Wildlife Protection and other similar organizations.

[Moderator:] Now the news conference has ended. Thank you all.

D. Minorities

94
Xinjiang Party Secretary Says Situation "Excellent"

Source: Hong Kong, *Ming Pao,* March 29, 1992, p. 24, *FBIS,* April 1, 1992.

Song Hanliang, secretary of the Xinjiang Uygur[1] Autonomous Regional CCP Committee, denied yesterday that national separatist activities are going on in Xinjiang's border areas. Describing the current Xinjiang "situation as excellent," he held that so long as Xinjiang's economic construction is genuinely boosted, the "voice" of the Western forces of infiltration and national separatists will be stifled.

Song was interviewed by reporters here yesterday. Asked about the recent national separatist activities in Xinjiang in the wake of the Soviet disintegration, he said: Although there is one force abroad adopting unfriendly acts and uttering unfriendly remarks toward China's Xinjiang, this does not affect the situation as a whole; . . . Xinjiang will not split with China.

He said: There are various voices in any society. The dissenting voices are insignificant and, with the development of economic construction, will disappear spontaneously.

He stressed: The current situation in Xinjiang Region is excellent. The nationalities are united, the economy is developing, the living standard of the people is improving. The people of Xinjiang do not want to lose the achievements they have attained through decades of development. . . .

---

[1]One of China's largest ethnic minorities, Uygurs are Muslims who generally reside in the western regions.

95
Bomb Part of "Antigovernment Attack" in Xinjiang

Source: Tokyo, Kyodo, June 24, 1993, *FBIS,* June 24, 1993.

A bomb ripped a huge hole in a Kashgar city government building in the remote western Chinese Xinjiang Uygur Autonomous Region last week, in what was believed to be an antigovernment attack, sources said Thursday [June 24].

The bomb, which exploded around 4 P.M. on June 17, killed and wounded up to ten people, the sources in the city of Kashgar said.

According to local Chinese sources, the four-story building belonged to the city municipal government and housed the offices of the agricultural machinery division.

Public Security Bureau forces have already arrested one person allegedly involved in the bombing and are continuing their investigations, they said.

The sources said that the bombing could be related to antigovernment sentiments in the region, which is a predominantly Muslim-minority, non-Han, area of China.

Minority peoples often take to the street to express their antigovernment feelings, the sources claimed, adding that peasants have recently been dissatisfied with the government's tax policy.

An officer of the foreign affairs department of the Kashgar city government confirmed that the incident took place, but refused to answer journalists' questions.

"The incident is still under investigation, so we are unable to comment at this time," he said.

The building, located in downtown Kashgar, is across the street from the Seman Guesthouse, a hotel popular with Western tourists.

Sources said that the bomb was placed on the third floor of the building, next to the offices of a private company involved in the purchase and sale of agricultural machinery.

The company is owned by the city government. . . . Employees at the Seman Guesthouse estimated that between two and five people were killed in the blast.

Kashgar is close to the border of Pakistan and several former Soviet republics.

Peasants, predominantly Muslim, mainly depend on farming and sheep-rearing for their livelihood.

In late May, citizens in Lhasa, the capital of Tibet, rioted over price rises, while other such incidents have reportedly occurred in Sichuan, Hunan, Henan, and Jinan provinces.

96
Tibet's Deputy Party Secretary Raidi Discusses "Antisplittist Struggle"

Source: Lhasa, *Tibet People's Radio Network,* August 11, 1993, *FBIS,* August 24, 1993.

Speaking at a recent work meeting held by the autonomous regional party committee and people's government, Raidi, deputy secretary of the autonomous regional party committee and chairman of the autonomous regional people's congress standing committee,[1] pointed out: Tibetan people of various nationalities have waged resolute struggles against domestic and foreign splittist forces in recent years. They have achieved very considerable results in their antisplittist struggle and in their work to stabilize the situation. We must further strengthen our understanding of the protractedness, complexity, and arduousness of the antisplittist struggle; crack down, with a clear-cut stance, on splittist activities; and firmly maintain our initiative in the struggle.

Raidi pointed out: Party organizations at various levels should correctly and properly handle the relationship between economic construction and stabilizing the situation. They should understand that we must have a stable social environment if we are to take economic

---

[1]Under the Chinese state constitution, autonomous regions are theoretically "autonomous" from the central government, but in reality are under tight central control. Conflicts between Chinese government authorities and local Tibetans involve local access to Tibetan religious shrines, training of young Tibetans in the area's traditional Lamaist religion, and the large number of Han Chinese migrants to Tibet.

construction as our central task and if we wish to enhance economic progress. Without stability, we cannot possibly seize opportunities, develop social productive forces, or raise people's living standards. Therefore, issues concerning the situation's stability are major issues that concern the country's unification, the unity of nationalities, and Tibet's development and progress. Therein lie the basic interests of people of various nationalities in China, including Tibet's people. We must uphold the policy of grasping two links at the same time and of attaching importance to both. While properly enhancing economic construction, we should specifically, firmly, and realistically carry out antisplittist struggles and work to stabilize the situation.

Raidi stressed: The broad masses of party members and cadres should resolutely stand at the forefront of the antisplittist struggle; safeguard, with a clear-cut stance, the motherland's unification; strengthen the unity of nationalities; enhance social stability; self-consciously resist various infiltrations of hostile forces; and withstand the test of antisplittist struggles. We should persistently attach importance to teaching the history that Tibet has been an inalienable part of the motherland and to publicizing and promoting Tibet's future. We should enable the masses of various nationalities to profoundly understand that only by following the CCP's leadership and taking the socialist road can Tibet have a bright and splendid future. Only by living in the motherland's large family can Tibetan people have a rich and happy tomorrow. We should realize that no attempts can restore Tibet to its former state. The schemes of domestic and foreign splittist forces will never succeed. Their activities to split the motherland can only fail totally in the end.

Raidi said: Strengthening the administration of temples and religious activities has a special practical significance in comprehensively implementing the party's policy on religion, in better resisting the splittist forces that conduct splittist activities and sabotage under the pretext of religion, and in stabilizing Tibet's situation. Religious activities can only be conducted within the realm of the law. Normal religious activities should be protected by law; however, no one is allowed, under the pretext of religion, to oppose the party's leadership or the socialist system, or to carry out crimes that violate the law, including splitting the motherland's unification.

In conclusion, Raidi stressed: Strengthening antisplittist struggles and properly performing work to stabilize the situation are the current important tasks for party and government organizations at various levels in Tibet. All party and government organizations should uphold the party's basic line and persistently pursue the policy of grasping two links at the same time and of attaching importance to both. While upholding the central task of economic construction and properly carrying out reform and opening up, we should regard launching antisplittist struggles and work to stabilize the situation as important parts of our agenda. Party and government leaders should personally attend to work to stabilize the situation, should inspect and study new circumstances in their localities and departments, should soberly understand the trends in their localities, should study and formulate plans on antisplittist struggles, and should resolutely crack down on splittist forces to score new victories in the antisplittist struggle.

E. Intellectuals, Journalism, and the Arts

97
Scholars Xing Bensi, Ru Xin, and Su Shuangbi[1] Discuss "Double-Hundred Policy"

Tao Kai and Li Chunlin

Source: Beijing, *Guangming ribao,* June 20, 1990, p. 2, *FBIS,* July 12, 1990.

Over the last thirty-four years, we have achieved some successes in implementing the policy of "letting a hundred flowers blossom and a hundred schools of thought contend," but the work was less satisfactory in some respects. Would you mind giving your opinions about the matters to which we should pay special attention in implementing the "double-hundred" policy?

[Su Shuangbi:] The "double-hundred" policy was put forward in 1956, when the socialist transformation was basically accomplished and the economic situation took a turn for the better. At that time, the whole party was pondering a problem: How should China build socialism? Before 1956, the ideological field witnessed criticism of the movie *Biography of Wuxun*, discussions on the classic novel *Dream of the Red Chamber,* and the "Hu Feng case," which are events from which we should draw lessons.[2] At the same time, the debate on the Lysenko and Vavilop schools also took a turn.[3] The situations at home

---

[1]See glossary.

[2]A Marxist literary critic and writer, Hu Feng was purged by Mao Zedong in 1955 for advocating an independent literature. The campaign against a purported "Hu Feng clique" of writers and artists followed and spread throughout the country, even into remote areas, and set the stage for the full-scale assault on intellectuals during the 1957 Anti-Rightist campaign.

[3]In the mid-1950s, Chinese geneticists were forced to follow the bogus theories of the Soviet geneticist Lysenko. See *Lysenkoism in China: Proceedings of the 1956 Qingdao Genetics Symposium*, ed. Lawrence Schneider (Armonk, NY: M.E. Sharpe, 1986).

and abroad put a new question before us: How should we provide correct guidance for the struggle in the ideological field? It was under this special historical situation that Comrade Mao Zedong put forward the "double-hundred" policy.

[Xing Bensi:] The "double-hundred" policy was properly implemented in several periods after it was advanced. The first period was from 1956, when the policy was put forward, until the start of the Anti-Rightist struggle. During that period of about one year, the ideological and theoretical front was brisk. Intellectuals had no reservations and often engaged in heated debates. The second period was around 1964, that is, before the Cultural Revolution [1966–1976], when the three-year difficult period [following the disastrous 1958–60 Great Leap Forward] was just over, and the economic situation changed for the better. Again, since the Anti-Rightist struggle, a fierce political struggle several years back, had gradually faded from people's memory, intellectuals had ease of mind and the ideological field came to life again. The third period began some time after the Cultural Revolution. The discussion on the criterion for truth,[4] and the [1978] Third Plenary Session in fact brought about a movement for ideological emancipation, facilitating academic and cultural activities. But generally speaking, the work of carrying out the "double-hundred" policy has left much to be desired over the last thirty-four years. To successfully implement the "double-hundred" policy calls for a congenial social environment, but such an environment has been constantly disrupted and interrupted, by the "left" ideology in particular. During the years when "class struggle was taken as the key link," different schools of thought were unable to contend because academic issues were invariably seen as a matter of political principle.

[Su Shuangbi:] Under the influence of the "left" guiding ideology, contentions between different academic viewpoints were described as struggles between different classes. As a result, those who attended academic discussions were considered as representing this class or that. That being the case, who dared take part in such discussions?

[Xing Bensi:] Under such political conditions, even if some discussions were held in the academic field, they were abnormal. Take, for example, the contention between the propositions of "one divides into

---

[4]The campaign begun in the late 1970s by then CCP leader Hu Yaobang to free Chinese intellectual life from the shackles of leftist ideology.

two" and "two combines into two."[5] Though there was a heated debate, the participants were inclined toward one side, resulting in the latter being criticized from the higher plane of political principle and two-line struggle. This was abnormal. During the years when bourgeois liberalization ran wild, the interference came from the right. Only a few people were in favor of bourgeois liberalization, but they were in control of many departments and prohibited publication of many articles that were not to their taste. During that period, too, the "double-hundred" policy could not be properly implemented.

[Su Shuangbi:] The "double-hundred" policy had been hampered by interferences from the "left" and right since its introduction. The [1978] Third Plenary Session stopped the interference with the "double-hundred" policy from the "left," that is, from dogmatism, and the [June 1989] Fourth Plenary Session of the Thirteenth CCP Central Committee put an end to the interference from bourgeois liberalization.[6] The present period is the most favorable time for carrying out the "double-hundred" policy.

[Guangming ribao:] In the process of carrying out the "double-hundred" policy, we have been coming up against a knotty problem, that is, should we separate academic issues from political ones? If the answer is positive, how should we draw a clear line of demarcation between them?

[Xing Bensi:] I am in favor of separating academic issues from political ones. As far as the work of repudiating bourgeois liberalization is concerned, I am of the opinion that the work should be divided into two categories. The first category deals with the theory of wholesale Westernization, the theory asserting that Marxism is out of date, opinions advocating a multiparty system and private ownership, and so on. These viewpoints are against the Four Cardinal Principles. They are political issues instead of academic ones. They should come under repudiation rather than be considered as academic viewpoints to be allowed to contend with other schools of thought. The second category

---

[5]The philosophical debate that became a hot-button political issue during the Cultural Revolution. "One divides into two" was advocated by radical political forces in China as the essence of the Marxist "law of the unity of opposites" that applied to the political realm justified "uninterrupted revolution." "Two combines into one" was attacked by the same radical forces for purportedly justifying class reconciliation, class cooperation, and the elimination of class struggle.

[6]This plenum followed the June 4, 1989, military crackdown in Beijing.

includes erroneous viewpoints formed under the influence of bourgeois liberalization. They can only be corrected through "letting a hundred schools of thought contend." If we should regard them as bourgeois-liberalization thinking, we would create confusion by changing the "contradictions among the people" into "contradictions between ourselves and the enemy."[7] If we can solve these problems through "letting a hundred schools of thought contend" and criticism and self-criticism, we will be able to win over those who hold these erroneous views and other intellectuals like them to our side. This is a very important policy-related matter, and newspapers should pay special attention to it.

[Ru Xin:] There is no denying that some articles are related to bourgeois-liberalization thinking. In my opinion, we should see them as academic issues as far as possible, trying our best to unite with the majority. If we can straighten things out through discussion, will it not be better than upgrading them to the political level? We should adopt a down-to-earth manner in criticizing these articles rather than making inferences in a roundabout way or arbitrarily raising them to the higher plane of principle.

[Su Shuangbi:] To really encourage "a hundred schools of thought to contend," a very important thing to do is to take a correct attitude toward academic viewpoints and people who are affected by bourgeois liberalization. We should deepen their understanding and raise their consciousness through discussion and arouse their enthusiasm. In helping intellectuals solve their ideological problems, we should not try to solve the problems by resorting to radical measures, seeking momentary gratification. If we fail to do a good job in this respect, many people will stand aloof from us. We should handle the matter with great care and should never be careless.

[Ru Xin:] At present, the living and working conditions for large numbers of intellectuals remain poor. These problems should be solved steadily and in a proper way. For the majority of intellectuals, however, their greatest concern is not material benefits, but rather whether they can enjoy academic freedom, openly expressing their opinions.

---

[7]A Maoist ideological rule of thumb for distinguishing between conflicts that can be decided by argument and debate ("contradictions among the people") and conflicts that demand the exercise of proletarian dictatorship against "enemies" ("contradictions between ourselves and the enemy").

They are worried whether their creative mental labor can enjoy political protection and whether their research results are acknowledged by society. Therefore, whether or not the "double-hundred" policy is carried out is of great importance to the broad masses of intellectuals. At present, preservation of the country's stability is a matter of paramount importance, and correctly carrying out the "double-hundred" policy will play a significant role in stabilizing the contingent of intellectuals and bringing their enthusiasm and creativeness into full play. It should be acknowledged that in the preceding period, many intellectuals had misgivings about whether and how the "double-hundred" policy would be carried out after the repudiation of bourgeois liberalization. Comrade Jiang Zemin's speech delivered on May 4 [1990] came at the right time, dispelling misgivings from their minds. Comrade Su Shuangbi said just now that the present is most opportune for implementing the "double-hundred" policy. I agree with him. Since conditions are ready and Comrade Jiang Zemin has once again encouraged "different schools of thought to contend" in his speech, what matters is how we will actually act in carrying out the policy.

[Xing Bensi:] In the field of social sciences, it is really difficult to separate political issues from academic ones. But if you do not separate them, it will be out of the question for us to carry out the policy of letting a hundred schools of thought contend, making the academic field flourish, and building a major contingent of Marxist theoretical workers. At present, to separate political issues from academic ones, we must give an exact definition of bourgeois liberalization as a political concept, thoroughly repudiating it. In the meantime, any ideological viewpoints that are not against the party and socialism should be allowed to contend as academic viewpoints.

[Guangming ribao:] Marxism should serve as guidance and the Four Cardinal Principles as preconditions in letting a hundred schools of thought contend. How should we correctly interpret this and apply it to practice?

[Ru Xin:] Both the proletariat and the capitalist class can make use of the policy of "letting a hundred schools of thought contend." Our party's purpose in putting forward the "double-hundred" policy is very clear, that is, to develop socialist sciences and arts. Naturally, Marxist guidance and socialist orientation must be preserved in carrying out this policy. Therefore, we should reject bourgeois liberalization and "left" dogmatism because they prevent Marxism from playing a guiding role in "letting a hundred flowers blossom and a hundred schools of thought contend."

[Xing Bensi:] Those who favor bourgeois liberalism direct the spearhead of the criticism at the guiding role of Marxism, negating its principal role. They believe that truth is pluralistic. This is not correct! Because history has shown that Marxism remains a universally applicable truth. Upholding Marxism as the guiding principle will help all schools of thought to seek the truth rather than otherwise. This does not mean that non-Marxists are not allowed to take part in academic discussion or that self-styled Marxists are allowed to stifle differing opinions. . . . By regarding Marxism as a guide, we mean setting up a political rule that everyone is expected to follow. Under this rule, nobody is allowed to oppose the Four Cardinal Principles. With this as a precondition, many issues are open to discussion.

[Su Shuangbi:] Regarding Marxism as a guide is not contradictory to stressing holding discussions on an equal footing. So long as everyone takes part in discussion with a view to making socialist culture flourish, they enjoy equal status, but this does not mean their views should receive the same treatment because they are not necessarily correct ones. We can only distinguish correct ideas, which conform to Marxism, from erroneous ones, which run counter to Marxism, through conscientious and calm discussions, and then correct ideas will enjoy support and erroneous ones will be corrected. How to treat non-Marxist viewpoints also poses a problem in letting a hundred schools of thought contend while upholding Marxism as a guide. It is a normal phenomenon that some people adhere to non-Marxist viewpoints in discussions. Those who hold non-Marxist viewpoints are different from those who hold anti-Marxist viewpoints. Those who hold anti-Marxist viewpoints are conscious of the nature of their stand, while those who hold non-Marxist viewpoints tend to regard themselves as pure Marxists. Though the problem with those who hold non-Marxist viewpoints is a matter of recognition, we can only make them correct their viewpoints through discussions, that is, through "letting a hundred schools of thought contend."

[Ru Xin:] We should combat pluralism on the problem of the truth, but we should encourage diversity. Those who apply the same Marxist method to studying the same subject do not necessarily arrive at the same conclusion. Take, for example, historians of the elder generation such as Guo Moruo, Fan Wenlan, and Jian Bozan. They were Marxists, but they founded different schools of thought because they held different academic views. This practice should be encouraged because this helps make the academic field prosper. Again, some old experts such as historian Chen Yinke and the philosopher Feng Youlan are not Marxists and do not apply the Marxist method to their research work, but their academic achievements can be assimilated and made use of by Marxists. Therefore, we should interpret Marxist guidance in a broader sense: Different schools of thought are allowed to contend with each other, and those who are allowed to take part in the contention do not necessarily have to be Marxists. We hope that everyone will study Marxism and that they will regard Marxism as an ideological weapon. But we cannot impose this on those who pursue a particular research. We can only encourage them to do so. Take religious research, for example: We cannot force religious people to give up their belief and change their research approach. In short, Marxism is an intellectual achievement created by mankind over several thousand years, but we should also assimilate various research results to enrich and develop Marxism. Marxism itself should be an open-ended theory. Through "letting a hundred schools of thought contend," we can absorb useful research results of other non-Marxist schools of thought; otherwise, Marxism will not be enriched and developed for lack of new nutrients. Therefore, we should make a clean break with non-Marxist schools of thought, and on the other hand should absorb their valuable research results in a critical way. We should try to achieve this through letting a hundred schools of thought contend.

[Xing Bensi:] In letting different schools of thought contend, we had better set a political prerequisite so that it will be easy to separate political issues from academic issues, that is, those who do not oppose the Four Cardinal Principles are allowed to take part in academic contention. . . .

[Guangming ribao:] "Letting a hundred flowers blossom and a hundred schools of thought contend" is not a theoretical issue, but rather a principle or a policy. Therefore, what is of great importance is how to put the policy into effect. You three comrades talked about matters that we should pay attention to in implementing the "double-hundred" principle just now. Will you talk about specific matters such as the style of study?

[Ru Xin:] The style of study really merits attention. It is necessary to combat proneness to boasting and exaggeration. We should not be overanxious for quick results in engaging in scholarship. We must devote a lot of time and energy to research and should not take part in academic contention before we found a school. Several years ago, some people who took part in academic contention did not even have rudimentary knowledge, let alone personal experience from study. They only sought "sensational effect" by doing something unconventional or unorthodox. This is "arbitrary contention" rather than "academic contention."

[Xing Bensi:] Arbitrary contention can only serve to vulgarize academic discussions. Another unhealthy phenomenon is that some people are keen on reversing verdicts.[8] It seems that the more fantastic the way in which they try to reverse verdicts, the stronger repercussions they will cause. Such a practice is seemingly sensational at the time, but in fact it is meaningless. Of course some verdicts must be reversed. To rectify the style of study, we must first of all encourage our comrades to integrate theory with practice. In his summary report for the meeting to discuss ideological guidelines, held in 1979, Comrade Deng Xiaoping stressed that we should go deep into the realities of life and make a thorough study. We should continue to follow his instructions at present. Without going deep into the realities of life and making a thorough study, we cannot push academic discussion to a higher level. Some people discussed the subjects that had been discussed in the 1950s. It was all right if they could advance new ideas. There should have been some new ideas and new research results in the wake of the great change over the last several decades. But it turns out that what they said in the 1980s was hardly different from what other people had said in the 1950s. What is the use of holding such a discussion? Therefore, only after we have gone deep into the realities of life and made a thorough study can academic contention be of high quality and really contribute to developing Marxist theoretical studies.

[Ru Xin:] Furthermore, in the academic field, criticism and self-criticism should become a regular practice. In the past, we practiced criticism in a radical way at one time, but forgot all about it at another. As a result, intellectuals became nervous of criticism. In fact, criticism is a normal practice during academic discussions.

[Su Shuangbi:] To my recollection, there were a number of major heated debates in the 1950s, such as the debates over how many histor-

---

[8]That is, reversing negative judgments by the CCP leadership on political events, such as the labeling of the 1989 democracy movement as "turmoil."

ical stages China's feudal society should be divided into and over the land ownership of the feudal society. Though the participants were greatly divided and they named names when leveling criticism at each other, they were calm, so everyone felt at ease. This shows we can do a good job in "letting different schools of thought contend" so long as wise guidance is given.

[Ru Xin:] I can cite the debate over logic as another example. The two sides engaged for several rounds and both sides used bitter language, but nobody misunderstood the harsh criticism as making them submit by force. Later Chairman Mao gave his opinions. No one said that those opinions that were not identical with Chairman Mao's were mistaken. The debate merely served to distinguish right from wrong on the question of logic. Other examples are heated debates over the stages of China's ancient history and over whether Lao-tze [the founder of Taoism] was a materialist or an idealist. On these two topics too, Chairman Mao expressed his opinions. Neither debate brought about negative results. If criticism and self-criticism becomes a regular practice, we will improve intellectuals' mentality. . . .

98
Shanghai Professor Criticizes Economic Policies

P. N. Kandinsky

Source: Hong Kong, *Eastern Express,* February 24, 1994, p. 6, *FBIS,* February 24, 1994.

Professor Li of the Shanghai Academy of Social Sciences wasn't impressed when a Communist Party newspaper invited him to write an article on the "socialist market economy" in late 1992.

"Those people have gone on preaching about their kind of socialism for the last three years," he said. "Who knew what they really wanted?" Li didn't write anything for it, but he continued to publish articles about his market theories in other media. "Publications on the lower levels of the official hierarchy have a better reputation," he said.

"Intellectuals of my generation no longer have any hope of working with this regime."

But the newspaper kept asking him, most recently late last year, shortly after the party's central committee held its annual plenary session, which adopted a decision to embrace more economic reforms. "I finally agreed, thinking this time it might be different," he said. "But once again, I was being stupid."

The editor of the newspaper called Li not long after the article had been submitted. "I'm sorry, but we can't use your piece," he said. "Why?" Li asked. The editor explained: "Didn't you recently write an article for a Hong Kong newspaper? According to the responsible authorities, you did, and that article raised some problematic points."[1]

And so, the professor's article was killed. "Every time the government fails, it is because it has refused to listen to its best critics," Li said.

China's best-trained economists, including those in the government think tanks, are predicting that the regime's single-minded pursuit of high growth will have disastrous consequences, according to Li. But Chinese leaders have yet to mend their relations with the intellectuals, which were rent asunder after the Tiananmen Square crackdown in 1989.

The party's "policy on intellectuals" is still one of deep distrust. Soon after Tiananmen, the regime convened a series of meetings to "sum up the experience" of how the party had won that "historical victory." The central issue was explaining the spread of "bourgeois liberalism," which had almost toppled the communist regime. Their conclusion: It was still necessary to continue the class struggle in the Stalinist and Maoist sense. Class analysis, not economic development, should remain the "lifeline of the party."

The class enemy, the party ideologues declared, was the middle class, represented by troublemakers among the intellectuals. Their theory, according to Li, is that intellectuals know how much more their counterparts in the West are paid. Their resentment has corrupted them into refusing to work for the party and attacking the proletarian state.

"Examine the speeches and articles by people like Deng Liqun—the party's leading hard-line ideologue—or Wang Renzhi, who was direc-

---

[1]Publication in the foreign press is still considered treason by the CCP leadership and can result in severe political persecution.

tor of the party's propaganda department after the 1989 crackdown," said Li. "From their speeches, you can see clearly that the middle class is the enemy and intellectuals are its representatives."

There were open clashes between party bosses and intellectuals at the meetings to sum up the lessons of 1989, he said. At one session, he recalled, Wu Jinglian—one of China's leading economists—challenged the party speaker by saying that no government could hold itself up without support from intellectuals, nor could society become stable without a large middle-income population. "Of course, they rejected this kind of criticism," he said. "They don't believe that a middle class is necessary to sustain stability. They think that because they have the Army, their guns and tanks will be enough for them to rule China forever."

Since the mid-1980s, economists have been strenuously advocating many of the reform ideas that the regime is now tentatively considering. The proposal for a genuinely independent central bank, for instance, was rejected by the Premier, Li Peng, many times. At one State Council meeting in 1991, Li became furious when banking reform was mentioned. "The People's Bank [China's nominal central bank] is nearly the last bit of power that I have left," Li yelled at the proponent. "If you want to rob me of this too, why don't you just proclaim yourself premier?" It may not be coincidental that the new banking reforms were approved only while Li was on sick leave after a heart attack last year.[2]

"I no longer care whether they use my ideas or not," a professor at Beijing University said. "These are the same ideas that we put forward back in the mid-1980s and that they condemned as 'bourgeois liberalism'—if they don't use my ideas, they themselves will pay the price."

Relations between the regime and intellectuals were different, he said, from the time "when we were enthusiastic about the reform and optimistic about its success. Now, it is more like a business relationship: You place an order, and I'll deliver the goods—if I feel like it."

There were several thousand Chinese graduate students with economics majors in Western countries. But the regime had never listened to their opinions, he said. "This is a terrible waste of human resources at a time when China is faced by all sorts of dangers."

---

[2]See Document #49.

As one cultural critic said: "China [will] fall apart. But if it reaches that point, it will be because of the regime's policy blunders. The worst mistake is to label those whose help is most needed as the enemy."

99
Party's Leadership over Arts Stressed

Source: Beijing, *Beijing Domestic Radio Service,* January 4, 1991, *FBIS,* January 8, 1991.

[From the "News and Press Review" program]

According to a report carried in *Renmin ribao,* the party committee of the Shanxi CCP Committee and the Shanxi provincial government[1] persist in the policies of party leadership over cultural undertakings, of literature and art serving the people and socialism, and of letting a hundred flowers blossom and a hundred schools of thought contend, thus enabling cultural undertakings in Shanxi to thrive in the correct direction. In recent years, a large number of literary and artistic works popular with the masses have emerged in Shanxi, which enliven the cultural life of the masses, enrich the spiritual food of the masses, exert a favorable influence on the sentiment of the masses, and promote the building of socialist spiritual civilization.

In this connection, today's *Renmin ribao* frontaged a commentator's article, entitled: "Persist in the Principle of Literature and Art Serving the People and Socialism." The article pointed out: The problem of policy is an issue of guidance and of political direction. Only by persisting in the correct policy of serving the people and socialism can literature and art thrive and develop. Deviating from the party's correct policy and taking a wrong direction will only lead to

---

[1]Located in north China, this backward province has a political leadership that is one of the most conservative in China.

extensive growth of poisonous weeds,[2] not the thriving of literature and art. Since we build socialism with Chinese characteristics, we should cultivate socialist literature and art with Chinese characteristics. This kind of literature and art should only be one that serves the people and socialism.

The article stressed: On the issue of the principle for literature and art, there have been controversies and struggles in recent years. The controversies and struggles are one of the most conspicuous indications of the confrontation between the Four Cardinal Principles and bourgeois liberalization. Literary and art workers in some areas and units had for some time lost their direction and gone astray. It has been a profound lesson. The article pointed out: To implement the party's correct policy and rectify the direction of literature and art, we should strengthen the party's leadership. Abandoning the party's leadership means abandoning position and allowing the proliferation of thought associated with bourgeois liberalization. Of course, strengthening the party's leadership does not mean the party will interfere with the actual writing of a book or staging of a play.[3] Generally speaking, the party's leadership means ideological and political leadership and leadership over principles and policies, which include the implementation of the principle of letting a hundred flowers blossom and a hundred schools of thought contend, organization of sessions of criticism and self-criticism, and helping people differentiate between right and wrong and truth and falsehood. In the past, the party committed the mistakes of leftism as well as rightism in literary and art work. . . . At present, the main thing is to continuously carry out an in-depth criticism of the thought of bourgeois liberalization and continuously do a good job in rectification. We should, through a comprehensive implementation of the party's policy on literature and art, bring about an even greater thriving of China's socialist literature and art.

---

[2]"Poisonous weeds" *(ducao)* was the term used by leftist leaders, especially Jiang Qing, to vilify politically unacceptable literature and art throughout the Cultural Revolution. The works criticized included traditional Peking opera and piano works by Beethoven.

[3]In contrast to the censorship system of the former Soviet Union, censorship over the arts in China is generally exercised after a work is created. Paintings, books and films are produced largely free of official interference. But if judged to be politically inappropriate, the work is summarily banned.

100
Yang Baibing Attends
"Song of the Long Rockets"

Source: Beijing, *Beijing Central Television Program,* November 6, 1991, *FBIS,* November 15, 1991.

The "Song of the Long Rockets," a large song and dance drama that depicts the history of the Second Artillery Corps and eulogizes the heroic achievements of rocket soldiers, has been widely acclaimed in the capital recently. Leaders of the Central Military Commission and the three general departments of the People's Liberation Army watched and highly praised the show on separate occasions. (Video opens with a large red flag being raised on the stage. A number of performers dressed in uniform kneel and look up at the flag, which has a golden star and the words "August 1" [army day] patched on its upper right corner and the characters for the "Second Artillery Corps" in the middle. Video then shows two unidentified ranking military officers talking to each other.)

The drama's choreographer and director employed dance solo, chorus, and other theatric forms to represent the arduous development of the Second Artillery Corps from various angles, and to extol the spectacular, heroic achievements of rocket soldiers. (Video alternates shots of performers singing and dancing with those of the audience.)

After watching the performance, Yang Baibing, secretary general of the Central Military Commission, praised the song and dance drama for its creativity and called it an excellent representation of revolutionary heroism and realism. (Video ends with shots of Yang Baibing and other ranking military officers shaking hands with performers and speakers.)

101
Media Ordered to Toe Line Regarding Plane Crash

Source: Hong Kong, *Hong Kong Standard,* October 4, 1990, *FBIS,* October 4, 1990.

Chinese media groups in Canton have been told to toe the official line of the Xinhua News Agency when reporting the air crash [that recently occurred there].[1]

Media sources said yesterday that the Propaganda Department of the party's Central Committee issued the instructions on Tuesday.

According to the instructions, news groups had to strictly follow reports released by Xinhua and should "play down" the news.

Sources said the official policy was ordered by Premier Li Peng, who flew to Canton on Tuesday and visited crash victims in the hospital.

However, Chinese authorities have apparently adopted a flexible attitude toward Hong Kong and Macao journalists.

A seven-point rule announced last November required Hong Kong and Macao journalists to apply for interviews and reporting assignments fifteen days in advance.

The rule has widely been seen as a new measure to tighten control over reporting after the June 4 crackdown last year.

Most Hong Kong news organizations sent reporters to Canton a few hours after the disaster without submitting written applications.

It is understood that arrangements for press coverage are being handled by a high-powered team.

---

[1]China severely restricts its domestic media coverage of natural and man-made disasters.

102
Calls for Press Reform Reappear in China

Ho Po-shih

Source: Beijing, *Tang tai,* #16, July 15, 1992, pp. 24–26, *FBIS,* July 23, 1992.

Having laid low for a few years, the Chinese press circles have seemingly shown some vigor in recent days. It can be said that, after summing up the experience of being kept under control for over forty years, some observant and conscientious people in the Chinese press circles have, in recent years, mastered a set of brand-new skills to "parry" conservative government figures in charge of the press circles. These skills have surpassed the previous practice of playing "touch ball" (namely, striving for space within the scope permitted by the policy), and further efforts have been made to take the initiative carefully.

Turning "Internal Reference" into News

One method is to "take the internal line." In addition to open newspaper reports, there is more nonopen "internal reference" in China. Whatever journalists learn from abroad that the government deems inappropriate for publication in newspapers is relayed to the higher levels through "internal reference." For this reason, for a long time, the status and influence of "internal reference" have far outweighed those of open reporting. Knowing this truth, Chinese journalists have also sought action along this line. Some time ago, through "professional study and exchange," a number of journalists offered advice to the CCP hierarchy—to take the press initiative, the contents of some "internal reference" can be made public in light of the circumstances and turned into press reports, lest they end up being distorted after being spread here and there by word of mouth. . . .

The Tide of Expanding Newspaper Editions
Emerges in China

Another method is to legally expand information volume. Since the beginning of this year, a high tide of expanding newspaper editions has emerged in China. To date, over 200 newspapers have expanded editions. This is a popular demand and the outcome of efforts by press workers.

Since the beginning of this year, by expanding editions to eight pages, *Wen hui pao* in Shanghai, *Fujian Daily,* and *Heilongjiang Daily* have begun forming the ranks of a small number of provincial-level newspapers published in eight pages. *Beijing Daily* (provincial level) will also be expanded to eight pages this year. Moreover, by expanding to twelve pages, *Canton Daily* has become the first Chinese newspaper with twelve pages every day.

Of course, the government can publicize government things in this expanded space. However, because of the trend of the times, the expanded edition generally deals with information, counseling, and pastimes. In other words, the government propaganda contents have correspondingly decreased in proportion. Following its expansion of its editions, sales of *Cankao xiaoxi [Reference News]*[1] jumped 13 percent early this year over the same period last year. In the words of a person in the Chinese press circles, "We can also compare our material with theirs (referring to officials controlling public opinion direction)." Breaking a path with nonsensitive information, avoiding the important and dwelling on the trivial, and waiting for the opportune moment to go into action—these are chess moves coincidentally adopted by people in Chinese press circles.

The Need to Respect the People's Right to Know What Is Going On Is Raised Again

Moreover, Chinese press circles have recently reissued the call for press reform. The formulations (such as "respect the people's right to know what is going on" and "allow the people to know the major state of affairs and to discuss major events") raised in the 1978 Chinese press reform have reappeared, and a momentum of advancing press reform again has emerged in media guidance.

Recently, two former *Renmin ribao* directors, Qin Chuan and Hu Jiwei, wrote articles criticizing *Renmin ribao*'s ultra-leftist conduct in recent years; the former even launched a verbal attack on current *Renmin ribao* Director Gao Di at a National People's Congress Stand-

---

[1] An "internal" newspaper that carries articles from the foreign press.

ing Committee meeting. Earlier, at an international press circles meeting in Beijing, China Journalism School Professor Xu Zhankun (also a senior Xinhua reporter) affirmed the previous press reform, saying "it was the press reform that lasted the longest and was the largest in scale in the history of Chinese press development." This is something high-level Chinese officials in charge of propaganda have refrained from saying. He put "renewal of ideas and concepts" first in Chinese press reform, saying that what should be renewed are "those outdated concepts that are not suited to the development of socialist modernized press undertakings." He also put forward the need to "foster the concept of press openness; overcome the closed concept; and report major international and domestic events in a truthful, objective, and comprehensive way so that the people can promptly know the major state of affairs and the people's right to know what is going on is respected." These remarks were incorporated in the report to the [1987] Thirteenth CCP National Congress after numerous efforts were made in those years, but, after the June 4 [1989] Incident, CCP General Secretary Jiang Zemin said that the news' affinity to the people must be subordinated to the party's character. Apparently, the people's character has not [sic] been overlooked by journalists.

In another seminar, Gan Xifen, professor of the People's University of China, pointed out more sharply the crux of the current Chinese press reform. He said: "The media undertaking has developed rapidly on the Chinese mainland over the past four decades, but the struggle between power and right in the media has not ended. A handful of people attempted to draw the mainland's media in the direction of bourgeois liberalization, but the media power is solidly in the Chinese government's hands. After fighting for freedom for decades, Mao Zedong vehemently tried to turn the country he had founded into the freest paradise in the world, but he was also challenged, and this challenger was sometimes himself." "This has proved true: Right is weak, but power is tough. The former should be vehemently fought for, while the latter is monopolized and compulsory. The conflict between power and right often results in the appropriation of right."

The Path of Integrating with Publication Circles

Integrating with the publication circles is also a path the Chinese press circles have been experimenting with in recent years.

Due to market law and competition, a tendency of paying attention only to market effect has emerged in publication circles in recent years. They vie with each other in publishing books that can bring in money and refuse to publish those that cannot. This is not good, but it has provided an action space for the press circles.

Precisely because nobody wants to publish books that cannot bring in money (such as engineering and technological books), the China Press and Publications Administration stipulated a few years ago that people can freely find publishing houses to print such books with money they raise themselves. This has provided a relatively wider space and played a positive role in the past few years, ensuring that some books with no market effect can be published. In 1988, Dai Qing and others published a book entitled *Yangtze! Yangtze!* (which reported views opposing construction of the Three Gorges Project) with money raised by themselves.[2] They precisely took advantage of the space to integrate the press and publication circles and publish in the form of books what cannot be published in newspapers. Books such as *Western China's Large Prisons* by Jia Lusheng are examples of breakthroughs sought by the press circles.

In recent years, news printed in the form of books has appeared from time to time. If only we carefully read some books, we can easily find a lot of valuable news slipping through censorship. The *Trend of History* [a 1982 attack on leftism in China], which the authorities recently banned, also contains the shadow of integration between press and publication circles.

Strive to Establish Contact with International Press Circles

In recent years, Chinese press circles have also constantly fought for resumption of contacts with international press circles and increased opportunities for external activities. Usually, the Chinese government attaches importance only to China's good aspects reported in international media circles, and does not welcome "intervention by way of reports" from overseas media circles. For this reason, it has not taken an active part in international press organizations. But journalists do not agree. In recent years, they have vigorously opened up international relations and invited foreign press academics to international

---

[2]See Document #34 for an excerpt.

news conferences held in China. This was previously rare. The International Journalists Federation recently approved a new resolution to resume overall contacts with China's press circles (including government ones) at all levels. This momentum will also be conducive to China's continued contact with and opening up to the outside world.

103
Tibet Announces Rules against "Paid Journalism"

Source: Lhasa, *Xizang ribao (Tibet Daily),* November 16, 1993, p. 1, *FBIS,* November 18, 1993.

Following the issuance of the "Circular Concerning Strengthening the Construction of Professional Ethics of Journalists and Banning 'Paid Journalism'" by the Propaganda Department of the CCP Central Committee and the State Press and Publications Administration, *Xizang ribao*'s Editorial Committee immediately organized study and discussion sessions for editors and reporters, and adopted effective measures to correct unhealthy practices in the profession. The rank-and-file journalists have considered the ban on "paid journalism" and the cultivation of sound professional ethics as an important task of the anti-corruption drive in journalistic circles. To further implement the guidelines of the "circular" and to accept effective supervision by the masses of readers and various sectors of society, *Xizang ribao* hereby announces the following regulations banning "paid journalism":

1. *Xizang ribao,* the organ of the Tibet autonomous regional party committee, is the mouthpiece of the party, the government, and the people. Staff members of the newspaper must maintain unity with the party Central Committee and the regional party committee politically and in action; uphold the principle of party spirit in journalistic work; persist in serving the people and socialism; strictly observe journalistic ethics; regard social benefits as the supreme criterion; take economic construction as the central task; promote reform and opening; safe-

guard the motherland's unification, national unity, and social stability; and be devoted to duty and work hard.[1]

2. While gathering news, journalists of the newspaper are not allowed to accept monetary gifts or negotiable securities, nor are they allowed to solicit money or goods, or exchange the publication of articles and news coverage for money and goods.

3. While selecting and editing stories, it is necessary to base their actions on their journalistic and propaganda values and to uphold the principles of objectivity, fairness, and truthfulness. It is also necessary to guard against publishing stories based on "special connections" or "special human relations."

4. "Paid journalism" in any form is forbidden. Stories endorsing quizzes, essay contests, and special joint columns with prizes for publicity purposes must be examined and approved by the Editing Committee.

5. Advertisements must be strictly separated from news reports. Advertisement for a unit in the form of news reporting is forbidden. No one should be allowed to collect fees for news reports on units and individuals. A paid story should be clearly indicated as an "advertisement."

6. Journalists are not allowed to take up a second profession, nor to engage and participate in business activities.

7. Leading newspaper cadres at and above the county level should set a good example in honesty and self-discipline. They should regularly conduct education on journalistic ethics, the legal system, and discipline among journalists, and they should do things strictly according to the regulations. It is necessary to go all out in commending collectives and individuals who are outstanding in performing their duties honestly and in observing the law, discipline, and professional ethics; and to severely punish violators.

Xizang ribao sincerely hopes that various sectors of society and the masses of the readers will supervise the enforcement of these regulations.

Telephone hot lines: 36440 and 22758.

---

[1]This wording elliptically admits that the paper's own reporters had not followed party guidelines in their news stories.

104
New Style in Broadcast: Telephone Hot Line

Xu Guoping

Source: Beijing, *Zhongguo jizhe (China Reporter),* #6, June 15, 1993, pp. 20–22, *FBIS,* July 22, 1993.

In the wake of the popular trend of the expansion of pages and editions by newspapers and of the inauguration of weekend editions, our country's broadcasting circles have also been silently undergoing a change in recent years. The fruitful results of this change are increasingly apparent as large numbers of listeners have returned to the use of radios. Its main features are comprehensive reform through the introduction of telephone hot lines and opening telephone call-in programs. The telephone call-in has played an extremely important role in new programs and has had a profound influence on the method, function, and effects of broadcasting. It is like a powerful spring wind, and it has opened "splendid vistas" for broadcasting circles.

History and the Current Situation

It has now been thirty years since the development of the telephone hot line. Initially, it was a kind of special communications method and usually used for emergency communications between heads of governments or between high-level military commands. Since the 1960s, government organizations and social establishments in some countries have started to obtain information from the society and installed open telephone lines to provide public services for the people. The people also called this a "telephone hot line." Later, the telephone call-in hot line was used extensively by broadcasting stations all over the world and has become an integral part of radio broadcasting.

Since the [1978] Third Plenary Session, radio stations in China have adopted an active "policy of introducing" the telephone call-in hot line.[1] In 1985, the English division of China Radio International twice

---

[1]This reflects the recent rapid growth of private phones in China, although acquiring a residential line is still extraordinarily expensive. Before the 1978 reforms, private telephones and public phone booths were virtually unknown in China.

broadcast programs that were not prerecorded and answered listeners' questions from abroad through international phone calls then and there. However, the earliest regular telephone call-in program broadcast was the "Telephone Hot Line" of Guangdong's Zhujiang Economic Radio, which started broadcasting on December 15, 1986. Currently, there are a considerable number of economic radio stations in various localities. Most of them have set up different types of telephone call-in programs and columns.

In terms of the mode of propagation, call-ins may be directly broadcast or prerecorded. In direct broadcasting, a telephone hot line may be installed in the studio; by keeping the line on during the program, it carries telephone conversations live or broadcasts them a few seconds after they have been recorded. Most radio call-in programs are broadcast live. In prerecorded mode, a telephone hot line will be installed out of the studio—in the editorial room, for example. The host or the editor will receive and record incoming calls during a designated time and air the edited telephone conversations during the program.

Judging from the content of conversations, call-in programs may be divided into two categories:

Cultural and Entertainment. . . .

Public Services. This category may be further subdivided into four:

1. Psychological consultation: The host, through heart-to-heart telephone conversations, may play the role of providing spiritual enlightenment and psychological consolation to listeners by helping them clear psychological barriers and solve knotty problems in interpersonal relations. . . .

2. Expressing feelings: Knowing well that people tend to have a desire to express their feelings, radio stations provide listeners with an opportunity to express their feelings openly. The "Call-In Lovers' Island" . . . provides lovers in different places a way to express their inner feelings through call-in. Via the "Air Message," a listener in one place may convey his or her sincere regards to a listener in another place.

3. Community services. . . .

4. Voicing complaints: Hosts of Nanning [City] Station's "Consumers' Complaints," the "Hot Line for Patrons of Health Services" program once introduced by Anhui Provincial Station, and Nanjing City Economic Station's "Citizens and Public Servants" help listeners solve problems.

As vehicles of public opinion, radio stations have been more convenient and effective in providing supervision. There are two main patterns of using call-in telephone services for providing supervision through public opinion, with the first being the introduction of call-in programs for listeners to voice their complaints. Listeners can directly raise their problems, criticisms, and pleas. For these programs, radio stations normally invite relevant leaders to their studios to handle complaints from telephone calls. As announcements have been made of the leaders to be invited, listeners' questions are relevant and easily solved. As the two parties talk in an atmosphere of interpersonal exchange, it is easy to achieve communication and understanding. Second, criticisms made during call-in programs are from the listeners, not from the stations, and so they are genuine and reliable. Disputes of right and wrong are avoided. The Tianjin Economic Radio's "Good Morning, Tianjin" program introduced a "call-in telephone" service so that the municipal leaders could directly answer listeners' questions. It helped to solve some 120 problems of the masses in just fifteen days. Since its inception more than a year ago, the Guangdong Radio's "Social Forum" program has successively introduced topics such as "When will Canton's traffic congestion end?" and "Startling wastefulness" to arouse listeners' discussions. It has achieved very good social results. . . .

Call-in telephone service programs have played special roles in guiding and educating the masses. The Nanjing Economic Radio's "Tonight's Guest of Honor" program frequently invites heroic models who have made selfless sacrifices for society, such as Jin Qingmin, the first woman scientist to reach the South Pole, and Shi Guang, who became disabled by bravely fighting off criminals. These reports are usually very moving. During an interview with Zhou Chao, a model people's police officer, and his wife, a listener asked his wife: Do you complain when Zhou Chao has to work many hours of overtime in a year and has very little time for home? She replied: "I am the wife of a people's police officer and an ordinary woman. My greatest wish is that the three family members can eat a meal together, but even this is impossible." She could not continue at this point, and the studio was very quiet except for the sound of her sobs. Moments later, the listener said: On behalf of my wife and all my relatives and friends, I would like to thank you. These true and moving incidents have subtly influenced listeners, and it is hard to achieve the effects of self-education for the people in other programs. Some telephone discussion programs on the radio have also played a very prominent role in providing spiritual guidance to the masses. Various viewpoints are vigorously exchanged in programs, with hosts firmly guiding discussions in correct directions. When everyone has finally obtained a common understanding, the correct concept is then deeply entrenched in the people's hearts. The Guangdong Radio's "Social Forum" has introduced a series of discussions such as "Is Lei Feng's spirit obsolete?" and "How to be a civilized Canton resident. . . ."[2]

Although the use of call-in telephone services has only seven or eight years of history in our country's broadcast circles, it is worth pondering the influence they have brought to the circles.

---

[2]See Document #74 for a description of Lei Feng.

105
Academic Works "Blacklist" Reportedly Compiled

William Brent

Source: Hong Kong, AFP, January 15, 1992, *FBIS,* January 15, 1992.

The Chinese government is compiling a blacklist of academic works advocating Western ideas and democracy in an attempt to purge reformist intellectuals, Chinese sources said.

The ministry-level State Education Commission issued a document ordering top universities and the Chinese Academy of Social Sciences (CASS)[1] to check all dissertations written in the last five years for "political problems."

It said the institutions would be barred from accepting any graduate students in the future if the directive is ignored, according to the

---

[1]A government-run "research" center that has often been embroiled in ideological and political controversies in China.

sources, who include Chinese professors, researchers, and journalists.

The sources added, however, that the effort is meeting passive resistance and would likely fail.

China is trying to intensify ideological control after the collapse of communism in Eastern Europe. The intended purge seems to have been engineered by Communist Party hard-liners who harbor a deep distrust of intellectuals.

The education commission, overseen by conservative party elder He Dongchang, sixty-seven, has especially targeted the four Beijing universities most active in the 1989 pro-democracy movement.

They are Beijing University, Chinese People's University, Beijing Foreign Languages University, and China Politics and Law University.

University graduate student advisers in each department are going over dissertations written since 1986 for signs of "bourgeois liberalization," the official term for harmful Western influences.

After advisers review the works, they are to hand a list of all dissertations to university presidents for submission to the education commission. The commission is then to review a random sampling of papers from each school.

But dissertation advisers are using the vagueness of the commission document to avoid fingering any of their students, university teachers said.

"It's a stupid move on the part of the government. All it will do is further antagonize intellectuals," one professor said. "I said nothing about political content when I reviewed the dissertations."

A CASS official predicted that the intended purge would fail because the government did not have the manpower to go over thousands of dissertations and because intellectuals have learned to look out for one another.

"If they say my work has political problems, my boss will say it is a scholarly pursuit of facts. Or he will say I am too young and need to improve my understanding of Marxism, and that will be it," a CASS researcher said.

"A big thing will become a small thing, which will then disappear," he said.

The main aim of the purge, the sources said, was to make sure that intellectuals remained scared. Many Communist Party conservatives blame intellectuals for past antigovernment movements, including the 1989 protests.

"It has been a historical trend in China for the rulers to lop the heads off of intellectuals not in their ideological camp," one orthodox party member said. "The party wants to do the same thing."

It was unclear what would happen to those academics whose works were deemed harmful to China. The most likely targets of the crackdown would be students of law, politics, the humanities, and social sciences, the sources said.

Since the 1989 crackdown, the enthusiasm of university students has fallen dramatically due to the oppressive political atmosphere on campuses.

The authorities have replaced the heads of leading universities with loyal Marxists since the 1989 unrest, and freshmen have been required to take a year of military training before starting their studies.

Further Readings

Banister, Judith. *China's Changing Population* (Stanford, CA: Stanford University Press, 1987).

Barmé, Geremie, and Linda Jaivin. *New Ghosts, Old Dreams: Chinese Rebel Voices* (New York: Random House, 1992).

Barnett, A. Doak. *China's Far West* (Boulder, CO: Westview Press, 1993).

Brugger, Bill, and David Kelly. *Chinese Marxism in the Post-Mao Era* (Stanford, CA: Stanford University Press, 1990).

Committee to Protect Journalists, *"Don't Force Us to Lie": The Struggle of Chinese Journalists in the Reform Era* (New York: Committee to Protect Journalists, 1993).

He Bochuan. *China on the Edge: The Crisis of Ecology and Development* (San Francisco: China Books and Periodicals, 1991).

Henderson, Gail, and Myron S. Cohen. *The Chinese Hospital: A Socialist Work Unit* (New Haven, CT: Yale University Press, 1985).

Huang Shu-min. *The Spiral Road: Change in a Chinese Village through the Eyes of a Communist Party Leader* (Boulder, CO: Westview Press, 1989).

Kristof, Nicholas D., and Sheryl Wu Dunn. *China Wakes: The Struggle for the Soul of a Rising Power* (New York: Random House, 1994).

Kuan Hsin-chi, and Maurice Brosseau, editors. *China Review* (Hong Kong: The Chinese University Press, yearly).

Link, Perry. *Evening Chats in Beijing: Probing China's Predicament* (New York: W.W. Norton, 1992).

Luo Zhufeng, editor. *Religion under Socialism in China* (Armonk, NY: M.E. Sharpe, 1991).

Pepper, Suzanne. *China's Universities: Post-Mao Enrollment Policies* (Ann Arbor: Center for Chinese Studies, University of Michigan, 1984).

Smil, Vaclav. *China's Environmental Crisis: An Inquiry into the Limits of National Development* (Armonk, NY: M.E. Sharpe, 1993).

Watson, Rubie S., and Patricia Buckley, editors. *Marriage and Inequality in Chinese Society* (Berkeley: University of California Press, 1991).

Whyte, Martin King, and William L. Parish. *Urban Life in Contemporary China* (Chicago: University of Chicago Press, 1984).

IV

Science and Technology

In China nothing is free from politics, including science and technology. During the Maoist era, Chinese scientists who challenged Communist Party orthodoxies on scientific issues were persecuted. Today, censorship in the scientific realm is limited, although Chinese scientists are still provided "guidance" by Deng Xiaoping's "theories" on science and technology (Document 106). An advocate of scientific modernization since the mid-1970s, Deng has consistently supported large-scale scientific projects in high technology and nuclear research (Documents 108 and 109). Yet just as Deng has imposed his vision on China's scientific establishment, young Chinese scientists supportive of democratic reforms have taken their revenge by introducing a "June 4" computer virus into the country's computers (Document 107)!

106
Deng Xiaoping's Theories on Science and Technology

Zhou Peirong

Source: Beijing, *Guangming ribao,* June 2, 1992, pp. 1, 4, *FBIS,* July 1, 1992. (Originally published in *Dangjian (Party Building)* #6, 1992: "Chief Designer and Primary Productive Forces—On Comrade Deng Xiaoping's Concern for, and Attention to Scientific and Technological Work.")

People will not forget March 18, 1978, the extraordinary day on the eve of China making its policy decision to reform and open up to the outside world. Comrade Deng Xiaoping, the chief architect of reform and opening up, elaborated on a very simple but profound theoretical issue at the National Science Conference opening ceremony: "Science and technology are productive forces. This has always been a Marxist point of view."

Comrade Deng Xiaoping's thesis shook the great earth of China like the spring thunder, proclaiming the arrival of the most charming scientific spring in Chinese history. The theory of science and technology being productive forces has guided the practice of reform and development in science and technology. It has also withstood tests and trials in practice and continued to develop.

A decade later, in reviewing the role played by science and technology in China's economic and social development since reform and opening up, and the above Marxist viewpoint that he creatively developed, Deng Xiaoping advanced the theory that science and technology were not only productive forces, but primary productive forces. On September 12, 1988, he said meaningfully, after listening to work reports: "Marx said science and technology were productive forces. This is very correct, but it seems not enough now to put it this way. I think, perhaps, they are primary productive forces." After that, he repeatedly expounded the theory of "science and technology being primary productive forces."

A major leap in theory was recorded in the process from "science and technology being productive forces" to "science and technology being primary productive forces." This process also reflected the historical change of the scientific and technological status in real life.

The Breeding and Advancing of the Theory Concerning
Science and Technology as Productive Forces

In fact, the breeding and developing of this theory occurred much earlier than the National Science Conference. As early as the pioneering years of "two bombs and one satellite," Comrade Deng Xiaoping made a number of brilliant expositions on developing science and technology. As a member of the then central special committee, together with Mao Zedong, Zhou Enlai, and other comrades, he took charge of the dynamic pioneering cause, concretely attending to and handling some important affairs. In 1973, when the nation stood up to the calamity of the Cultural Revolution and the national economy was on the verge of collapse, Deng Xiaoping was entrusted to take care of the routine work of the central authorities, and, on different occasions, he repeatedly stressed that scientific work must go ahead of the national economy.[1] He gave many instructions to bring into play the initiative of scientific and technological personnel and create better conditions for them to enable them to conduct research with concentrated attention. While taking charge of drafting the "Outline of the Academy of Sciences Work Report," which was later labeled by the [leftist] "Gang of Four" as one of the "three big poisonous weeds," he again stressed the need to trust scientific and technological personnel, to have successors to scientific and technological undertakings, to expedite industrial technological transformation on the strength of science and technology, and to enhance labor productivity. After the "Gang of Four's" downfall [1976], he volunteered to take charge of scientific and technological work personally, conducted investigation and study extensively and thoroughly, inspected scientific research organs, kept informed and looked into the future of the world's scientific and technological development trends, frequently met with scientific and technological experts, and had repeated discussions with experts to consult them on the major plans for developing science and technology as well as the economy through application of scientific and technological advances. He said: "Without taking firm hold of science and technology and education, there would be no hope for the four modernizations."

---

[1]This followed Deng Xiaoping's return to power near the end of the Cultural Revolution at the behest of Mao Zedong. In April 1976, however, Deng was purged again by Mao following the outbreak of the Tiananmen Incident on April 5, 1976.

At the National Science Conference opening ceremony, Comrade Deng Xiaoping said: "The means of production were integrated with certain branches of science and technology in history, and, similarly, the labor forces in history were those who mastered certain scientific and technological know-how. We often say that man is the most positive factor in productive forces. Man here refers to one who has certain scientific knowledge, production experience, and labor abilities to use productive tools to bring about material means of production." From the profound changes in science and technology and the emergence of burgeoning science and technology since World War II, he clearly expounded that science and technology had directly embodied productive forces in many facets, and that a series of new and developing industries had been established on the foundation of the burgeoning sciences. "Being productive forces, science and technology have increasingly displayed their enormous usefulness" and "are becoming more and more important productive forces." . . .

Deng Xiaoping's remarks carried great weight, which aroused endless echoes in the hearts of the country's 8 million scientific and technological workers, and became the theoretical foundation guiding the ensuing scientific and technological reform and development.

107
Sichuan Province Uses Card against "June 4" Computer virus

Source: Chengdu, Sichuan, *Sichuan jingji ribao (Sichuan Economic Daily),* January 1, 1993, p. 1, *FBIS,* March 10, 1993.

[Summary] At the end of last year, the Sichuan Provincial Public Security Office and the Shenzhen Huaxing Science and Technology Company announced that that company's microcomputer virus immunity card would be promoted throughout Sichuan. Computer crime and viruses are an increasing problem. According to Sichuan's investigation begun last year of 3,549 computers in 37 province-level departments, 1,013 machines (28 percent) were found to be infected with the "June 4" virus.[1] . . .

As a result, the Sichuan Public Security Office has forbidden any department or unit to do computer virus research, sell virus-prevention devices, or publish items on computer virus programs without the approval of the Public Security Office Computer Security Supervisory Department. It has also decided to promote the Shenzhen Huaxing microcomputer virus immunity card throughout Sichuan. The card entered the market in January 1990, and is one of the world's first hardware-software combinations designed to prevent viruses. It has had good social and economic results in use by domestic and overseas consumers. In June 1992, the card underwent tests by U.S. computer virus specialists using 800 types of virus without a single failure.

---

[1] A computer virus introduced into China's computer network evidently by pro-democracy students after the June 4, 1989, massacre.

108
"863" Plan Promotes High Technology Application

Yang Zhaobo and Yang Ning

Source: Beijing, Xinhua, August 16, 1993, *FBIS,* August 27, 1993.

According to the State Science and Technology Commission, China's "863" plan, which was put into effect six years ago, has stimulated the development of related sciences and promoted the application of advances in high technology in related areas.

It has been learned that the "863" plan is China's intermediate and long-term plan for the study and development of high technology. Its aim is to render service to national economic construction at the end of this century and the beginning of the next century, to create conditions for the development of high technology and the formation of industries employing high technology, and to bring up a new generation of highly skilled technicians. The implementation of this plan has stimulated the development of high-technology industries and the transformation of traditional industries, promoted social progress, and yielded economic results. Some laboratory achievements have been transformed into products, while others, still in the intermediate stage of experimentation, will soon be applied in industry. Most of the projects have made smooth progress. High technology has played an initial role in stimulating the transformation of traditional industries and in optimizing their structures; it has also stimulated the development of genetic engineering, intelligence technology, optoelectronic science, industrial automation, advanced nuclear energy technology, and materials science technology. Many high-technology advances have also spread to other scientific fields, creating fairly noticeable social benefits.

Meanwhile, a number of high-technology research bases have been set up. With the help and efforts of the relevant state ministries and commissions, fifteen important research bases or centers in the fields of biology, information, automation, new materials, and energy have been established; a number of experimental networks are being constructed according to the original schedule; and some have been completed. The construction of these bases and centers has facilitated high-technology research, the tackling of many kinds of scientific research projects, the attraction and training of personnel, exchanges and cooperation with foreign countries, single-item technological experiments, and the continued production and development of new products in China, which have created good conditions for further advancing high-technology research and development in China.

In the course of implementing the "863" plan, experiences in reforming the science and technology management system have been applied, foreign management methods for high technology have been borrowed, and the operating mechanism of employing experts and reforming the appropriation system has been implemented, thus discovering a management model suitable for the development of high technology in China. The management mechanism of employing experts has fully embodied the dominant status of experts in scientific and technological work and has played a role in making policy decisions scientific, democratic, and highly efficient. The appropriation system has reformed the traditional practice of departments carving a big portion for themselves. The appropriation of funds according to the requirements of the task has heightened efficiency and the rational use of funds. With unremitting efforts from all sectors, management and operating mechanisms for high technology have continued to improve, thus giving rise to an initial management system by which policy decisions are made by experts in coordination with relevant departments, supervision and appraisal is carried out by experts, and information services are provided. The planned implementation of this system in five sectors has yielded initial results.

109
Thermal Nuclear Fusion Experiment "Satisfactory"

Source: Beijing, Xinhua, November 23, 1993, *FBIS,* November 23, 1993.

Scientists have achieved "satisfactory results" in experiments on China's first controlled nuclear thermal fusion experimental device, a spokesman for the China National Nuclear Corporation [CNNC] told Xinhua today.

While declining to specify, the spokesman noted that this has prepared China to catch up with countries "most developed in the nuclear sciences" in searching for "the source of energy after the twenty-first century."

The device, known to experts as the "reverse-field pinch experiment device," was installed in May 1991 at the Southwestern Institute of Physics of Chengdu, a subdivision of CNNC.

Using the device, scientists are trying to break a new path for the search based on the theory that deuterium, a substance abundant in sea water, could be used in thermal nuclear fusion to generate electricity, the spokesman said.

According to the spokesman, nuclear fusion is a process of deuterium, tritium, and other light atomic nuclei "fusing" into heavier nuclei, in the course of which a huge amount of heat is released.

If the process is well controlled, the human race could use the heat to generate electricity. The oceans contain enough deuterium to fuel controlled thermal nuclear fusion reactors the world over for at least 100 million years.

"That means that seas and oceans could become an inexhaustible powerhouse for the human race," the spokesman said.

He added that scientists have been inspired to pursue the experiments by solar light and heat, which result from nonstop thermal nuclear fusion in the sun.

Further Readings

Lampton, David M., editor. *Policy Implementation in Post-Mao China* (Berkeley: University of California Press, 1987).

Lewis, John Wilson, and Xue Litai. *China Builds the Bomb* (Stanford, CA: Stanford University Press, 1988).

Saich, Tony. *China's Science Policy in the 80s* (Atlantic Highlands, NJ: Humanities Press, 1989).

Selected Works of Deng Xiaoping (1975–1982) (Beijing: Foreign Languages Press, 1984).

Simon, Denis, and Merle Goldman, editors. *Science and Technology in Post-Mao China* (Cambridge, MA: Council on East Asian Studies, Harvard University, 1989).

Suttmeier, Richard P. *Science, Technology and China's Drive for Modernization* (Stanford, CA: Hoover Institution Press, 1980).

Government of the People's Republic of China*

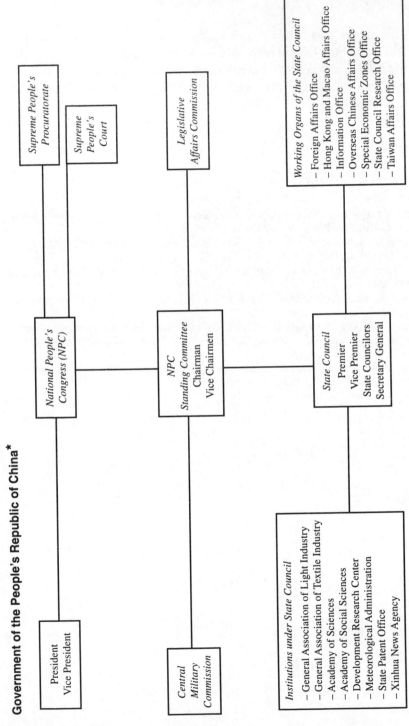

Commissions

- Science, Technology and Industry for National Defense
- State Economic and Trade
- State Education
- State Family Planning
- State Nationalities Affairs
- State Physical Culture and Sports
- State Planning
- State Restructuring of the Economic System
- State Science and Technology
- People's Bank of China

Ministries

- Agriculture
- Chemical Industry
- Civil Affairs
- Coal Industry
- Communications
- Construction
- Culture
- Electronics Industry
- Finance
- Foreign Affairs
- Foreign Trade and Economic Cooperation
- Forestry
- Geology and Mineral Resources
- Internal Trade
- Justice
- Labor
- Machine-Building Industry
- Metallurgical Industry
- National Defense
- Personnel
- Posts and Telecommunications
- Power Industry
- Public Health
- Public Security
- Radio, Film, and Television
- Railways
- State Auditing Administration
- State Security
- Supervision
- Water Resources

Organizations under the State Council

- Civil Aviation Administration
- Counsellors' Office
- General Administration of Customs
- Government Offices Administration Bureau
- National Tourism Administration
- Administration for Industry and Commerce
- General Administration of Taxation
- Environmental Protection Bureau
- Land Administration Bureau
- Legislative Affairs Bureau
- Press and Publications Administration
- Religious Affairs Bureau
- Statistical Bureau

*Prepared by Nancy Hearst.

293

Chinese Communist Party Organizations*

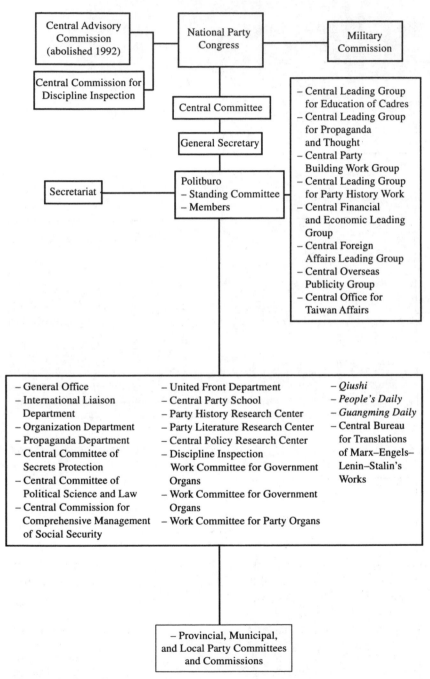

Central Advisory Commission (abolished 1992)

Central Commission for Discipline Inspection

National Party Congress

Military Commission

Central Committee

General Secretary

Secretariat

Politburo
– Standing Committee
– Members

– Central Leading Group for Education of Cadres
– Central Leading Group for Propaganda and Thought
– Central Party Building Work Group
– Central Leading Group for Party History Work
– Central Financial and Economic Leading Group
– Central Foreign Affairs Leading Group
– Central Overseas Publicity Group
– Central Office for Taiwan Affairs

– General Office
– International Liaison Department
– Organization Department
– Propaganda Department
– Central Committee of Secrets Protection
– Central Committee of Political Science and Law
– Central Commission for Comprehensive Management of Social Security

– United Front Department
– Central Party School
– Party History Research Center
– Party Literature Research Center
– Central Policy Research Center
– Discipline Inspection Work Committee for Government Organs
– Work Committee for Government Organs
– Work Committee for Party Organs

– *Qiushi*
– *People's Daily*
– *Guangming Daily*
– Central Bureau for Translations of Marx–Engels–Lenin–Stalin's Works

– Provincial, Municipal, and Local Party Committees and Commissions

* Prepared by Nancy Hearst

Historical Chronology, 1989–1994*

1989

June 3–4: People's Liberation Army troops force their way into Tiananmen Square in central Beijing and outlying parts of China's capital city, killing several hundred or perhaps thousands of students and city residents.

June 23–24: Fourth Plenum of the Thirteenth CCP Party Congress votes to strip General Secretary Zhao Ziyang of all his posts for having supported the pro-democracy movement and appoints Jiang Zemin as the new general secretary of the Chinese Communist Party.

November 6–9: At the Fifth Plenum of the Thirteenth Party Congress, Deng Xiaoping resigns as chairman of the Central Military Commission, his last formal position of authority. He remains president of the Chinese Bridge Association.

November 7: More than two million private rural enterprises are shut down.

December 22: Ceausescu government in Romania is overthrown.

1990

January 1: New Year's address by CCP General Secretary Jiang Zemin emphasizes social stability and national unity to overcome the nation's "temporary difficulties."

---

*Sources used in preparing this Chronology include: the annual editions of *China Briefing*, 1989–90, and 1991–92, 1994, Tony Kane and William A. Joseph, eds., respectively (Boulder, CO: Westview Press), and "Quarterly Chronicle and Documentation," *The China Quarterly*, School of Oriental and African Studies, London.

January 2: Two-year economic austerity program announced.

January 6: Chinese police put on alert following the collapse of the communist government in Romania.

February 2: United States Export-Import Bank resumes aid to China.

February 16: Hong Kong Basic Law governing the future political status of the colony after its return to China in 1997 is ratified in Beijing.

March 20: At the Third Session of the Seventh National People's Congress (NPC), Premier Li Peng calls for tighter control of "hostile elements" in China.

March 22: Finance Minister Wang Bingqian in speech to NPC announces a 15 percent increase in military spending for the PLA.

April 3: Jiang Zemin named as chairman of the state Central Military Commission.

April 22: China reports twenty-two dead and thirteen wounded in an armed rebellion in the northwest province of Xinjiang in early April.

May 22: China rejects Taiwan's offer for reconciliation as an attempt to create "two Chinas."

May 24: U.S. President George Bush announces renewal of China's Most Favored Nation (MFN) status for one year.

June 3: Hundreds of students at Peking University (Beida) throw small bottles (*xiaoping*) from balconies of student dormitories as a symbolic expression of antigovernment feeling on the first anniversary of the Beijing massacre.

June 6: Chinese government releases 97 pro-democracy demonstrators bringing the 1990 official total releases to 881.

June 23: Vice President Wang Zhen attacks moderates in Chinese government as hostile antiparty forces.

July 16: China opens negotiations with the USSR for purchase of military technology.

September 20: China reportedly violates United Nations embargo by selling Iraq large quantities of a chemical that can be used to manufacture nuclear weapons.

October 1: Administrative Procedure Law goes into effect, giving Chinese citizens the power to sue governmental officials.

October 2: A hijacked Chinese airliner crashes at Guangzhou (Canton) city airport, killing 127 people.

October 9: Premier Li Peng publishes a lengthy speech outlining cautious economic growth for the next five years.

October 23: *People's Daily* announces new campaign cracking down on crime and "liberalizing" influences such as pornography.

October 26: Agriculture Ministry announces plan to raise state-controlled grain prices for the first time in forty years.

November 1: Nationwide price increases for foods, energy, and other staples go into effect.

November 29: Asian Development Bank grants China a $50 million agriculture loan—its first loan to China since the June 1989 crackdown.

December 30: Communique issued at end of CCP Central Committee meeting outlines cautious blueprint for the 1990s stressing "stability" and self-reliance in implementing the Eighth Five-Year Plan.

1991

January-February: Trials are held of various 1989 democratic movement participants for "conspiracy to overthrow the government."

March 2: Communications Minister Qian Yongchang and Construction Minister Lin Hanxiong are removed from their posts by the Standing Committee of the NPC for graft and corruption.

March 3: At a national meeting on economic reform, Li Peng supports further reforms to decentralize the economy.

March 17: Eight Tibetan monks and nuns are arrested after protest in front of Jokhang Temple in Lhasa, Tibet.

March 25: Premier Li Peng at Fourth Session of the Seventh National People's Congress says Chinese socialism remains "rock solid," prices must be freed up, and market forces should play a greater role.

April 8: Shanghai Mayor Zhu Rongji and Minister of the State Planning Commission Zou Jiahua appointed vice-premiers by the NPC.

May 6: New press code approved by the All-China Journalism Federation encourages journalists to spread Marxism-Leninism.

May 11: China refuses to renounce use of military force against Taiwan.

May 26: New protests erupt in Lhasa, Tibet, three days after fortieth anniversary celebration of the Chinese "liberation" of Tibet in 1951.

May 27: President Bush pledges renewal of MFN for China but decides to ban export of missile technology and equipment to China.

May 29: Secret emergency decree is issued to all Party and government offices to guard against hostile forces seeking to overthrow the government.

June 1: Three reformist government leaders who were ousted after the 1989 Tiananmen pro-democracy movement (Hu Qili, Yan Mingfu, and Rui Xingwen) are appointed to vice-ministerial positions.

June 7: China says that it is willing for the first time to send CCP officials to Taiwan for talks.

June 10: China announces that it has no intention of intervening in the administration of Hong Kong before 1997.

June 14: Li Peng asserts that a multiparty system would bring misery to China.

July 1: On official anniversary of the founding of the CCP in 1921, General Secretary Jiang Zemin views the country's "central political task" to be opposition to alleged Western plots against China.

August 20: The Chinese government issues a statement giving tacit support to the anti-Gorbachev coup in the Soviet Union.

August 28: The Xinhua News Agency reports that China will move ahead on plans for the controversial Three Gorges Dam project along the Yangtze River.

September 7: Central Committee Document #4 blames the collapse of socialism in the USSR on the poor choice of successors by the Soviet communist leadership.

September 9: Chen Yuan, son of economic czar and arch-conservative Chen Yun, reportedly draws up document titled "Realistic Responses and Strategic Options for China Following the Soviet Union Upheaval."

September 15: Landslide victory by the liberal United Democrats of Hong Kong over candidates supported by the PRC in elections to Hong Kong's quasi-democratic Legco (Legislative Council).

October 19: China's Foreign Ministry denies involvement in developing Iran's nuclear weapons program.

October 25: Internal CCP document accuses U.S. President George Bush and the U.S. Congress of attempting to bring about the collapse of communism through a strategy of "peaceful evolution."

December 29: The Standing Committee of the NPC approves signing of the Nuclear Nonproliferation Treaty to limit international transfers of nuclear materials.

December 31: China announces it will export a nuclear power plant to Pakistan.

1992

January 10: Premier Li Peng announces plans to speed up market reforms.

January 19–21: Deng Xiaoping tours the southern Special Economic Zone (SEZ) of Shenzhen and calls for further economic reforms.

January 30: U.S. intelligence reports that China is continuing to sell missile technology to Syria and Pakistan.

February 21: U.S. lifts sanctions on the sale of high-technology equipment to China in exchange for a Chinese agreement to restrict sale of missiles and missile technology.

February 23: *People's Daily* attacks hard-line views and calls for bolder economic reforms.

March 14–15: Supporters of economic reforms attack conservative attempts to reverse economic reform policies.

March 20: Li Peng vows in speech to NPC to pursue economic reforms but warns that political changes that challenge CCP rule will not be tolerated.

March 21: Finance Minister Wang Bingqian reveals a projected budget deficit of $3.8 billion for 1992 and announces a 13 percent increase in military spending.

April 1: Long-standing government subsidies of food costs for urban residents are terminated.

April 3: The NPC approves construction of the Three Gorges dam on the Yangtze River, though an unprecedented number of delegates abstain or vote "no" on the final resolution.

April 14: *People's Daily* renews its call for a national campaign against "bourgeois liberalism."

May 22: Deng Xiaoping tours the Capital Iron and Steel Corporation in Beijing's suburbs, seeking to advance his efforts to shake up inefficient state-run industries.

June 13: China announces that more than one million workers have been laid off in 1992 as part of government campaign to turn around money-losing, state-owned factories.

July 5: Liberal scholars hold unofficial forum to condemn continuing power of the hard-liners in the CCP.

July 16: Taiwan lifts ban on cross-straits contacts with China.

August 3: Chinese government confirms outbreak of protests by industrial workers.

August 10: CCP Politburo Standing Committee member Li Ruihuan declares that art and literature can be more than just tools of the party.

August 29: Authorities in Tianjin city auction off for the first time a bankrupt joint-venture company.

October 7: Newly appointed Hong Kong governor Chris Patten outlines plan to broaden democracy in the territory prior to the 1997 takeover by China.

October 12–19: Fourteenth Party Congress and its first plenum are held and vote to replace one-half of Central Committee members while shake-ups in the Politburo and its Standing Committee are announced. Congress also enshrines "socialist market economic system" for China's future development and abolishes Central Advisory Commission. Yang Shangkun is dropped from the Central Military Commission.

October 23: China warns that if Britain pushes ahead with plans for further democracy in Hong Kong, China will install its own government in the territory after 1997.

November: Deng Xiaoping gives speech admonishing people to follow the "three don'ts"; that is, don't revise the political interpretation of the 1989 Beijing crackdown, don't tolerate "bourgeois liberalism," and don't replace any more leading leftists.

December 4: The United States postpones decision on the sale of computers to China after it reportedly delivered new ballistic-missile technology to Pakistan.

December 20: Hard-line acting Minister of Culture He Jingzhi is ousted.

1993

January 5: Xinhua News Agency threatens economic harm to Hong Kong if Britain's plans for democratization continue.

February 11: The provincial governor of Taiwan, Taiwanese-born Lien Chan, is nominated by President Lee Teng-hui to be the prime minister of the Republic of China.

March 12: Vice-President Wang Zhen dies in Beijing at age of 85.

March 15: After Li Peng attacks Britain for trying to create disorder in Hong Kong, the territory's stock market, the Hang Seng Index, drops 5.1 percent in one day.

March 27: CCP General Secretary Jiang Zemin is appointed PRC president.

March 28: Li Peng is reelected as premier by NPC, despite opposition by 11 percent of the body's delegates.

April 21: Peng Peiyun, minister for family planning, announces that the birthrate in China dropped in 1992.

April 23: World Bank announces that China is now the world's fastest-growing economy, estimated at 12 percent a year.

May 7: China's Foreign Ministry denies selling medium-range M–11 missiles to Pakistan.

May 25: Chinese police in Lhasa, Tibet use tear gas to disperse Tibetan demonstrators.

June 6: Thousands of peasants riot over taxes and other fees in Renshou county, Sichuan province.

July 13: Tibetan spiritual leader, the Dalai Lama, sends official team to Beijing for talks with Chinese officials.

July 24: Foreign Minister Qian Qichen accuses the United States of fabricating evidence that China had sold missile technology to Pakistan.

August 14: A central government directive is issued limiting private land speculation.

August 22: The *South China Morning Post* in Hong Kong leaks a People's Bank report of the biggest scandal in PRC history involving embezzlement of $28 billion in state funds.

August 25: The United States imposes trade sanctions on China and Pakistan, charging Chinese companies with selling missile technology to Pakistan.

August 27: Yu Zuomin, former leader of the model village of Daqiuzhuang, is sentenced to twenty years in prison for "corrupt feudal practices."

September 2: The Ministry of Radio, Film, and Television warns that films with "attitude problems" will continue to be banned.

October: Political crisis in Russia erupts that pits defenders of communist old order against President Boris Yeltsin, ending with assault by pro-Yeltsin troops against Russian White House.

October 6: Hong Kong governor Chris Patten says that his efforts to get China's approval for democratic political reforms in Hong Kong have failed.

October 29: A mayor, police chief, and a local official are executed in China on charges of corruption.

November 8: China indicates it will accept some of Chris Patten's proposals on new government election procedures for Hong Kong.

November 10: Clinton administration proposes to cancel recent trade sanctions against China if it agrees not to sell long-range missiles to Pakistan in the future.

November 24: Managers of 100 state-owned factories in China will assume full responsibility for the success or failure of their enterprises beginning in 1994.

December 2: Chris Patten reports that he will submit proposals for political reform in Hong Kong without China's approval.

December 26: China marks 100th anniversary of birthday of Mao Zedong.

1994

March 15: At the Second Session of the Eighth NPC, Ren Jianxin of the Supreme People's Court reports significant increase in serious crimes—murder, robbery, and rape—and also economic crimes.

March 25: "Outline of State Industrial Policy in the 1990s" issued by the State Council calls for strengthening the role of agriculture as the foundation of the economy, giving greater priority to construction of China's poor infrastructure, and accelerating growth of the "pillar industries"—electronics, machinery, and petrochemicals. At the same time, it is reported that fully 41 percent of all state-operated industries had lost money in 1993, a 5 percent increase over the previous year, and totalling 17 billion yuan ($3 billion). One half of all enterprises—state and private—and individual business households, engaged in tax evasion.

March 31: Twenty-four Taiwanese tourists are robbed and murdered on a pleasure boat on Qiandao Lake in Zhejiang Province precipitating a crisis in Taiwan-PRC relations.

May 3: *Legal News* (*Fazhi ribao*) notes that strong peasant discontent has precipitated "chaos" in some areas and caused major breakdowns in public order.

May 5–7: In his report to the Seventh Session of the Eighth NPC Standing Committee, Tao Siju, minister of public security, expands the list of punishable crimes in China to include "damaging people's health through religious activities" and "inciting separation of nationalities."

May 26: Led by recently released student dissident Wang Dan, Chinese intellectuals address petition to CCP leadership calling on the government to reappraise the 1989 democracy movement, compensate the families of victims of the military crackdown, and free all those under arrest for involvement in the June 4th "incident."

May 27: Clinton administration extends MFN to China for 1994–95 and breaks previous link between human rights and trade. At the same time, the Foreign Relations Authorization Act passed by the U.S. Congress refers to Tibet as a "country," bringing an official protest from China. Twelve-thousand U.S. companies now operate in China with total bilateral trade of $28 billion.

June: In the midst of the crisis over North Korea's possible development of a nuclear weapon, China's Foreign Ministry urges North Korean government to desist from "fruitless military conflicts" and to seek a settlement of the crisis on the basis of consultation.

October: Confrontation between an American aircraft carrier battle group and a Chinese submarine and aircraft occurs in the Yellow Sea off China's eastern peninsula of Qingdao.

November: Deng Xiaoping's health is rumored to have suffered a serious deterioration. Chinese journalist Gao Yu is sentenced to six years in prison for reporting data on China's increasingly difficult economic situation.

December: In a continuing wave of political repression, a lecturer at the Beijing Languages Institute is sentenced to twenty years in prison for "spreading counterrevolutionary propaganda." International negotiations continue over China's entry into the newly-created World Trade Organization. Conservative economist Yao Yilin passes away at age seventy-seven.

Biographical Glossary*

Chen Jinhua: From 1979 to 1983, Chen Jinhua was vice mayor of Shanghai. In 1993, he was minister in charge of the State Planning Commission.

Chen Junsheng: A native of China's northeastern province of Heilongjiang [Black Dragon River], Chen Junsheng served from 1949 to 1973 in various county level and provincial posts in the province. From 1974 to 1979 he was the deputy director of the Policy Research Center under the Heilongjiang CP and in 1980 became Party secretary of the Qiqihar City CP. In 1982 he was identified as a secretary of the Heilongjiang CP and in 1984 became secretary of the All-China Federation of Trade Unions and in 1985 the organization's vice president. In 1986 Chen was appointed head of the State Leading Group for Economic Development in Poor Areas and in 1987 headed the Leading Group for Housing System Reform. In 1988 he became a deputy secretary at the first session of the Seventh NPC and was appointed a state councilor.

Chen Yuan: Son of Chen Yun, China's economic czar and perennial political conservative, Chen Yuan was trained as an engineer at China's premier technical university, Qinghua University in Beijing, and became a CCP Party secretary in a west Beijing district. He was appointed to the Standing Committee of the Beijing city CP in 1984 and became a vice governor of the People's Bank in 1988 and a member of the Science and Technology Commission in 1990. In September 1991, Chen Yuan re-

---

*Thanks to Westview Press, Boulder, CO, for permission to reproduce parts of this Glossary from Ruan Ming, *Deng Xiaoping: Chronicle of an Empire,* translated and edited by Nancy Liu, Peter Rand, and Lawrence R. Sullivan, 1994. Additional sources consulted in preparation of this glossary include: *Who's Who in the People's Republic of China,* ed. Wolfgang Bartke, 1st ed. (Armonk, N.Y.: M.E. Sharpe, 1981), 2d and 3rd ed. (Munich: K.G. Saur, 1987 and 1991), and Donald W. Klein and Anne B. Clark, *Biographic Dictionary of Chinese Communism, 1921–1965* (Cambridge, Mass.: Harvard University Press, 1971).

portedly joined other members of China's so-called "crown princes" faction (the adult offspring of a number of senior CCP officials) in composing a neoconservative document titled "Realistic Responses and Strategic Options for China after the Soviet Union Upheaval."

Chen Yun: Born in 1905, Chen Yun became active in the early 1920s in the trade union movement and joined the CCP in 1925. Trained in the Soviet Union, Chen emerged after 1949 as a major proponent of China's Soviet-style system of economic planning and led the Party's effort to establish state control of the rural and urban economies. Throughout the 1950s and 1960s, he served in the CCP Politburo and in various posts dealing with the economic planning system and was a member of the Central Committee during the Cultural Revolution (1966–1976). In the late 1970s, Chen opposed Maoist radicals and endorsed Deng Xiaoping's proposals for limited reforms in the economy. Throughout the 1980s, however, Chen led the CCP faction that was opposed to wholesale economic liberalization, and called instead to limit market reforms in rural and urban areas and to maintain a strong role for economic planning. In ill health for several years, Chen Yun has, nevertheless, remained the leading opponent of radical economic reform and a staunch critic of any and all political reform measures that would undermine the CCP's political power.

Deng Liqun: Born in 1914 in Mao Zedong's native province of Hunan, Deng Liqun worked in the early 1950s in China's northwestern province of Xinjiang, where he assisted in putting down Muslim resistance to Chinese Communist rule. Deng was purged in the Cultural Revolution but returned in 1975 to serve on the State Council and in 1978 as vice president of the Academy of Social Sciences. In the early 1980s, he headed the Policy Research Center under the Party Secretariat and was a member of the Central Commission for Guiding Party Consolidation. From 1982 to 1985 he was director of the Party Propaganda Department. Following the June 1989 Beijing massacre, Deng Liqun emerged as a major "leftist" opponent of political reform and an outspoken critic of "bourgeois liberalism" in the CCP and among intellectuals.

Deng Pufang: The son of China's paramount leader Deng Xiaoping, Deng Pufang, a graduate from the physics department at Beida (Peking University), in 1968 was crippled by Red Guards. Throughout the

1980s and early 1990s he served in various national and international organizations for disabled persons.

Deng Xiaoping: Born in 1904 in Sichuan Province, Deng Xiaoping was the eldest son of a landowner. In 1920 he traveled to France as a work-study student and joined a Chinese socialist youth organization. Upon returning to China, in 1924 he joined the CCP and assumed his first position as an instructor at the Xi'an Military and Political Academy. During the 1945–49 Civil War with the Nationalists, Deng was a member of the Second Field Army in the Crossing the Yangtze River and Huaihai battles. In 1952, he was appointed a vice premier and in 1956 a member of the Politburo Standing Committee and head of the Party Secretariat. He was condemned in the Cultural Revolution for having previously criticized the personality cult of Mao Zedong and for his "liberal" agricultural policies. He first appeared after the Cultural Revolution in 1973 as vice premier and in 1975 was reappointed to the Politburo Standing Committee, only to be dropped again in 1976 following the April Tiananmen Incident. Deng reappeared in July 1977 and assumed all previous posts, plus PLA chief of staff, and in 1981 became chairman of the Central Military Commission. In November 1987 he "retired" from all posts, except the Military Commission, a position he finally yielded in November 1989. In February 1992, Deng toured the southern provinces where he openly sided with reformists in resisting conservative attempts to stall economic reform.

Ding Guan'gen: Trained as railway engineer in the early 1950s, Ding Guan'gen served from 1952 to 1983 as a technician in various bureaus of the Ministry of Communication and Ministry of Railways. In 1983, he was appointed deputy secretary general of the NPC Standing Committee and in 1985 became the minister of railways. He was appointed to the Central Committee of the Chinese Communist Party in 1987 and became an alternate member of the Politburo. In 1988, he resigned on his own request as minister of railways as a result of three major train accidents. In 1989 he became a member of the powerful Secretariat of the CCP Central Committee where he generally sided with conservative leaders against further economic and political reforms.

Dong Fureng: Trained in the early 1950s in Marxist economics at the Moscow State Institute of Economics, Dong Fureng joined the Economic Institute under the Chinese Academy of Sciences and in 1978 became deputy director of the Economic Institute of the Academy of Social Sciences, established in 1977. In 1982 he was identified as the vice president of the Graduate School under the Academy of Social Sciences and in 1985 became the director of the academy's Economics Institute and a consultant to the World Bank. In 1988 he became a deputy to the NPC from Zhejiang Province and a member of the NPC Standing Committee.

Fan Wenlan: An intellectual who joined the CCP in 1926, Fan Wenlan was appointed as the president of the Central Research Institute in the communist redoubt of Yan'an in 1939. This institute—whose members translated the works of Marx, Lenin, and Stalin into Chinese and provided Mao Zedong with a "Sinified" version of Marxism-Leninism for his political struggle with opponents in the Party—was the scene of the first CCP attacks on the intelligentsia, in which Fan Wenlan was deeply embroiled. In 1958, Fan was appointed as an alternate member of the CCP Central Committee and served as the director of the Institute of Modern History in the Academy of Sciences from 1950 to 1969. He died in 1969 during the Cultural Revolution.

Gao Di: Beginning in the 1950s as a county Party secretary in China's northeastern province of Jilin, Gao Di in 1983 rose to become Jilin's provincial Party secretary and in 1985 a member of the Central Committee. In 1988 he was appointed vice president of the Central Party School in Beijing and visited North Korea. In 1989 following the Beijing massacre, he became director of the *People's Daily* until his dismissal in 1992.

Guo Moruo: One of the premier intellectuals in the CCP, Guo Moruo was educated in classical Chinese and in Japan at Kyushu University. He joined the CCP in 1927 but dropped out after the brutal April 1927 Nationalist coup against the communists in China's urban areas that cost the CCP nine out of ten members. Guo rejoined the CCP in 1958 and played a leading role in CCP front organizations established to maintain control over the intelligentsia, such as the Federation of Literary and Art Circles and the All-China Writers' Association. Guo was also the president of the University of Science and Technology (1958–64) and of the prestigious Academy of Sciences from 1949 until his death in 1978.

He Dongchang: During the 1950s, He Dongchang served as the Party secretary of Qinghua University and was director of the Department of Engineering Physics. Branded as a "counterrevolutionary" during the Cultural Revolution, he reappeared in the late 1970s and served once again as Party secretary at Qinghua. In 1978 he became a member of the CCP's Central Commission for Discipline Inspection, the Party's internal disciplinary organ, and in 1982 became minister of education and a member of the CCP Central Committee. In 1986 he headed the State Education Commission and in 1987 was appointed to the presidium of the CCP Thirteenth Party Congress. He is a frequent critic of excessive "westernization" in Chinese education.

He Xin: A college dropout, He Xin joined the Chinese Academy of Social Sciences and in 1982 became a research fellow at its Institute of Modern Chinese History. A constant critic of excessive attraction for "westernization" among many Chinese intellectuals, he has emerged as the intellectual darling of China's conservative leadership, especially since June 1989. He Xin is also a specialist in Chinese fine arts and has written several books on Chinese cultural history and western philosophers, such as Sir Francis Bacon.

Hu Jintao: A graduate of Qinghua University with a specialty in hydropower, Hu Jintao served in the late 1970s and early 1980s as the director of the State Construction Commission in the northwest province of Gansu, one of China's poorest regions. In 1982 he was appointed to the Central Committee and in 1983 became the president of the Society of Young Pioneers, the CCP-run organization for children (ages 7–13). In 1985 he became Party secretary in the southwestern province of Guizhou and in 1988 was appointed Party secretary of the Tibet Autonomous Region, where tensions between Han Chinese and Tibetans intensified throughout the 1970s and 1980s. Hu is a Han Chinese originally from Anhui Province.

Hu Jiwei: In 1954 Hu Jiwei became deputy editor and then in 1958 deputy editor in chief of the *People's Daily*, the official organ of the CCP Central Committee. Purged during the Cultural Revolution, Hu reappeared in 1977 and emerged as a staunch advocate of press reform and liberalization in China and a strong supporter of the reformist political ideas of the then CCP general secretary, Hu Yaobang, whose sudden death in April 1989 set off the student demonstrations that culminated in the June 1989 Beijing massacre. Appointed director of the *People's Daily* in 1982, Hu was summarily terminated from his position in 1983 during the Anti-Spiritual Pollution Campaign. In June 1989 he was criticized for soliciting NPC members' signatures to convene a special NPC meeting to rescind martial law and dismiss Li Peng.

Hu Ping: In 1983, Hu Ping was appointed governor of China's coastal Fujian Province (directly opposite Taiwan) and in 1985 became deputy secretary of the Fujian Province CP committee. A major proponent of radical economic reform, Hu in 1987 became vice minister of the State Economic Commission and in 1988 minister of commerce.

Hu Qili: A mechanical engineer and long-time active Communist Youth League member, Hu Qili, during the Cultural Revolution, was branded a follower of Liu Shaoqi (Mao Zedong's first heir apparent whom Mao later purged). Hu Qili returned to prominence in the mid-1970s and was appointed vice president of Qinghua University. In 1982, he became director of the General Office of the CCP and in 1985 a member of the CCP Politburo and later its five-member Standing Committee. In 1988 he was put in charge of the Leading Group for Propaganda and Thought under the Central Committee. In June 1989 Hu lost his position on the Politburo Standing Committee and other posts for having allowed Chinese journalists free rein during the student demonstrations. Hu Qili reemerged in April 1990 at a meeting of the NPC and in 1991 became a vice minister.

Hu Yaobang: Appointed Party chairman and then general secretary of the CCP in the early 1980s following Deng Xiaoping's return to power, Hu Yaobang led China's truncated effort at liberal political reform until his dismissal in 1987. His death in April 1989 sparked the student demonstrations that culminated in the June 4, 1989, Beijing massacre.

Hua Guofeng: Appointed to the CCP Politburo in 1973 and minister of public security in 1975, Hua became premier in 1976 and was personally designated by Mao Zedong to succeed him as Party chairman, a post Hua assumed in October 1976 soon after Mao's demise.

Outflanked by Deng Xiaoping at the watershed Third Plenary Session of the Eleventh Party Congress in December 1978, Hua was replaced as Party chairman in September 1982, though he retained his position on the Central Committee. Since then he has been a virtual political recluse.

Jian Bozan: An historian of Chinese history, Jian Bozan was attacked during the Cultural Revolution for opposing the use of historical research to serve present-day politics and ideological struggles, especially in the historical interpretation of "peasant uprisings." Persecuted to death by radicals during the Cultural Revolution, Jian was posthumously "rehabilitated" in the late 1970s.

Jiang Zemin: In 1994 the general secretary of the CCP, president of the PRC, and chairman of the Central Military Commission, Jiang Zemin is the third successor chosen by Deng Xiaoping, following Hu Yaobang and Zhao Ziyang, both of whom were purged. Jiang is from Shanghai and has a degree in electrical engineering. Early in his career Jiang worked as a trainee in the Stalin Automobile Factory in Moscow and in the 1950s and 1960s was director of a number of industrial plants in Shanghai. In 1971 he entered the central government in the First Ministry of Machine Building and in the early 1980s headed the Ministry of Electronics Industry. In 1985 he became mayor of Shanghai and in 1987 a member of the CCP Politburo. During the June 1989 student demonstrations in Shanghai, he averted violence, mollifying students by reading them Lincoln's Gettysburg address in English! Following the massacre in Beijing, he was appointed by Deng Xiaoping as the "core" of the third generation of leaders.

Li Guixian: A specialist in electron vacuum chemistry who was trained and then conducted research at the Mendeleyev Chemical Technology Institute in Moscow, Li Guixian worked throughout the 1960s and 1970s in China as a researcher for the Ministry of Public Security, evidently in the field of electronics. In 1985 Li was appointed leading secretary of the Liaoning Province CP and became a member of the CCP Central Committee in the same year. In 1988 he became a state councilor and was appointed governor of the People's Bank of China, the country's central bank, and a member of the State Planning Commission. In 1989 he was China's representative to the Asian Development Bank and the World Bank. In 1993, he was forced to resign as head of the People's Bank because of a financial scandal that reportedly involved losses of several billion dollars.

Li Peng: In 1994 the premier of China in charge of the state administration, Li is the "adopted" son of Zhou Enlai. From 1948 to 1954, Li was trained as a power engineer in the Soviet Union and from 1955 to 1979 worked in China in numerous positions in the power industry. In 1982 he became vice minister of the Ministry of Water Resources and Electric Power and in the same year became a member of the Central Committee at the Twelfth Party Congress. In 1985 he was appointed to the Politburo and in 1987 to its Standing Committee. He became premier in 1988 and in June 1989 reportedly issued the order for troops to use force against prodemocracy demonstrators. In the early 1990s, Li led China's effort to restore its reputation in the international arena after the 1989 crackdown with visits to India, Europe, Japan, Vietnam, and the United Nations in New York where he met briefly with U.S. president George Bush. In June 1993, Li suffered a mild heart attack but returned to work later in the year. A strong proponent of the controversial Three Gorges Dam project, Li led the successful effort to overturn previous opposition to the dam and win NPC approval in early 1992 for the projected eighteen-year construction project.

Li Rui: Previously Mao Zedong's secretary on industrial affairs, Li Rui was in the 1950s vice minister of the Ministry of Water Resources and Electric Power. Purged as a "rightist" in the 1957 Anti-Rightist Struggle and as an "anti-Party element" during the Cultural Revolution, Li Rui returned to prominence in the late 1970s. He was elected to the Central Committee in 1982 and led the effort to halt plans for construction of the massive Three Gorges Dam project on the Yangtze River. Since the 1989 crackdown, Li has acted as an adviser to the Energy and Resources Research Institute in China and has remained an outspoken opponent of the Three Gorges project.

Li Ruihuan: Trained as a construction worker in the 1950s, Li Ruihuan cut his teeth during the 1958–60 Great Leap Forward as a member of the young carpenters' shock brigade building the Great Hall of the People in Beijing's Tiananmen Square, one of the world's largest buildings. In 1976 Li was made director of the work site constructing the Mao Zedong Memorial Hall in Tiananmen (which contains Mao's corpse encased in a crystal sarcophagus). In 1982, Li became mayor of Tianjin city and helped to clean up the city's notoriously polluted water supply. In 1987 he was appointed head of the Tianjin city CP and entered the CCP Politburo. With little formal education, Li has since 1989 emerged as a major figure dealing with ideological and educational issues in China on which he has taken a fairly moderate line.

Li Xiannian: Born in 1909 to poor peasants in Hubei Province, Li Xiannian joined the CCP in the late 1920s and later rose to the top of the CCP hierarchy as a military commander. In 1945 he became a member of the Central Committee and in 1949 served as mayor of Wuhan city located in the central Yangtze River valley. In 1956 he was appointed minister of finance and served throughout the Cultural Revolution with great influence over financial and economic affairs. From 1983 to 1988 he was president of the PRC. Li Xiannian died in 1992.

Li Ximing: A graduate of Qinghua University in civil engineering and architecture, Li Ximing served as vice minister in the Ministry of Electric Power in the late 1970s and vice minister of the power industry from 1979 to 1982. From 1982 to 1984 he was minister of urban and rural construction and environmental protection, and in 1984 became the "leading" secretary of the Beijing city CP and the first political commissar of the Beijing military garrison. In 1987 he was appointed to the Politburo. Following the June 1989 military crackdown in Beijing, which he championed, Li Ximing's political star faded somewhat. In 1994, he became titular head of the Three Gorges Dam project.

Liu Huaqing: A military veteran with close ties to Deng Xiaoping, Liu Huaqing attended a naval academy in the USSR in the early 1950s and in 1965 became deputy political commissar of the PLA Navy. During the 1960s, Liu weathered the Cultural Revolution and in 1978 became vice minister of the State Science and Technology Commission. In 1980 he became deputy chief of the PLA General Staff and in 1982 was appointed commander of the Navy. In the late 1980s Liu became vice chairman of the Central Military Commission and in 1992 was appointed to the Standing Committee of the Politburo as China's top military man.

Liu Huaqiu: A specialist on American political affairs, Liu Huaqiu in 1994 was China's vice minister of foreign affairs.

Liu Shaoqi: Mao Zedong's first heir apparent, Liu Shaoqi was attacked very early during the Cultural Revolution as "China's Khrushchev" and as the "Number One Party person in authority taking the capitalist road." Replaced as Mao's heir by Lin Biao (who himself would later die in an ill-fated attempt to kill the chairman in 1971), Liu Shaoqi died ignominiously in a solitary cell in 1969.

Liu Zhongli: From 1973–84, Liu Zhongli served in the planning commission of Heilongjiang Province and in 1988 became a vice minister of finance in the central government. In 1992, he replaced Wang Bingqian as minister of finance following Wang's apparent involvement in a financial scandal.

Lu Ping: A 1947 graduate of the Agricultural College of St. John's University in Shanghai, Lu Ping served in the 1950s as editor in chief of the magazine *China Reconstructs* and then disappeared during the Cultural Revolution. In 1978 he was made secretary general of the State Hong Kong and Macao Affairs Office and in 1985 was deputy secretary general of the Basic Law Drafting Committee for Hong Kong. In 1987 he was appointed deputy director of the Hong Kong and Macao Affairs Office.

Lu Youmei: Trained as a hydrologist in the 1950s, Lu Youmei served as an engineer from 1956 to 1970 at the Liujia Gorge Hydropower station on the Yellow River and then from 1978 to 1984 in the Ministry of Water Resources and Electric Power. In 1988 he was appointed vice minister of energy resources and in 1992 became the president of the Three Gorges Project Development Corporation, the quasi-private organization charged with constructing the Three Gorges Dam on the Yangtze River in central China.

Lu Xun: China's premier fiction writer of the twentieth century, Lu Xun authored such classic works as "The True Story of Ah Q" and "A Madman's Diary." A critic of the Nationalist Party and a founder of the League of Left-Wing Writers, Lu Xun died in 1936.

Peng Zhen: One of the "eight old cadres" of the CCP, Peng Zhen became a member of the Central Committee and Politburo in the 1950s and the mayor of Beijing until his purge during the Cultural Revolution. He reappeared in 1979 and was reappointed to top Party posts, but "resigned" his positions in 1987. In June 1989 he played a major role in sanctioning the crackdown on pro-democracy demonstrators.

Qian Qichen: In 1994, China's minister of foreign affairs, Qian Qichen spent many years in the foreign service of the PRC as ambassador to Guinea (1974–76) and the director of the Information Department of the Ministry of Foreign Affairs (1977–82). He was vice minister of foreign affairs from 1982 to 1988 and has been minister since 1988.

Qian Zhengying: Born in the United States, Qian Zhengying returned with her family to China where she studied civil engineering and in 1941 joined the CCP. From 1958 to 1974, she served as a vice minister in the Ministry of Water Resources and Electric Power and was a member of the Grand Canal Commission and the Huai River Harnessing Commission. In 1973, she was elected to the CCP Central Committee and in 1975 became minister of water resources and electric power and in 1988 became minister of water resources where she strongly supported construction of the Three Gorges Dam.

Qiao Shi: Leader of the Shanghai student movement in the 1940s, Qiao Shi in the 1950s and early 1960s worked in the Communist Youth League and in the steel industry. In 1982 he was appointed director of the International Liaison Department of the CCP and in 1984 a director of the CCP Organization Department. In 1985 he became a member of the Politburo and the Party Secretariat and in 1987 a member of the Politburo Standing Committee with responsibilities for maintaining internal Party discipline and ideological control. In 1989 he was appointed president of the Central Party School and assumed overall responsibility for China's internal security.

Raidi: A member of the Tibetan "minority" and a graduate of the CCP-run Central Nationalities Institute in Beijing, Raidi is a long-time member of the Tibet Autonomous Region CP. In 1985 he became the deputy secretary of the Tibet CP and chairman of the autonomous regional people's congress standing committee.

Ren Jianxin: A graduate in chemical engineering from Beida, Ren Jianxin worked in the 1950s for the Political and Legal Affairs Committee under the Government Administration Council and the Legal Affairs Bureau under the State Council. In the late 1950s, he became involved in international trade issues and after the Cultural Revolution became vice chairman of the China Council for Promotion of International Trade. In 1988 he was appointed president of China's Supreme People's Court and became a member of the CCP Central Secretariat.

Ru Xin: A 1949 graduate of St. John's University in Shanghai and later a student at the Institute of Philosophy of the Academy of Sciences, Ru Xin became vice president of the Academy of Social Sciences (established in 1977) in 1982. In 1989 he became director of the Institute of Philosophy and published the *History of Western Aesthetics*.

Rui Xingwen: A chemical engineer and in the late 1970s a vice minister of the military-related Seventh Ministry of Machine Building, Rui Xingwen became a vice minister of the State Planning Commission and member of the Central Party Secretariat. In 1988 he became deputy head of the Leading Group for Propaganda and Thought under the CCP Central Committee but was dropped from power after the June 1989 pro-democracy demonstrations. He returned to government service in the early 1990s.

Shen Daren: A former director of the textile industry in Jiangsu Province, Shen Daren served in the early 1980s as mayor of Changzhou city, Jiangsu Province, and in 1983 became deputy secretary of the Jiangsu provincial CP. In 1987, he was appointed secretary of the Ningxia Autonomous Region CP and in 1989 became Communist Party secretary of Jiangsu Province.

Song Ping: In the late 1950s Song Ping was appointed vice minister of the State Planning Commission and during the 1960s was put in charge of defense construction projects for inland areas (the so-called Third Front). He was active in the northwestern province of Gansu during the

Cultural Revolution and in 1983 became a state councilor and minister of the State Planning Commission. In 1987 he assumed the director-ship of the CCP Organization Department and in June 1989 became a member of the Politburo Standing Committee in the midst of the political crisis stemming from pro democracy demonstrations.

Song Renqiong: A Long March veteran, Song Renqiong organized the "Death Corps" in Shanxi Province and in 1945 was appointed to the CCP Central Committee. In 1954, Song became a member of China's National Defense Council and in the early 1960s he became deputy secretary in chief of the Central Committee and minister of the Third Ministry of Machine Building. Throughout the Cultural Revolution he was repeatedly attacked by Red Guards but returned in 1979 to become director of the CCP Organization Department. In 1982 he was elected to the Politburo and in 1985 resigned to become the vice chairman of the Central Advisory Commission.

Su Shuangbi: A graduate of Beida in history in 1961, Su Shuangbi was director of the Theoretical Department of *Enlightenment Daily*. In the early 1990s he became deputy editor in chief of the journal *Seeking Truth (Qiushi)*.

Tao Siju: A graduate of the Beijing Institute of Diplomacy, Tao Siju served as a section chief in the Ministry of Public Security from 1968 to 1976 and as secretary of the General Office of the Central Military Commission from 1978 to 1979. In 1984, he was appointed vice minister of public security and in 1990 became minister of public security.

Wan Li: A Party elder and long-time supporter of economic and political reform, Wan Li was purged during the Cultural Revolution and reappeared in 1971, only to be dismissed again, along with Deng Xiaoping, after the April 1976 Tiananmen Incident. In the late 1970s, he reappeared as first secretary of the Party committee in Anhui Province, one of China's poorest regions, where radical reforms in agricultural policy were initiated, apparently with Wan's blessings. In 1982 Wan Li was appointed to the Politburo and in 1988 he became the chairman of the seventh NPC Standing Committee. In May 1989 he cut short his visit to the United States and Canada and returned to China. During the 1992 NPC session that passed the Resolution approving construction of the Three Gorges Dam project, Wan, despite his credentials as a reformer, summarily cut off debate and effectively prevented dam opponents from mobilizing opposition among the delegates.

Wang Bingqian: A long-time specialist in finance and economics, Wang Bingqian became minister of finance in 1980. He also served as a governor of the World Bank representing the PRC and was China's delegate to the IMF and meetings of the China-U.S. Joint Economic Committee. In September 1992, he was forced to resign under pressure as minister of finance.

Wang Renzhi: A member of the Policy Research Office under the State Council from 1978 to 1982, Wang Renzhi became deputy editor in chief of the CCP's leftist-oriented theoretical organ, *Red Flag* (*Hongqi*). In 1987, Wang assumed the directorship of the CCP Propaganda Department and in 1988 became a member of the Leading Group for Propaganda and Thought. Wang was one of the last Chinese leaders to visit the former USSR before its political demise.

Wang Zhen: A military man, Wang Zhen was appointed by Mao Zedong in the 1940s to oversee and ultimately persecute intellectuals in the CCP's mountain redoubt of Yan'an. After 1949 Wang was stationed in Xinjiang Province in China's northwest, where with Deng Liqun he helped put down local Muslim resistance to CCP rule. In 1956 Wang was appointed minister of state farms and reclamation and became a member of the CCP Central Committee. Wang retained his posts throughout the Cultural Revolution and in 1978 became a member of the Politburo and the Central Military Commission. From 1982 to 1987 he headed the Central Party School in Beijing where he acted as Deng Xiaoping's "bazooka" in ferreting out advocates of radical political reform. In 1987 he became the vice president of China. In 1989 during the PLA crackdown on pro-democracy demonstrators he reportedly rode in an army tank. Wang died in 1993.

Wei Jianxing: A graduate of the Dalian Engineering Institute in China's northeast, Wei Jianxing became mayor of Harbin city in Heilongjiang Province in 1983. In 1984 he became the deputy director of the CCP Organization Department and served as its director until 1987. In 1987 he became minister of supervision and a member of the presidium of the Thirteenth Party Congress.

Wu Yi: A graduate of the Beijing Petroleum Institute, she became a vice mayor of Beijing in 1988 and in 1994 was China's minister of trade.

Xie Fei: After joining the CCP in 1949, Xie Fei served in various posts in China's southern province of Guangdong, since 1978 the fastest growing region in the country. In 1983, he was appointed secretary of the Guangdong Provincial CP and in 1986 became the secretary of the Guangzhou (Canton) city CP. In 1987, he was appointed to the CCP Central Committee at the Thirteenth Party Congress and in 1988 became a member of the NPC.

Xing Bensi: In the 1950s and early 1960s, Xing Bensi was trained in Russian language and served as a researcher at the Institute of Philosophy under the Academy of Sciences. In 1979, he became the director of the Institute of Philosophy under the Academy of Social Sciences and spent a year as a visiting scholar at Columbia University in New York. A hard-line intellectual critic of "bourgeois liberalism," in July 1989 he became the vice president of the Central Party School in Beijing following the June 4 massacre. Xing is a specialist on the philosophy of Ludwig Feuerbach and Saint Simon.

Yan Mingfu: A graduate of the Harbin Foreign Languages Institute, Yan Mingfu became a cadre in the General Office of the CCP in the late 1950s before disappearing in the Cultural Revolution. In 1985, he became director of the United Front Department of the CCP Central Committee and a member of the CCP Secretariat. He was purged following the June 4, 1989, Beijing massacre for involvement in the pro-democracy student movement, but returned to government service in the early 1990s.

Yang Baibing: A full general in the PLA, Yang Baibing was a key figure in the late 1970s and early 1980s in the strategic Beijing Military Region where he served as political commissar until 1987. At the November 1987 Thirteenth Party Congress, Yang was appointed director of the PLA General Political Department, the key central organ responsible for maintaining loyalty among the troops to CCP leaders. In 1988, Yang also became a member of the Central Military Commission and in November 1989 was appointed to the Secretariat of the

CCP Central Committee and became secretary general of the Central Military Commission. Yang Baibing and his half brother, Yang Shangkun, China's former president, lost their positions on the powerful Military Commission at the October 1992 Fourteenth Party Congress as Deng Xiaoping apparently became concerned with the rising power of the "Yang family clique." Yang Baibing, however, remained a member of the Politburo and the Central Committee.

Yang Rudai: A native of Sichuan Province, China's most populous, Yang Rudai rose through the ranks from a county Party secretary to the vice chairman of the Revolutionary Committee of Sichuan Province during the Cultural Revolution and, finally, became secretary of the Sichuan CCP in 1980. In 1982 he was appointed to the CCP Central Committee at the Twelfth Party Congress and in 1984 became the political commissar of the Sichuan Military District. In 1987 he was appointed to the CCP Politburo. He has the equivalent of a middle school education, while his wife, a peasant woman, worked in a street factory in the Sichuan city of Chengdu until 1988.

Yang Shangkun: Trained in Moscow in the 1920s and early 1930s and ostensibly a military man, Yang Shangkun became head of the CCP General Office in 1945, a post he held until the Cultural Revolution. He became a member of the Central Committee in 1956 but fell out of favor with Mao Zedong in the early 1960s, purportedly after bugging the chairman's residence (a fact apparently discovered by one of Mao's many mistresses). In 1966, Yang was branded a "counterrevolutionary" and did not reappear until 1978. In 1982 he was appointed to the Politburo and became a permanent vice chairman of the Central Military Commission and in 1988 became president of the PRC. Yang lost his positions in the October 1992 Fourteenth Party Congress, allegedly after Deng Xiaoping caught wind of the plans by Yang and his half-brother Yang Baibing to place all the blame for the 1989 Beijing massacre on Deng following his death. Although in his eighties, Yang is described as being in "robust" health.

Yao Yilin: Trained in chemistry, Yao Yilin became a vice minister of commerce in the early 1950s and negotiated trade agreements with the Soviet Union. In 1958 he was appointed to the Bureau of Finance and Commerce under the State Council and in 1960 became minister of commerce. Criticized during the Cultural Revolution because of his close association with Peng Zhen, Yao returned to prominence in 1973 and became involved in foreign trade issues. In 1980 he became director of the State Planning Commission and in 1985 was appointed to the Politburo. An influential figure supporting the Three Gorges Dam project, Yao was generally considered a conservative on economics. He died in December 1994.

Zhao Ziyang: A deputy secretary of the Guangdong CP in the 1950s and early 1960s, Zhao Ziyang was paraded through the streets by Red Guards during the Cultural Revolution. He reappeared in 1971 and in 1973 became Party secretary in Guangdong and in 1976 took over the Sichuan CP where he supported reformist policies in agriculture. In 1979 he was appointed to the CCP Politburo and in 1980 became premier. Following the dismissal of Hu Yaobang in 1987, he became general secretary of the CCP and tried to steer the Party along the twin paths of both economic and political reform. In June 1989 he was dismissed from all posts because of his refusal to endorse the use of force against pro-democracy demonstrators. Since 1989 he has been the subject of many official "investigations" of his political errors, but has retained his Party membership.

Zhu Rongji. A graduate of Qinghua University, Zhu worked in the State Planning Commission from 1951 to 1966. After the Cultural Revolution he worked in the Ministry of Petroleum and then in 1983 was appointed vice minister of the State Economic Commission. In 1987 Zhu became a member of the Central Committee and in 1988 was made mayor of Shanghai. After a stint in the China International Trust and Investment Corporation (CITIC), in 1991 he became vice premier. In 1993 he was made governor of the People's Bank of China and was put in charge of cooling down the Chinese economy. As China's new economic "czar," Zhu Rongji is considered a top candidate to become China's paramount leader after Deng Xiaoping's death.

Zou Jiahua: A graduate of the Moscow Engineering Institute, Zou Jiahua served in the 1950s and 1960s as a director of a machine tool plant in Shenyang city in China's northeast and then worked in the First Ministry of Machine Building. In 1974 he was identified as a member of the PLA's Science and Technology Commission for National Defense and in 1977 was elected as an alternate member of the Central Committee. In 1983 he became a vice minister in the Commission of Science, Technology, and Industry for National Defense and in 1985 minister of ordnance industry. In 1988 he was appointed a state councilor and minister of machine building and the electronics industry and in 1989 became head of the State Planning Commission and in 1991 a vice premier.

Index

Lawrence R. Sullivan is an associate professor of political science at Adelphi University. Author of numerous articles and books on contemporary Chinese politics and the history of the Chinese Communist Party, his latest works include co-editing and translating *Deng Xiaoping: Chronicle of an Empire* by Ruan Ming (1994) and co-editing *Yangtze! Yangtze!* by Dai Qing (1994).